Little Girl
Big War

A Refugee's Memoir

Life is good.

婷婷 ☺

Ting-Ting Chan-Burford, M.S.W.

ACKNOWLEDGEMENTS

So many of my friends and family have supported this project, even when others wondered why I would want to revisit my dark memories. This book of memories would not have been possible without the input and inspiration of these of my special people, along with scores of others who encouraged me and helped fill in the blanks in my childhood memories:

Dan and Franell Burford, who told me to write my story even before I remembered most of it;

Michelle and Dave Woldstad and the rest of the Joint Heirs who listened through my tears;

Steve and Christy Shepard, who befriended our family as newcomers;

Bob and Sandy G, who helped me put pen to paper;

Wanda Elliot, who forgave, and Papa Al, rest in peace knowing your sacrifice had value;

Peng and Ted Jones, who formed an unlikely friendship;

Chuck, Charie, Viola, and Steve Horne, who stuck by despite my craziness;

Jim and Lucille Mcleran, who opened up the floodgates and put words to memories;

Sue Henderson and Renée Pawlish, who helped with editing and formatting.

For Mother, who never gave up;
For my brothers and sister, who lived it too;
For David, who gave me the freedom to experience it all over
again.

INTRODUCTION

Growing up in the late sixties and early seventies, I was one of the richest, upper-class, Mercedes-chauffeured princesses in tumultuous Saigon, Vietnam. But on April 30, 1975, after watching from behind the gate as the last American helicopter full of refugees lifted off from Tan Son Nhut Airport, I was just another hopeless pedestrian walking back to the shack my family called home. I was one of the fortunate ones, however, because eventually I escaped Vietnam and found a home in America. It's time to tell my family's story in honor of the hundreds of thousands of us who were left behind the gate when the last, fortunate evacuees flew to freedom.

I can tell this story due in large part to the American GIs who struggled with their duties, their consciences, and even their own countrymen because of their fight for our freedom. If you are a Vietnam veteran reading this, thank you, thank you, and thank you. I know many Americans, veterans in particular, still feel guilty for what they did in Vietnam, or for leaving without accomplishing their mission to save us from communism. Likewise, many feel that getting involved in Vietnam's war was a mistake. I'm not a politician. I was just a kid during the war, but I do know that my family would not have had a future without the Americans' intervention.

My story is a journey told through the mental maze of Post-Traumatic Stress Disorder (PTSD). I still suffer the effects of tricks my mind played to help me get through some horrible situations. If you sense I am jumping from story to story, I do it purposely to distract myself from the stress overload of reliving traumatic events. Bear with me, and you will have a better understanding of the effect PTSD has and how I've learned to participate in the world around me without going crazy. There are many trauma victims and veterans whose minds are still dealing with the war and more soldiers coming home every day from wars with similar issues. I hope my story will help PTSD survivors see that there can be a good life beyond PTSD.

CHAPTER ONE:

TET

Any American Vietnam veteran who served in 1968 can tell you where he was before, during, and after the 1968 Tet Offensive. It was a turning point in the Vietnam conflict when the war moved from the jungles and villages to the capitol city. It was also a turning point in my family's history. We lived in northern Saigon, in Cho Lon, a mostly Chinese neighborhood which was the area of town hardest hit by the North Vietnamese attacks. I was five or eight years old, depending on who's telling the story.

My parents ran a restaurant and nightclub adjacent to Tan Son Nhut Air Force Base, which catered to military officers and government officials by invitation only. Because of its strategic and secure location, it was a "green zone" of sorts, where visiting dignitaries could hold meetings, celebrities could relax, and American officers could enjoy a fine meal cooked in French or Chinese style while unwinding with familiar entertainment.

We had a French kitchen with a French chef and a Chinese kitchen with a Chinese chef. One floor housed the restaurant and another held a nightclub. Bob Hope, Sammy Davis, Jr., and many other famous

American entertainers and officials visited our restaurant before and after the Tet Offensive. Of course, I didn't fully appreciate who these celebrities were, as I was only eight or nine years old. I wasn't allowed in the restaurant when we had important visitors, but I do remember hanging out in the kitchen or behind a curtain in the bar and catching glimpses of the famous people everyone was rushing around to impress.

I remember my curiosity at seeing the smallest black man I had ever seen because he was short and smiled a lot just like my dad. He jumped around and laughed when he talked with the officers and dignitaries in our lobby. He always had a cigarette in his hand or his mouth, and seemed to go from one to another, lighting a new one with the burning head of one he had smoked down to a nub. He jumped from one conversation to another, while amateur photographers got their pictures taken with him on their Kodak Instamatics. Mr. Davis worked the lobby like a dancer, with each small group the next act of his dance. He was a man who was used to attention, and he knew how to act as though he was a friend of each person he met, just like my dad … and what a smile. All the other black men I had seen were big soldiers wearing green and carrying guns. This one wasn't so scary.

The restaurant and nightclub were wildly successful and made our family wealthy beyond our imagination. We had the best of everything from around the world. Aside from the staff of over a hundred, we had our own cooks, servants, and nannies at home. For a while, my father took us around Saigon, nicknamed "The Little Paris of Asia," in a chauffeured Mercedes. As the war came closer to Saigon, my mother, always the practical one, convinced him that driving one of the few such cars in the country at the time displayed our wealth and made us a big target. We switched to a less noticeable Toyota sedan, but kept the driver.

Tet is the Vietnamese word for Chinese New Year. Traditionally, families stocked up on groceries and gifts of fruit and tea for neighbors and friends who came to visit during this two-week long holiday, much like Christmas here in the States.

In the days before the 1968 Tet Festival, Mother and Father had sent most of our household servants home to their families, everyone but Chi-Hoa, our cook, who chose to stay with our family. Chi-Hoa's mother, whose husband had abandoned her, sold her to our family as a slave when she was fourteen. Her mother was a chronic gambler and opium user, and had sold her once before, before she came to us.

Chi-Hoa was only eight years old when she was first sold. That family abused her terribly. She was punished for every childish action, imperfection, or mistake, usually by being beaten with a bamboo pole. Sometimes she was forced to go days without food. She must have been in such bad shape that her owners feared they would get into trouble for her poor condition, so she ended up on her mother's doorstep again. Once she reached puberty, her mother put her up for sale again, hoping to get a good price. Fortunately, she didn't end up in a brothel, because she was only average looking, and the brothels had plenty of pretty young girls to choose from in those days. Her mother heard that my mother was looking for help with her soon-to-be three children. She reluctantly approached Mother, and a modest bargain was struck. Chi-Hoa came to live with my family in 1956.

Mother was good at planning kind solutions to cruel situations even before she became wealthy. Though she was still just a poor seamstress herself, she paid the price for Chi-Hoa and took her into our home out of need and also out of pity for her mother. Rather than keep her as a slave or adopt her as a daughter, Mother insisted that she must be paid the same wages as the neighbors' servants. Her salary was paid before Mother's own needs were met. Chi-Hoa could be free, having already been purchased, and due to her employment she could support her mother's family with her income.

Chi-Hoa stayed with us until 1970, when she was an old maid at twenty-eight years of age. (Most Vietnamese girls had their marriages arranged at sixteen and were married by twenty.) A local tailor, who had been widowed and had two young children, approached Mother for Chi-Hoa's hand in marriage. Although they had not courted, he saw what a special relationship Mother and Chi-Hoa had (and it didn't hurt that Mother was rich by this time), and he decided to ask Mother to give her away rather than her own mother.

Chi-Hoa was willing to go, so Mother sent her off with a large traditional dowry, as extravagant as she would have given her own daughter. In addition to an entire wardrobe of traditional dresses, linen tablecloths, and bed sheets, she gave her several 24 carat gold chains, gold rings, gold and diamond earrings, ankle bracelets, huge natural pearl earrings and stickpins, traditional Vietnamese gold leaf-embossed red plaques, several jade necklaces and bracelets of the highest quality, and a ceremonial quilt for the couple's marriage bed. The quilt was bright red silk, embroidered with gold thread, portraying a dragon and a phoenix, gold lace trim, and was quilted and stuffed with pure white cotton. My grandmother criticized Mother for being so generous to a slave girl marrying a greedy old tailor. Mother said that Chi-Hoa had been with us longer than all the other servants. She came to live with us during the time we were poor and stayed with us as a loyal and hard worker. She deserved a good send-off with gifts for a lucky start in her new life.

Chi-Hoa was sleeping with us when we were awakened in the pre-dawn hours of the second day of Tet. Warning sirens blared throughout the city, church-bells rang, and explosions boomed all around us. No sooner had we been awakened by the loud noises that warm February morning, than the fighting was right in our own neighborhood. The North Vietnamese communist forces were lobbing mortars into the city and, at the same time, their soldiers were fighting our South Vietnamese and American soldiers in the streets.

Trucks with mounted loudspeakers traveling the streets ordered us to stay inside our houses and hide as well as possible to protect ourselves from the dangers outside. Frantically, my father and brothers dragged the heavy, black ironwood dining table my grandmother had brought from China into an interior room. Mother told us to bring all the New Year's holiday food and buckets of water into that room, and we blocked the door and walls with other furniture from all over our house.

We set up a makeshift kitchen on a bench, with a bucket and a coal-burning clay stove. Another bucket behind a blanket strung on wire across a corner of the room served as a toilet. When we heard a "wheeee" or a "tet-tet-tet" outside, the ten of us huddled together under that ironwood table and waited for the "boom." For several days, the sound of artillery was our only clue as to what was going on outside that room. The ground shook so violently that we didn't know whether or not the rest of our house was still standing.

After several days, the shelling had died down and my parents reluctantly let us come out of the fortified room a few hours at a time during the day. I was so stir-crazy from being cooped up inside the safe room that I jumped at the chance to explore. A round-the-clock curfew meant no one was allowed to leave the house.

One of my traumatic memories comes from the first few hours I was allowed to escape the safe room. While Mother and Father searched the house to retrieve food, water, valuables, and important papers, I sneaked out. I was told not to leave the house, but I remember sneaking out.

I figured I was not really leaving the house because I didn't have to go out through the door. Half of the concrete kitchen wall was blown to bits and I could see out into the street. Big rocks and chunks of concrete were everywhere, spilling into the street and the living room. I looked outside and down the alley. All the standing walls were pocked with little craters created by bullets and flying rocks and concrete, and the sunlight and shadows in the little craters made the walls look like they crawled with bugs. The air was thick with concrete dust, wood smoke, and gunpowder.

As I stood in the hole in the wall that separated the kitchen from the alley, surrounded by the haze and rubble and debris, I heard a loud "BAM!" from a grenade and felt the concussion from the explosion. I recoiled as a little sponge slammed against the wall, then watched it quiver and fall down the wall. It dawned on me that it wasn't a sponge, but brains. I recognized brains because I had sometimes seen our cook preparing pig, cow, or monkey brains with herbs for medicinal purposes. Thankfully, I was too young at the time to connect the brains with someone's death. Looking back on it now, I imagine that a dog took the force of the blast for me and it was his brains on the wall. That's how I can cope with the gruesome scene in my mind.

People ran through the alley and the street, crying for help. Children were crying for their parents. Adults were screaming hysterically for their children to come home, but they were too afraid to go out into the street and look for them.

As I stood, frozen and transfixed by the chaos around me, a man dressed in a black uniform I had seen before only on television, ran through the broken wall from the alley into the kitchen. He ran past where I was standing, and on into the dining room on my right. He had a rifle in his hands. Then I saw another man, dressed in a familiar green camouflage uniform, run after the man in black. He caught up with him and hit him very hard on the back with his rifle. The man in black fell to his knees and dropped his rifle on the ground beside him. The man in camouflage made him put his hands on top of his head, took his gun and walked behind him out the metal, scissor-folding security gate that protected the front of our house. It was the kind of sturdy gate seen on the front of jewelry stores, which are popular everywhere in the world in all sorts of neighborhoods now, but were seen in Asia only on homes in wealthy neighborhoods back then. It was torn away and hanging by one upper corner.

The human mind has a funny way of filling in the gaps of what we perceive, so that what we see can be interpreted and sorted and processed to allow us to respond appropriately. But sometimes our mind can play tricks on us by filling in too many of these gaps when there is an information overload. As I discussed my memories with my family in preparation to write my story, my mother and sister said, "No, our house was not bombed, but our neighbors to the right and left were." Mother says I was a very curious and nosy child, and after the boredom of staying in the hiding place for so long, I couldn't be kept still any longer. My two older brothers and sister had better sense, and my little brothers were too small to be so curious. As soon as Mother and Father felt they could get out of the safe room to search the house for food and charcoal, I ran outside to investigate what was happening around the neighborhood. The bombing I witnessed actually happened at my next-door neighbor's house.

My mind helped me get through many traumas to come by playing these kinds of tricks. For years afterward, I thought I was crazy. I was at war with my mind, and I struggled every day to determine whether my perceptions of events around me really existed. Not just traumatic memories of the war and of the jails and abuse, but almost anything could throw me off balance. Did that boy walking in front of me on his way to class really just fall down, or is he still walking? Is that car going to hit me, or is it waiting to turn? In college, I learned that these coping mechanisms were hard-wired into my subconscious mind as a child. They numbed me to the reality of desperate circumstances and put the memories on time-release to process later, bit by bit, as I could accept and acknowledge the trauma. To this day, I cannot watch a suspenseful or gory movie, spend the night in a tent, shoot a gun, ride in a boat, or even watch the neighborhood kids playing "Cowboys and Indians." The old feelings come back to all my senses, too terrifyingly strong and all too real.

My PTSD makes every emotion exaggerated, every adrenaline-rush a life-or-death event. In 1990, when I was newly married, my husband's college roommate, Rhys, paid us a visit and took us to Marriott's Great America, an amusement park in California's Silicon Valley. After a couple of hours in the park, we stood in line to get on a white water raft ride. As soon as the rocking and splashing began, I started screaming, "We're gonna die!" "Get me off!!" "Stop!" I screamed in every language I knew, until David finally stopped the raft to let me off in the middle of the watercourse.

In the days following September 11, 2001, almost two thousand miles from Ground Zero and thirty-three years after my first traumatic experiences, I smelled concrete dust and decaying bodies as I listened to the radio reporting the World Trade Center attacks. I was driving to work and had to pull over to the side of the road to regain my composure and convince myself that this would not affect me like before.

Back to the Tet Offensive: the twenty-four hour curfew was on for more than a week. Everyone was stuck inside their homes, no one allowed on the street. The open market was closed (picture an indoor farmers' market crossed with a supermarket in the United States, the only source of meat and vegetables in the city at that time.). People had to make do with whatever they had in their homes. Slowly, the curfew was lifted for a few hours each day. We could go out of the house, but the stench of rotting corpses and concrete dust didn't invite us out to play. It took months before life returned to normal. During the day, curfew was off at 6:00 a.m., and people were allowed out to do business. The nighttime curfew started at noon in the beginning, and then slowly moved to 10: 00 p.m. After curfew, only people with special permits were allowed on the street, and anyone on the street without one could be shot.

While we had to stay in the house, we invented games to play, like shooting bugs with rubber bands and folding paper frogs and cranes to "eat" the bugs. We also played card games. The electricity remained on most of the time, but our black and white television only showed the news. It was just pictures of bombings, bodies, and stories about how the daily battles were being won by the "good guys," meaning the South Vietnamese and American troops, accompanied by the mournful melody of "What a Wonderful World". The news droned on and on with no relief from the war all around us. We entertained ourselves and tried to ignore the chaos by inventing stories to tell Mother and Father about how this brother or that sister had done something more terrible than the last story. We wrote, produced, directed, and acted in our own theatrical productions. We giggled and laughed and carried on as though death was not camped out on our front doorstep.

Probably the best product of that isolation was the sense of family we developed as we listened to Mother and Father tell us stories, which gave us an understanding of who we were. I learned that my parents, born in China, were both brought to Vietnam by their parents when they were toddlers. My grandparents had immigrated to North Vietnam to escape communism and economic turmoil in China. Later, as the communists advanced from China into Vietnam, the families migrated to South Vietnam to escape the extermination of their merchant class. Grandma told us stories about how she had come to Vietnam with her parents and young children, and who our ancestors had been back in China. We had accountants, mayors, and other learned and accomplished ancestors in our family tree.

My grandparents' generation was the last to suffer from the cruel custom of foot binding. Grandma's feet were bound tightly with bandages when she was two or three years old, so they would stay small as she grew. She had to be carried around town by servants on a litter, a fancy cart without wheels, to show the family was high class. Grandma's feet were very, very small, no bigger than a Coke can from the tips of her toes to the tops of her ankles. They were always very sore.

Our family huddled together for the most severe bombings, but we generally tried to ignore sporadic gunfire. It was a very scary time, but we drew closer together than we had ever been. We kids didn't fight as much after Tet. We listened and absorbed our grandmother's illustration that our family was like a hand with each of us a finger, and the hand didn't look right or function properly without any one of us. To this day we stick by each other, not daring to cut off a finger no matter how angry we might be.

During the Tet Offensive, Mother and Father had long, whispered conversations, unlike the short, business-like communication they had before. We knew they were planning for us and would figure out a way for the family to survive. We still didn't know whether our restaurant had survived the attacks, which we heard were very heavy around the airport. But our grandparents had nothing except what they could carry or push on a wheelbarrow when they moved to North Vietnam from their village in Fujian Province, and our parents had started over with only a sewing machine when they left North Vietnam for Saigon. Little did we know that our generation would have to start over from scratch as well. We had so much wealth, it seemed impossible.

After Tet, my parents realized that we would be targets wherever we went or however we lived, so we moved to the security of the restaurant grounds. Although we hid our wealth and lived very modestly, Mother and Father secretly sent millions of dollars to my uncle in Hong Kong to be invested for us. My parents knew the war would not last forever. They realized that since we were so dependent on the American military for our wealth in Vietnam, we would have to leave the country eventually no matter who won the war. They just didn't know how close to home it would come until the bombs had already landed in our neighborhood.

As the curfew lifted, people bought whatever food was available. No matter what it was, they paid the price requested. Sometimes a customer would offer double or triple the price on the last item just to get something to eat. Soon, only the rich could feed their families. One morning, even my mother came home with nothing but a few small watermelons. She fed us the red fruit for a few meals, then shaved off the skin and used the white rind to cook soup for us, which kept us from going hungry.

Thankfully, the Tet Offensive began on the second day of the Lunar New Year, after the whole town had stocked up for two weeks of feasting. If it had come on a regular day or at the end of New Year's, many of us would have died of starvation.

The fighting didn't stay in Saigon after the Tet Offensive. An American Vietnam veteran friend told me that it lasted only six weeks. It spread to the countryside, into the jungle, and extended to the borders of Cambodia and Laos for years. After the Tet Offensive, there was a 10:00 P.M. curfew in all of Saigon which was strictly enforced. We heard the sounds of the war not only through our televisions and radios but actually by living in the war zone. The sound of bombing became more pronounced at night when the city was quiet. I could feel the concussions from the far-off bombing and continuous "tet-tet-tet" of automatic gunfire. I lay awake in bed, terrified by these sounds. I prayed before I went to bed that I would not wake up in the middle of the night. If I did, I covered my face very tightly with my pillow, hoping against hope for the noises to somehow disappear.

The nightmares started then, when I was a little girl. I dreamed I was above the mountains. It seemed as though I floated in mid-air somewhere between the jungle and the sky, or in a helicopter or an airplane flying over the mountains and looking down on them. Lying there in my bed in the darkness, I heard again the low-pitched booms I detested and felt the big guns reverberating in my bed. I always woke up in a sweat. Sometimes it became too much for me and I would grab my older sister, or nanny, or whoever was sleeping next to me in the girls' bed, and shove my head against her body. Again, I shut my eyes and covered my ears as tightly as I possibly could, hoping that if I did it long and hard enough the fear and booming would disappear. This dream and fear stayed with me the whole time I was in Vietnam and the first ten years I was in America. It still haunts me occasionally. When the war was over, I dreamed it less often, but with a new twist: I could see myself in the dream. I didn't hear the sounds of bombing and guns anymore, but the terror remained.

The sights and smells of war were all over the city. Wounded soldiers became beggars on the streets. Most of them had missing body parts due to land mines. Some had lost their families and there was no home to return to. The South Vietnamese government had no support programs in place for wounded soldiers, and they were left homeless and destitute. The more fortunate ones had accepting family members to be reunited with, but life was no longer the same. Gainful employment could not be found, and food was scarce. Very often, the wives of these wounded soldiers were the sole breadwinners for their families, and they worked as prostitutes. Their children went barefoot and their meager clothing—rags scrounged from the hospital trash, temples, or the city market—barely covered their bulging, malnourished bellies.

Young women had no young men to marry as the majority of them had been drafted. The rich ones could afford to pay for passage to escape being drafted. Their parents purchased fake identities for them to flee the country, and this was done for my two older brothers. Corruption was rampant. Poor boys tried their best to escape the draft by hiding in the countryside, in temples, or at a relative's home, but it was just a matter of time before they were conscripted. The South Vietnamese government did impromptu headcount checks on families at night on a random basis. All the young men who were of age were taken away to serve in the military. The only men left were usually older married ones or wounded and disabled. If a young woman was brave enough to marry a young man, she had to be prepared to provide not only for herself but her husband, who might very likely eventually be wounded or hiding in some money-hungry monastery.

The weather in Vietnam is always hot and humid with six months each of rainy and dry seasons. During the rainy season, children took their showers in the rain. The people lived in extremely poor conditions, and there was no healthcare available for the general population. The entire country was depressed. Even the music at that time was sad and melancholy. The lyrics of the songs were about poverty, loneliness, and the effects of war.

Prostitution was not a crime but a legal profession and means of survival. Thousands of biracial children were conceived by the local women with American servicemen and international residents. They were half black, half white, half Latino, or half Native American children. Others were half Korean, half Filipino, or half Japanese. These children were called "Con Bui Doi" (Children of the Dust). They were spat upon and lived and begged on the streets. They ate out of the trash. No one wanted to acknowledge their existence. The lucky ones ended up in orphanages, which normally housed only pure Vietnamese orphans that were plentiful at the time.

The majority of the Con Bui Doi children were severely neglected and abused. They were often left to survive on their own as young as age two. These children were lucky if they were left on the doorsteps of temples, churches, or orphanages. Most of those left on the streets didn't survive past age four or five. Very few were cared for by their own families. Their mothers usually were left with no choice other than prostitution because of their unfortunate situation. Their men came home from the battlefield disabled, unable to work to provide for their families. Likewise, the women were generally illiterate and had no marketable skills. Many relied on the Americans for their livelihood during the war. They prostituted themselves and bore marked children. They hid their shame and, in order to continue working to provide for their families, they abandoned their biracial children. The mothers who kept them were totally rejected by their own society after the war.

Even the American government forgot about these children until the war was long over. They were treated as slaves even if they were with their own families, and considered of less value than animals. At least animals were treated respectfully as laborers working in the fields and were fed. When America finally recognized the Con Bui Dois' citizenship, many of their families had left them behind during the great exodus and the children were exploited again. Almost overnight, the surviving street kids, who were teenagers by then, disappeared from the streets and instantly became beloved children of families hopeful for tickets to America.

Television was the only entertainment available during the war and even it was controlled and limited. There were daily reports of the war and the death toll and during these reports the songs "Home Sweet Home" or "It's a Wonderful World" played in the background. The news always showed how dead bodies were collected and put into black plastic bags and how they identified the bodies of Americans and South or North Vietnamese soldiers. The American bodies were placed in nice wooden boxes, the South Vietnamese stored in black bags with name tags, and the North Vietnamese burned in piles.

Before the bodies were identified, it was sometimes hard to tell which was which, because all the dead bodies looked the same. We couldn't tell the color distinctions on the black and white television screen when the remains were down to just tattered clothing, flesh, and bones. The only way to distinguish between a black or white body was if skin and hair were still attached to the skeleton, and the chances of this became slimmer as the body decomposed. It seemed they always scheduled such reports either during our dinner or at bedtime. As I viewed these stories daily, I realized that all humans are the same when it comes right down to the bones.

Our TV had only two channels. One was the local Vietnamese channel and the other the American English-speaking channel. Even though most of us didn't speak English, we normally watched the American channel unless it wasn't available. I remember watching when the first astronauts landed on the moon in 1969. We watched American shows: *Bonanza* with the Chinese cook, *Big Valley* with a grandma living with her family in a big house on a ranch, *Mission Impossible* with a different villain every week, *Lost in Space* with a robot and a stupid professor in outer space, *The Tonight Show* with Johnny Carson behind a big desk making jokes, *The Twilight Zone* with a different cast every week, *Gilligan's Island*, and *Star Trek*. We didn't understand what they were saying, but we made it up as we followed along and it helped to ease the tense evenings with laughter.

I have some pleasant memories from the war. After all, I was an elementary school kid who loved to have fun. During the daytime, after the curfew was set only at night, I could play outside and visit my friends in the neighborhood. Although my parents could afford them, toys were not available because of the war. For children it was a time for creativity because we had to make our own toys out of paper, tin cans, wood, rubber bands, ropes, strings, long dried grass, banana leaves, and coconut leaves. Coconuts and seashells were also hot items for creating toys. We used paper to make dolls, pistols, animals, kites, and cookware. We made sandbag forts and gathered sticks for arrows. Rocks and pieces of brick fallen from buildings made good soccer balls. We used rocks for boundaries and kicked "balls" in our makeshift fields in the street. We tossed slippers at tin cans, and the cans could really scoot if you hit them just right. We made hackysacks with knots of burlap filled with sand and chicken feathers tied on for balance and counted how many times we could kick them without letting them drop to the ground. We caught crickets and made them fight each other. We played tin-can telephone and made ant and beetle towns in sand-filled shoebox dioramas. My favorite thing to do was make my own paper kites, with chopstick bracing and string made from unraveled burlap bags tied together, and fly them as high as I could.

I was raised as a Chinese girl and wasn't allowed to play or fight with boys. In the Chinese culture, I was not allowed to do a lot of things because I was a girl. However, I wasn't a normal Chinese girl. I was very active and loved the outdoors. I was a tomboy. All my elders were concerned about me because I wasn't the gentle, sweet, submissive young lady they hoped I would be. My mother and grandmother were especially worried about my future, as I was too boyish for their liking. I caused them a lot of grief.

I was an ugly, chubby little girl no one wanted to play with. Girls called me names and boys bullied me. No one wanted to be my friend.

Later, I learned how to fight with boys, and I could beat them at all their games. I was so good at it they chose me to be on their team so that they would win. Sometimes, I got to pick which team I wanted to be on instead of them picking me. Boys disliked me but wanted me on their team at the same time. They sometimes double-dared me to climb trees. When they lost a race, they told on me. They knew my grandmother or mother would spank me for climbing trees.

I was also a know-it-all. I kept my family updated on the latest and juiciest neighborhood news and gossip. I was the very first in our family to know about anything and everything, from the newest babies and puppies in the neighborhood to who had sheets hanging in their back windows because someone had wet their bed.

At times, I also teamed up with the big boys to fight the Vietnamese children in the neighborhood. We threw rocks back and forth at each other while taking turns calling the other side dirty names. I grew up with racism and I can smell it a mile away. We couldn't talk about it, because there were laws to protect the Vietnamese kids, so fighting with them was a big no-no. After such fights, the Chinese adults had to give gifts as a peace offering and apologize to the brats who started it! If you think Asians all look alike and wonder how we knew who was Vietnamese and who was Chinese, the answer then was footwear. Vietnamese children were bare-footed outside while Chinese children always wore shoes. All children walked to and from school on the same streets.

Vietnamese children called Chinese children names like "Ba Tau" which translates to "the mud" because the average Chinese kid could speak more than one Chinese dialect and we mixed them with Viet-namese. Cantonese was spoken in social settings and Mandarin was spoken in school and business settings. Another dialect (depending on an individual's ancestral roots in China) was spoken at home. The Vietnamese children were unable to understand us. They only spoke and understood Vietnamese. They threw rocks, spat at us, and soon the fights began.

The streets were unsafe for us at all times. People were desperate and robberies were very common. You would be robbed or pick-pocketed if you carried a purse. Even when the victim yelled and screamed for help, no one dared try to rescue them. Some onlookers just watched the whole incident and even laughed at the victim's predicament. Sometimes the robbers were the police themselves. They pretended to conduct a search or investigation. Very often, the police were Vietnamese and the victims Chinese. Racism and discrimination were rampant. The Chinese in Vietnam were considered to be intruders and outsiders. They were not welcome because they had a monopoly on the businesses and pretty much ran the economy of the country. The Vietnamese government had military and political power and the Chinese people were often harassed at all levels.

It was unsafe for females, regardless of age or race, to be out alone in the streets. If we needed to go out, we always went as a group, when going to the movies for example. We never left home without carrying a safety pin for a weapon. It was especially handy when a stranger's hand groped your leg in a dark theatre. You needed to stab the hand as hard as you could without warning, or you might stab yourself. If you forgot your safety pin, you just had to pinch the hand as hard as you could. People around you would quickly notice the pain you inflicted as the groper jumped up and left. They had a good laugh and it added to the evening's entertainment.

Even old women were robbed in broad daylight. Robbers had no compunction about ripping jewelry right off of their bodies. One of my aunts forgot to take her jade bracelet off when she went to the market a few blocks away. On her way home, three men stopped her and they tried to rip the bracelet from her. She fought and yelled for help but no one came to her rescue. One of the men pounded on her jade bracelet until it broke off, and he stole the pieces. She came home with a big bruise on her hand and scratches on her body. She was very lucky the bracelet was all the pirates wanted.

CHAPTER TWO:

THE SEPARATION

During the aftermath of the Tet Offensive, it became clear to my parents that either side had a good chance of victory in the war. The publicity in America had turned the tide of public opinion against the American presence in Vietnam. Because our lives depended on the American presence, Mother and Father secretly began to make plans to leave the country as soon as possible. My two older brothers were close to draft age for military service. My parents knew that because they were Chinese, if they were drafted Joe and Henry would most likely be sent to the front lines for the duration of the war. This was the Vietnamese government's way of getting back at the rich Chinese merchant class that controlled so much of the economy … put their kids on the front lines as cannon fodder. It was little less than genocide.

Naturally, because of the pervasive racism of the Vietnamese culture and government, my parents felt no allegiance toward Vietnam. Given a choice, they would not stay and sacrifice their children for a country that had never accepted them.

Since my sister, Anna, was also near draft age, they decided to give her my birth certificate and name to make her appear younger. They gave me an arbitrary birthday, which is how I came to be nine years old

and in the third grade for three years. As a cover story, my mother gave
the school principal a handsome bribe and told him I was retarded and
had to repeat the grade. Talk about an identity crisis waiting to happen!
Even though I only progressed to the sixth grade before the communists
took over and shut down all schools, I could read and write in everyday
colloquial Vietnamese and Chinese. Although I hated school, I had an
appetite for learning languages, which I inherited from Father. He spoke
French and Japanese as well as six Chinese dialects and Vietnamese,
while I only absorbed four Chinese dialects from my family and friends,
along with Vietnamese.

An educated Chinese person can read a newspaper from any
Chinese province. Spoken Chinese language varies greatly from one
region to another, and within the various provinces many isolated
villages and cities developed their own spoken languages. The written
language, however, is universal. This universality was a natural
outgrowth of ancient traveling merchants' needs to communicate with
the various peoples they came across in order to trade with them. They
wrote in simple pictures, communicated the meaning of each picture, and
the resident people adapted those pictures to their own oral language.
Over time, the pictures became both more precise and more abstract,
blossoming into over five thousand characters in the written language
today.

My family came from a small village in southeast China, in Fujian
Province. My siblings and I were the first generation born and raised
outside that village. Our in-home spoken dialect was Fukenese (say
"Fookineze" with a long "u" sound, not a short one). In our neighborhood, the social language was Cantonese, so of course I learned that,
too. Once I started Chinese school, I learned Mandarin. I learned to read

and write Chinese characters and the Vietnamese alphabet-based language in elementary school. To make sure none of my friends could talk about me behind my back while standing in front of me, I picked up my fourth dialect, Chao-Chuo, from my best friends at school and some of our staff at home. Another motivation for learning Chao-Chuo was my sweet tooth. I charmed my best friend's grandparents, who could only speak this dialect, by learning to communicate with them. They were so pleased that I could communicate with them that they always included me when they brought treats to school during recess. The sweet sticky rice and hard candy motivated me to learn something new every day. Because I was the only kid who made the effort to speak to them, they spoke highly of me, and I was their granddaughter's favorite playmate.

I was sent to Chinese school, and my brothers and sister, in true overseas Chinese fashion, went to schools emphasizing different languages. One went to French Catholic School, and two went to Chinese/English school. The education system in Vietnam was very different from the system in the United States. Vietnam had no publicly funded schools, only private schools. All schools were privately funded directly by the students' tuition and gifts. The content of the education provided, other than language and some cultural arts differences, was dictated by government standards. All schools had to teach Vietnamese as their primary language.

My family's odds for a bright future increased because of our education in the languages and cultures of the world. This collective, rather than individual, view of the purpose of education is a big part of what has driven much of the success of Chinese families around the world. The other significant contributor is guilt. The personal responsibility for one's family name as it relates to honoring one's ancestors, as well as the responsibility to leave an honorable legacy, weighs heavily on every schoolchild's conscience and self-image.

To avoid the draft, my two older brothers left Vietnam for Hong Kong in the summer of 1970, when I was ten. My parents bribed the government with gold in exchange for my brothers' unmolested but unsanctioned exit. They walked across the border into Cambodia, where they stayed and purchased genuine Cambodian passports (through a family connection in a high government office there), and then flew to Hong Kong on temporary visas, where of course they stayed and became unofficial but welcome residents. For several days before Joe, age sixteen, and Henry, age fourteen, left Saigon; my parents filled our days with family activities. We went out for special meals together. We went to the Saigon Zoo, which was a special treat and the closest thing we had to a theme park in Vietnam. It was a very special time for the family. We took lots of pictures, which included all of us kids.

My parents tried hard to make some special memories for us. They knew our upcoming separation could be permanent. Joe and Henry might be conscripted by the armies of either North Vietnam or South Vietnam at any point in their journey. There was no assurance that the boys would reach China, much less Hong Kong. They could only offer incense in the temple, pray, bow to their ancestors to guide and protect the boys along their journey, and hope for the best. It was more desperation than faith, but the war was on and desperation was not in short supply. Faith was simply something for desperation to busy itself with while hope was still alive.

The plan was for Cousin Ho to take Henry first. He wasn't really a cousin as far as we knew, but he had our last name, so we naturally associated with each other as cousins. This was Cousin Ho's first time taking anyone across the border, and he wasn't too sure his plan would work. Not wanting to risk my parents' wrath at losing their firstborn son, Cousin Ho hedged his bets and took the second boy first. If Henry was caught, he planned to claim (to the authorities or to my parents) that he had wandered off in the jungle and was lost. If Henry successfully made it across the border, Cousin Ho would take Joe next.

Very early in the morning while we were all still asleep, Mother woke Henry. She made sure he dressed in warm clothing and fed him a good breakfast before he left the house. Only Grandmother got to say goodbye to him. Mother took him by cycle taxi to a bus stop a couple of miles toward the center of the city. She waited with Henry to meet Cousin Ho, and then watched them disappear into the crowd at the open marketplace. The marketplace in Vietnam was much like a gigantic farmers' market in the United States, but with live animals slaughtered while you wait. The American farmers' markets are ten times cleaner. It's funny that Americans eat so much meat, but their farmers' markets sell only vegetables. I've often wondered if the sheriff or some animal-rights activist would come after me if, rather than avocadoes, I brought a few live chickens to my local farmers' market and gave slaughtering demonstrations.

Cousin Ho took Henry to Tay Ninh, a small town on the border of Vietnam and Cambodia that was divided between the two countries. The government on each side opened the border once a week for merchants to exchange goods. People were free to come and go without being checked. Cousin Ho took Henry across the border on a bicycle on open-market day. After they crossed into Cambodia, Ho met his associates, left Henry with them, and returned to Vietnam. They took Henry into Phnom Penh, the capital of Cambodia, where my uncle kept him in his home while they waited for Joe.

Father had three brothers who migrated to Cambodia in 1955. Uncle Dua (big)-Be and Yi (second)-Be are father's first and second oldest brothers, and Xieo (youngest)-Jei is the youngest brother. These uncles became very successful businessmen in Cambodia. Each had five or six children.

Only three members of their clan survived the Khmer Rouge genocide. In 1993, a year before he died, Father learned that two of his sisters-in-law and one niece had survived and still lived in Cambodia. From 1975 until 1993, we had no communication with his brothers' families, and didn't know if they were alive or dead.

Many years passed before Henry told mother what really happened on the trip with Cousin Ho. He was left by himself in a shack in the Vietnamese countryside. Ho told him to stay put until he returned. Henry was alone in this run-down house all day without food or water and he was very scared. In the daytime it wasn't bad, but at night he was terrified. He heard what he imagined to be stray dogs barking, and every noise seemed like a wild animal about to come and eat him. He knew his fears were based on reality, not just imagination. He curled up in a corner and tried to make the world go away by willing himself to sleep. He was there a long time, not knowing when Cousin Ho would come to get him. Hungry, exhausted, scared, and alone, it felt like a lifetime had passed and he thought he wouldn't make it.

Finally, he heard Cousin Ho whisper his name. Another boy was with Ho, and they were going to walk across the border to Cambodia in the middle of the night. They arrived at a Cambodian marketplace just at the break of day and traveled by bus to the capital city. They met Yi-Be at another market and were taken by cycle taxi to his house. Later that evening, he walked to another cousin's house. Henry is still the only member of our family who got to meet some of our cousins in Cambodia. Cousin Ho left Henry with Yi-Be and returned to Vietnam. He left word with my father that Henry was safe, and my parents began to prepare for Joe's escape.

It was a normal day and I was playing in the yard with my two younger brothers. When I went in the house I found Grandmother crying in her room. She was busy sewing a very heavy jacket. I asked why she was crying but she didn't answer, shook her head, and continued with her sewing. I went to look for Mother in the other room. Just as I stepped out of Grandmother's room, I found Joe crying. I asked him why but he just kept on crying. I had never seen Joe cry unless he was spanked by Mother because of bad grades. It wasn't report card day. I went quickly to Mother's room and found her crying, too! I was confused and crying myself by then. I sat beside her on her bed, and between sobs she told me Joe was leaving us to go on a long trip and that both Joe and Henry were going to be gone for good. She said she was sorry she had lied to me when Henry left. He hadn't really gone to Nha Trang to visit my uncle. Now Joe would be leaving in the morning and we would not see him or Henry until we left Vietnam. I hadn't seen her cry when Henry left, but when her oldest son was about to leave, the reality hit her hard. Our long separation and uncertainty had begun.

Cousin Ho came for Joe early the next morning. The whole family stood around him in the family room, touching or hugging him but not saying a word. Cousin Ho went with my parents to their room. We couldn't hear what they were whispering. When they came out, Father put his hands on Joe's shoulder. Mother took his hands and no one said anything. She told us kids not to follow Joe and Cousin Ho out the front door. We had to say goodbye behind closed doors to avoid making the neighbors' suspicious. Joe left the house red-faced but trying to look as normal as possible.

Cousin Ho took him by bus to Tay Ninh, the same way he took Henry. Joe later described his trip to me. Cousin Ho took him on a motorcycle ride to Tay Ninh and ended up at a very rundown house. He didn't leave Joe alone in the house as he had Henry, but stayed with him in the hiding place until the next day. They walked across the border into the Cambodian market where they met my uncle Yi-Be and all went by bus to Yi-Be's house, where Henry was staying. Joe and Henry stayed at my uncle's house for about six months. Cousin Ho got them passports and fake IDs, and they bought plane tickets for Hong Kong. When they all arrived in Hong Kong, Cousin Ho excused himself to go to the restroom at the airport and none of us have heard from him since.

Mother later told us Cousin Ho's story. He came to my father for help in escaping from Vietnam. His parents were poor, and they had come to Father for loans before. Cousin Ho was at the age for con-scription into the army. He was much older than all of us kids. He was my father's distant nephew, a cousin's son technically, but he was just ten years younger. They played together when they were boys. When he told Father he needed money to escape, Father was planning to let Joe and Henry escape too, but hadn't made any plans. It worked out perfectly for them.

Mother said the gold bars they gave Cousin Ho for Joe and Henry's escape were intended for him to pay for his own escape also. He used the gold to bribe the officials for the fake IDs, passports, and plane tickets for the three of them. When they arrived in Hong Kong together, Cousin Ho would have had enough money to live on or invest in a business. When he disappeared, perhaps he had decided he could not repay his debt, thought he was getting away with a fortune in gold, or just had his own life to lead and didn't want to burden us any further.

Once they were in Hong Kong, Joe and Henry pursued their educations while the rest of us made plans to join them. Because they weren't legal residents, they lived with our uncle who was the custodian of their fortune. Mother had been mailing money, jewelry, and gold to Hong Kong for many years, and had saved a few million dollars that way. The money enabled Henry and Joe to go to school. They both learned English (Hong Kong was still a British colony at that time), and eventually one graduated from junior college and the other from the prestigious University of Hong Kong. They avoided the war and hardships we endured in Vietnam, but were treated as outsiders in Hong Kong. They were called Vietnamese, not Chinese, even though Vietnam did not accept them as Vietnamese. So they had their own identity crises as well.

Traditionally, China claimed persons of Chinese ethnicity all over the world as Chinese citizens. There are two reasonable explanations for the practice. Twenty-seven generations ago, when China was ruled as many kingdoms and not united by a central government, a king of one province was about to be taken over by an invading neighbor. Knowing he and his entire family would be killed, leaving no heirs or claimants to his throne, he devised a clever plan using an ancient poem as its basis. Each of his five sons was given a new last name from the first five words of the poem. He then sent them to be scattered throughout the whole of China and eventually the world. They carried the poem and each generation descending from the five sons maintained their rightful status as oldest to youngest children of the king by using as their middle name the next word after the first five in the poem.

For example, all the children born of the five sons would carry the middle name of whatever the sixth word of the poem was. Their children's middle names would be the seventh word in the poem, and so it went throughout the generations. Although this practice has largely been lost, it is still possible in many primarily expatriated Chinese families, to trace their lineage and status as a child of the king by simply providing a last name and a middle name, so that proper respect can be paid to one's "brothers" with the same last name who carry the word in the poem preceding their own as their middle name. Hence, a sense of identity as Chinese has been maintained by the ethnically Chinese populations throughout the world, and Chinese typically count their same surnamed cousins as big or little brothers.

Perhaps this sense of identity as Chinese also stems from a worldview that considers China the center of the world with the only "people," and views all others as "ghosts" or outsiders. The Chinese word for foreigners is literally "ghosts." It was natural for ethnically Chinese people to assume they would be treated as Chinese citizens wherever they came from. Unfortunately, this assumption and worldview clashed with the British colonial system in Hong Kong, where citizenship depended on place of birth, not ethnicity. Although we were certainly treated as second class citizens in the country we were born in, we overseas Chinese discovered that we were not Chinese in the eyes of the outside world. Joe and Henry dealt with this conflict in their daily lives in Hong Kong, but in June of 1974, as I will share later, it affected our whole family in a huge, frightening way.

One day in Hong Kong, Joe was walking down the street on the way to catch the trolley home from school when three or four, he won't say which, older teenage boys cornered him. They demanded his wallet and his shoes, and the smallest one showed Joe a knife under his jacket. Joe had studied judo in summer school, and he took a big chance. As he bent over, apparently to untie his canvas high-topped sneakers, he grabbed the closest, biggest one's jacket and dragged him down, shoving his right knee up into his assailant's nose. Then, he tripped him to the ground with his left leg, pushed his head down until it bounced on the concrete, spun around, and ran for his life. It was the only fight he had ever been in, and it was over in less than three seconds. He never knew if the word had gotten out in the neighborhood, but no one ever tried to rob him or Henry again.

Henry, on the other hand, took the path of the assailant for a while. He rose in the gangs' ranks until it was time for him to receive his tattoo. The Hong Kong gangs used teenagers in extortion schemes, street robberies, and petty theft. Like a biker's patch on his leather jacket or a Mafioso's ring, the tattoo would mean he had moved beyond the teens' jobs and had earned respect in the gang. It amounted to a license to kill and to be protected. He would be sold out to the gang and could never leave. He was seventeen and had a choice to make: become a gangster for life or stop now if he could. He approached his "big brother" about the possibility of leaving, and was surprised when the gangster told him he was free to leave. He had proven himself trustworthy enough to be let go without punishment, and he deserved a good education and a long life. Henry is proud that he never dedicated himself to the gang life by getting a tattoo, and he still walks around his house shirtless to prove it.

CHAPTER THREE:

THE CLUB

My father loved the story of the Kennedy family in America. An immigrant came with nothing to a new country and his grandchildren became the most powerful men in the nation. Father set about to build his own Camelot.

Father was willing to do nearly whatever it took to become rich and powerful but, in contrast to some powerful men, he was too kind to take advantage of people or allow himself to harm others along his way. He ultimately succeeded in becoming rich, but never really had any power. He aligned himself too closely with two partners who had the real control over his business affairs. Although they made him rich, in the end his riches were fleeting and he did not have the power to protect himself or his family from the outside world or assure his children's futures.

Father's Partner Number One was a businessman from Singapore. He came to Vietnam occasionally to do business and monitor his investments. South Vietnam was ripe for investment at that time due to many foreign companies setting up factories and utilizing the natural resources of the land, all under the protection of an American military presence. Partner Number One was not a Vietnamese resident, so he could not be the face of the business.

Partner Number Two was also an overseas Chinese businessman, but was involved in many illegitimate, underworld, mafia-type businesses. He had known my father since they were teenage prisoners of the Japanese during World War II. My father had decided to stay out of the gang life, and Partner Number Two felt he needed protection from the big, mean world, so he joined a Chinese gang and used his gang connections to climb the business-world ladder. He wanted to use his profits to invest in a legitimate business, so he joined with Partner Number One and looked for business opportunities. Partner Number Two needed to keep his interest in the business confidential to protect it from his enemies.

My father was a natural socialite and knew many influential people because of his work as a French physician's assistant. As patients waited for the doctor, Father struck up conversations and made friends with them in their native tongues. He spoke several dialects of Chinese, Vietnamese, Japanese, and French, and wanted to learn more. He eventually learned English and quite a bit of Spanish. After the French doctor fled the country in 1959 due to the burgeoning communist conflict, Father was out of work. He made his living as a door-to-door physician's assistant in poor neighborhoods, providing immunizations, first aid, suturing, and wound care. Often he was paid in rice, chickens, or pot-bellied pigs. Mother became a seamstress and had a steady but meager income. Father's growing family didn't always have enough attention or food to eat. When an old friend called on him in 1965 to use his social skills running a world-class restaurant and nightclub, it was the opportunity of a lifetime.

The site Father found for the restaurant took advantage of the American presence perfectly. Saigon's international airport had become a U.S. Air Force base. The club-to-be was a French-style home on three acres, surrounded by a high brick wall but adjacent on three sides to airport property. Open fields lay across the public highway. It was far away from the dangers of the city and protected by the U.S. military at its gates and borders. Father was able to negotiate with the Americans for use of the building. Outsiders would arrive at the front gate by invitation only, and be checked by armed South Vietnamese and U.S. Military Police. Personnel from the base, having already been checked at a base gate, could come in through a side entrance.

The restaurant's setting was classic French colonial. A long drive-way led past lush lawns from the front gate through a columned entry portico at the main building and circled back around two flowering Plumeria trees. Across from the front porch, past the entry portico, trees, and lawn, and across the returning driveway, stood an old military fighter jet airplane on a concrete pedestal.

Inside the main entrance to the restaurant, Father put slot machines around the huge lobby. Off to the right behind high doors was a saloon with a long, dark wooden bar. The two team kitchen and offices were to the left of the lobby. A wide, winding staircase next to the kitchen led to the second floor. Beyond the stairs on the second floor overlooking the lobby, large meeting rooms lined the front and right sides of the house. In the back was a huge nightclub room for entertaining, with a grand piano on the stage, a dance floor, and many tables. Downstairs, in back of the lobby, was another large eating room, divided with moveable planter boxes. On one side were round tables for Chinese cuisine and on the other were square tables for French dining.

Toward the rear of the property lay several buildings containing a massage and steam parlor, recreational room with Ping-Pong, pool, and foosball tables, and staff dormitories. Goats and ducks milled about a barn and corral in back of these buildings. Our three German Shepherds and two English Bulldogs had the run of the entire grounds. Outside the high brick perimeter walls, Military Police and trained guard dogs patrolled constantly. It was truly an oasis and a diplomatic showplace, with no visual hint of the war outside after entrance through the gates.

In the early seventies, as the war dragged on and the American presence was more and more unpredictable as to whether it would be possible to continue to repel the communist forces knocking at our door, the South Vietnamese government officials became increasingly corrupt in an attempt at self-preservation at any cost. The administration felt threatened by the communists, the anti-war Americans, and the Chinese within their borders. The Chinese among them would potentially have a very great influence on the governance of the country if North Viet-namese communists won the war and allied their new government with the mainland communist Chinese government. The Vietnamese did not realize most of the Chinese in South Vietnam had fled communism themselves and would not have aligned themselves with the communists no matter what ethnicity or language they had in common.

To keep the business running smoothly and maintain the delicate balance between the Americans, Vietnamese, and his own economic interests, my father had to please many military officers and government bureaucrats. For example, the restaurant had two big delivery trucks which were used to pick up groceries. When officials asked my father to borrow a truck for whatever purpose, he had to consent. Sometimes administrative personnel or officers wanted to hold meetings in the restaurant at Father's expense. The restaurant had to pay for their drinks and food and turn away potential customers during these meetings. At times government workers came to the restaurant for lunch and expected to eat without charge. My father had to capitulate in order to maintain a good reputation. During holidays, he offered presents to the military and government officials to stay in good standing with the government. He was an expert at determining just how much he had to give in order to garner favor or avoid the harm that any particular official could do to his family or business. He never appeared to be begging, although of course that was exactly what he was doing.

While Father managed the restaurant business, he came home late at night with a very strong smell on his breath. He had never particularly enjoyed drinking, but government officials often expected him to drink with them. He learned all he could about fine French wines and liquor so he could stock the best available, sparing no expense for his important guests.

I remember watching Mother take care of Father when he came home drunk. He sang songs, played his harmonica, and insisted that Mother join him. His favorite tune was "There's No Place like Home". He was a good harmonica player. He taught himself to play to entertain and console himself after he left home at the age of fifteen. The harmonica didn't take up much room in his pocket, so it was easy to have music as he traveled. Many nights, we were awakened and herded out of our rooms to listen to Father and Mother sing and play. He was a very gentle man when he smelled of alcohol, not mean and cruel like some are. Mother usually went along with his melancholy because she could get him to see the logic in and agree to just about anything she suggested or asked of him. Many of his better decisions were made when he was drunk, with her whispering in his ear. He could not refuse her requests because of his love for her, and he was too intoxicated to think clearly enough to argue with her.

Because Father owed his livelihood to his partners, he never questioned their requests. Partner Number Two, the gangster, often asked Father for favors. Father figured that if he didn't ask too many questions, he wouldn't be asked to answer many. So, in 1971 when Partner Number Two asked Father to be a tour guide for his mistress, who was coming from France for a visit, he didn't ask any questions. Because he spoke fluent French, he enjoyed the chance to exercise his linguistic skills and cheerfully hosted her during her stay. He showed her the beautiful beach towns and Little Paris nightlife. He didn't ask why she was visiting Partner Number Two.

While Father showed the French lady around, Partner Number Two borrowed one of the restaurant's vans and went to the airport. Because of the symbiotic relationship between the restaurant and the American military, Father's vans had no problems moving around the airport grounds or between the airport and the city. On the last full day of the French lady's visit, Father took her to dinner on a big boat in the bay, a version of the "Jumbo" boat still famously visible in Hong Kong's harbor. The staff took photographs to commemorate the event. Father took the French lady back to the airport the next afternoon.

After she had been gone for two days, the police came to see my father. They requested to "ask a few questions downtown." They showed him the picture that was taken with the French lady on the bay. Because he was willing to cooperate, and probably too because he bribed them well enough with his best liquor, the police let him stay at home so that he could come into the station on his own the next day. He had done nothing wrong, and he had nothing to hide. That evening, Partner Number Two called Father and told him not to worry because he didn't know any answers to the detectives' questions anyway, so to go ahead downtown in the morning. If the police wanted to keep him, Partner Number Two would have him bailed out.

Predictably, we never heard from Partner Number Two again. Even though Father didn't know the answers to the questions, after he went downtown he wasn't released or bailed out. No one dared step forward and vouch for him. Partner Number One came to Vietnam immediately when he heard Father was being held by the police. Through staff, Mother requested to see Partner Number One. By now, the police were following her very closely. They figured she probably knew nothing, but had to do their jobs. At the same time, Mother had been paying attention all those years. She paid the police to keep their mouths shut. Partner Number One and Partner Number Two had relatives working in the restaurant. When Father was arrested, none of them would look her in the eye. They knew he was in trouble for the smuggling they had done and were afraid the police or informants would see her with them and start asking questions.

Partner Number One secretly met with Mother in a café in Saigon to talk about Father's predicament and the need for the restaurant to continue under new management. As they sipped espresso with sweetened condensed milk over ice, a Vietnamese favorite, he told Mother to find a replacement manager. He probably figured that the ship was sinking anyway, that his investment was lost, and so he told her he didn't care whom she chose to manage the business. Since Partner Number Two had disappeared, he gave Mother the authority to make whatever arrangements she thought best. He knew she was illiterate, and wouldn't be a problem. "You have full authority to choose a successor," he told Mother. She was in charge of picking the man who would take her husband's job.

Mother's chauffeur drove her Mercedes sedan slowly, winding through town and back to the restaurant. Mother had learned to drive to oversee trips to the market to purchase groceries for the restaurant, but it was more convenient to have someone look after the car as she met Partner Number One in the café. A woman driving any car alone in Saigon would have made a fine target for a thief or a terrorist. If left unattended in the part of the city where their meeting took place, the Mercedes could have been stolen, vandalized, or even burned.

Mother was lost in thought as she rode back to the compound. She had become more independent since Father began managing the restaurant. She knew good merchandise by sight at the market, what ingredients went into the Chinese and French dishes, and how they were supposed to taste when prepared properly. Her father had been an accountant in China. Even though she couldn't read, she could count and keep records and information straight in her head. She knew that once she picked a successor, she would be out on the street with four dependent children and no provider. The jail tended to have a one-way door in from the street, and there might as well have been a graveyard in the back. It wasn't likely her husband would ever leave prison. As she rode, the gravity of the situation weighed on her. If Father was to get out alive, it would take a great deal of money to pay for his care while he was in jail, and to assure he received a fair trial resulting in acquittal.

The justice system in Vietnam was not like that in the United States. The U.S. system appoints an attorney for criminal defendants who can't afford to pay one. In Vietnam, in order to get Father out of jail and declare him innocent, she would have to hire an attorney and bribe the judge to influence the trial. She would need to pay for a private jail cell, pay the guards to treat him well, and pay off all the police, witnesses, and officials and clerks who handled the trial. She would also need to feed the family, including her foot-bound, crippled mother-in-law, four of her six children, and our nannies. She had to come up with a plan quickly, because it would take more than *three times* her former income to get them through the trial.

Back at the restaurant, both partners' loyal staffs were dying to know about Mother's meeting with Partner Number One. "Don't worry," she told the assembled staff, "the business will continue, but the management will change. Partner Number One has given full authority *to me*."

CHAPTER FOUR:
MOTHER TAKES CONTROL

I wonder which was worse for the staff ... total accountability for every penny received in each department of the business, or having a woman as boss. There was little to be done to change the situation in any event. If they left the safety of the restaurant's employment, they would likely be drafted and sent to the front lines of the war. The South Vietnamese army couldn't come to the restaurant looking for draftees because they would lose face with the Americans. Besides, they didn't have permission to enter the gates. So the staff reluctantly stayed and submitted to Mother's new rules. Prostitution had been a problem at the restaurant. Partner Number Two's relatives pimped out the massage parlor girls and waitresses and took a cut of their earnings. Some girls participated willingly, but others were forced or had no choice in order to provide for their families, whose fathers, husbands, brothers, sons, and even daughters were off fighting the war or had already been killed.

Mother decided that Partner Number Two was in hiding and dared not show his face after betraying Father, so he wouldn't mind a few changes at the restaurant. One by one, she fired all his relatives very nicely, giving them severance pay and job prospects elsewhere, or bought mechanics' jobs for them if they wanted to go into the military. She told the female staff they were free to hook themselves out if they wanted to and keep all their earnings, but she would not force them to participate or be part of their activities. She told them they would have to arrange their liaisons elsewhere, because she had children on the property. Of course, everyone on the outside thought she was the new madam, and rumors spread like wildfire.

The first obstacle to Mother's leadership was that she could neither read nor write fluently in either Vietnamese or Chinese, and she spoke no French. As a female, she had never been given the opportunity to obtain a proper education. She could not possibly manage the restaurant without help.

When Mother was growing up in Hai Phong, a primarily Chinese suburb of Hanoi in northern Vietnam, foot-binding had gone out of fashion, but the old attitudes about women's role in society had changed little. After all, if a girl would only grow up to be a wife and mother, what use did she have for an expensive education? Better to get some use out of her labor while she was still obligated to her parents and not yet married to her assigned husband.

Arranged marriages were the norm back then. Parents were often contractually obligated to give their children in marriage according to arrangements made while the children were still toddlers. Fortunately, Mother's father was open-minded enough to allow her to marry Father when they fell in love. After all, Mother and Father had been born in the same village in Fujian Province, China, and the families knew each other, so it was deemed an acceptable union.

Even though they were such a progressive family for their time, when Mother was eight years old, her father hung her by her wrists from the front porch rafters and beat her within an inch of her life when she was caught sneaking away from her chores and listening outside the schoolhouse window, trying to learn something. She stubbornly persisted in hanging around the school.

Some Catholic nuns came to town and opened a school in Mother's neighborhood when she was sixteen. Mother pleaded with her father to let her finish all her chores before and after school so that she could attend. Eventually, he relented and allowed her to sit inside the schoolhouse. She absorbed enough over the next few years to be able to read and write at the third grade level. She still couldn't make sense of a newspaper article, but the little Chinese she learned allowed her much more independence than she would have had otherwise. When she was eighteen, she met Father, who was twenty-six, at a friend's house and they were married nearly two years later by choice, not by arrangement or necessity.

Now that she had full authority, Mother decided to promote to her management team only staff members who were not related to either Partner Number One or Partner Number Two. The right hand man she chose was able to read and write in both Vietnamese and Chinese, and he had the skill of bookkeeping. He developed this skill because none of the relatives of Partner Number One or Partner Number Two wanted to do paperwork at a desk (they would be responsible for actually accomplishing something on a daily basis if they did that), and he got the job no one else wanted. He was known only as the office clerk while Father managed the restaurant, but he actually did all the bookkeeping and knew the finances of the business better than Father did.

Mother knew his good work habits from working in the kitchen, and knew he was neither a gambler nor a drinker. She could rely on him to be loyal. Her chosen left-hand man was the head of the custodial staff. He, too, was not related to either partner, and had a job that required labor and responsibility. Mother learned that he was very knowledgeable and skillful in the kitchen and was also fluent in French. She hired his wife to replace him as head custodian. The kitchen had two prep areas and two chef teams, Chinese and French. She took charge of the Chinese team and put the left-hand man in charge of the French team.

Mother decreed that all sales in every department must be reported to the management office within an hour of closing. The practice among the partners' relatives had been to report sales the next morning, after they had a chance to cook the books and pocket whatever they felt entitled to. This caused hard feelings and, as they began to complain, Mother had the excuses she needed to get rid of them. She promoted the people actually doing the work, and paid them the high wages their former supervisors had been paying themselves. Now she had a workforce loyal to her alone.

Rumors flew about the two men spending so much time with Mother, especially the right-hand man. But he taught her how to keep and audit the books and they took in the receipts personally after closing time (3:00 a.m.) every night. Except for the right-hand man, none of the employees knew that Mother could not read or write.

The South Vietnamese government wanted to keep Father in jail in order to prevent a scandal involving the highest levels of the government. When the shipment of black market goods and cash was picked up by the Vietnamese Air Force and the staff of Partner Number Two in Father's van, there was to have been a split of a percentage of the goods between the staffs of both sides. Apparently, one side tried to stiff the other, and someone decided to blow the whistle. No one knew that the shipment had been arranged at the highest level. When the story broke to the public, the government couldn't cover it up, so they had to charge someone.

My father was the perfect choice, because he wouldn't know what to tell and what not to tell. He spent time with the French lady who was on the plane that delivered the shipment. The government officials' involvement in illegal activities wouldn't be exposed to the public. It was the best possible outcome for all parties concerned. Even the judge who tried my father's case knew he was innocent, but he had nothing to lose in trying the case because Mother paid him big money. He also looked good to the government officials, because he was trying "the right man" for the crime.

While Father was in jail, he lived like a king. He made friends playing cards and drinking fine liquor with the guards. He had a private cell, and every three months he got to make a new set of friends. The staff of the jail, the prosecuting attorneys, even the judge and his staff would change so that a new set of officials would get the benefit of Mother's generosity.

Upon hearing that Mother had put herself in charge instead of hiring a manager, Partner Number One was furious. He gave up the business for lost, certain that she would fail. After all, the business now had a cloud of illegitimacy around it because of Father's arrest and Partner Number Two's disappearance. He never came back to Vietnam due to the instability caused by the war. He told his staff to leave Mother alone and gave her his portion of the partnership.

Partner Number Two was nowhere to be found. He was still in Vietnam, but he was not able to reveal his identity. By default, he also lost his partnership share to Mother. As she righted the sinking ship, the money which had been going out the back door ended up in her pocket instead. The business and our fortune flourished. Whatever cash wasn't needed to support Father, she hid. Even some of Father's own relatives and siblings became jealous of Mother's success. They spread rumors about her affair with the right-hand man, but my grandmother was my mother's biggest fan. She scolded the relatives for their gossiping and told them the proof of who was in the right was shown by the results. Mother was being blessed.

CHAPTER FIVE:
FATHER TAKES A LONG TRIP

For a year, Mother spent most of her money on Father's support, and what wasn't needed for that purpose was saved. By the time Chinese New Year of 1972 came, Mother had enough savings to bribe the guards to let Father out of jail to spend New Year's Eve with his family. Each guard on duty that night received five years' salary, because Mother knew they would not have jobs to come back to. She reserved a very fancy restaurant in Saigon for our private New Year's Eve dinner. For the past year, we had been told that Father was on a business trip out of the country, but she told us that night he was back briefly and would meet us for a special dinner. After that we might not see him again for a long time as he was a very busy man.

Dinner at the restaurant with him was very exciting. There were three adults' tables set together, and one big kids' table. When we arrived at the restaurant, Father had not yet arrived, but Grandmother and all my aunts, uncles, and cousins were there. No one among us except Mother knew the plan.

When Father finally came into the room, he wore a new tailored suit and was accompanied by a few well-dressed strangers. Mother arranged for them to sit at a table far from the family. She told us they were Father's assistants. One by one, as the meal progressed, they left to use the restroom or to step outside for a cigarette. By the end of the meal, the jailers were all gone, with five years' wages in their pockets. After hugging and kissing us all goodbye, and telling us kids to be good, Father left the restaurant alone.

Mother had arranged his safe passage out of the country. He and a couple of his "assistants" rode Vespas to the harbor and he was hidden inside a cargo container. The next morning, he was picked up by a Panamanian cargo ship headed for Hong Kong. After several days without food or provisions other than what he had with him when he got into the container, he was transferred to a small boat, which took him into Hong Kong Harbor. He changed into a fisherman's coveralls and walked off the boat with the crew. It was still New Year's holiday when he arrived in his dirty tailored suit at the front door of his brother-in-law's palatial home in Hong Kong and was reunited with Joe and Henry.

During all the time Father was in jail, Mother never let us kids know about it. Whenever we asked where he was, she always answered: "He is very busy, he is in Hong Kong on business" … or "Taiwan" … or "Malaysia" … or "Singapore." Her biggest support was her mother-in-law. When Mother came home to be with us during the day, Grandmother always told us not to bother her. She would say, "Let your mother rest! She works hard and is tired!" She would have Chi-Cam cook Mother special herb soup. After Chi-Hoa had gotten married, Chi-Cam came to work for us as our housekeeper and cook.

The business schedule in Vietnam was similar to the border towns in Mexico. Everything opened as early as sunrise, closed by noon, and reopened at 2:00 p.m. Business and residence were often in one house, the front for the business and the back for living quarters. Some had the business downstairs and the residence upstairs. During the lunch hour, the doors closed and people returned to their residence until 2:00 p.m. Shops, offices, and schools were closed for lunch.

Students started school at 7:30 a.m. We went home for lunch at noon and took a nap until 2:00 p.m. We left the house for school by 2:00 p.m. and started classes by 2:30 p.m. School ended at 6:00 p.m. and we were home by 6:30 p.m. When Father was in jail, Mother came home to have lunch with us no matter how busy her schedule was. I remember she was always very tired, but she managed to smile. She seemed to look forward to taking a nap with us after lunch. Sometimes we saw tears in her eyes when my younger brothers asked about Father. She would tell us that her eyes were watery due to being too tired.

After Father made it to Hong Kong, Mother told us: "Your father is staying with Joe and Henry. He is not coming back, but someday we will join them. Don't tell anyone; this is our secret! If people ask where your father is, you don't know!" Mother continued to manage the business, and when people asked where Father was, she always answered that she didn't know. After a while, she told people that Father left her. During those days, divorce was not very common. Men in general still had as many wives and mistresses as they could support. Father purposely had no contact with Mother, so she could stay away from the public eye and not arouse the suspicions of the local government officials. People believed the rumors about her affair with the right-hand man, and the rumor kept her from being harassed by the government.

People talked more and more about Mother making Father wear a "green hat" and that he abandoned her. In our little corner of Chinese culture, no man wore a green hat. It meant your wife was an adulteress.

It's a big insult to the family name and his manhood. People were jealous of Mother's success, and this became her worst enemy. They added more flavor to the rumors, and all the relatives came to Grandmother with their objections and complaints, which fell on deaf ears.

We used to have lots of visitors when Father was home, but the house became more and more quiet and empty. I got in frequent fights with the neighborhood kids.

I made a habit of going to the Christian Church down the block from my house with my best friend. Father and Grandmother always told me not to believe what I heard there. They believed that Christianity was not our religion. We were born to Buddhism for many generations, structured by Confucianism, and mystified by Taoism, which sees every man, every thought, and every action as *significant* – a small piece of a larger outcome. We believe in the afterlife and in reincarnation. Every living creature can be a god. Humans, and all life forms such as animals, can become gods in their next lives as long as they do good deeds, do not kill, and do not eat other creatures. There are gods for light, fire, earth, water, and wind. Christianity belongs to foreigners.

I didn't understand a lot of what I heard at the church, but I enjoyed the singing and being with my friend.

I was overweight and very boyish in comparison to other girls. There was no grace or beauty in my behavior nor my appearance. I was a hyperactive child and my behavior did not reflect how a lady should behave. People considered me unattractive and kids in the neighborhood didn't want to be my friend. I often had to fight with boys to be included in their games. Girls didn't want to play with me because I was too boyish and clumsy. I handled their toys very roughly and would break them. They thought I was too fat and loud to be a girl and boys thought I was too ugly to be a boy.

I did have two friends to play with at home and at school. Both of them had the same last name, Wong, and both their first names were Wei. Only their middle names were different. Wong-Kim-Wei was my friend at home. Wong-Xiao-Wei was my friend from school. They didn't know each other, but they were both Christians and their families came from the same province of China. Protestant Christianity in Vietnam was not popular and was not well known in comparison to Buddhism and Catholicism.

Wong-Kim-Wei's family did not like me, but she accepted me. She was the only girl in her family and had seven brothers. Wong-Xiao-Wei's grandparents loved me. They took turns coming to school during break time to bring a snack to Xiao-Wei. They always brought extra for her to share with me. Xiao-Wei had ten siblings so I had a hard time keeping track of their names. I only got along with two of her younger brothers. They were my classmates during my second and third times in third grade.

The rumors about mother's affair brought out the worst in me. I got in a fight with kids at the church one Sunday because they were saying Mother was a bad woman and I was an unclean child. I remember that day well. I went to church with Kim-Wei. We were walking upstairs for class and one of the girls came downstairs and blocked my way. She said very loudly to everybody, "Look! Here is an unclean child in our church. Her mother is a bad woman. She steals other women's husbands and leaves their kids with no daddy! She let her own husband wear a green hat and he left her for good!" At first, I thought she was talking to someone else. I ignored her and didn't hear what she was saying. As I walked past her and kept going upstairs, I realized all eyes were on me.

She repeated what she had said. I heard her the second time and realized what she said was directed to me. I told her to take it back or else.

Kim-Wei knew I could hurt the girl, because she had seen me fighting with boys. She grabbed my hand, started to tug me back down the stairs, and told me not to say anything. She wanted me to talk to the pastor. But this girl would not stop talking. She talked in a louder voice to get more attention. I didn't hear what she said by this point, but I heard the people around me laughing. I brushed away Kim-Wei's hand, took one big step down toward the girl, and gave her a hard punch in the face. She fell down the stairs and tore her dress. Everyone on the stairway was screaming. I ran away from the crowd, turned back, and yelled at them with all my strength, "I will never come back to church. You are not my friends ever!" As I turned to run toward the front gate, I almost ran into someone. It was Kim-Wei trying to stop me. She had tears in her eyes. I gave her one last angry, hard look and ran around her. That was the end of our friendship.

I never told Mother what happened at church, but I told my grandmother that church days were over for me. I said, "I never understood what I learned at church any way." I didn't tell her I got in a fight because I would have been in deep trouble with her for fighting. I may not have learned a lot in my church-going days, but I remembered one prayer and three songs in Chinese. The prayer was from Matthew: "Our father in heaven may your holy name be honored. May your kingdom come on earth as it is in heaven. Give us today the food we need. Forgive us the wrongs that we have done, as we forgive the wrongs that others have done to us. Do not bring us to hard testing, but keep us safe from the evil one." The three songs were "Jesus Loves Me", "Jesus Loves the Little Children", and "Silent Night". I didn't understand the meaning or depth of this prayer or the simple songs, but somehow the words stuck with me and are still deep in my memory.

Grandmother had been taking me to the Buddhist temple since I was six years old. She dedicated me into the service of the monks when I was seven. When she heard that I was not going to church anymore, she did not push the issue. She didn't care whether I went to church or not. She knew I was lonely when my friends went to church and let me go because she knew I just wanted to be with them and wasn't interested in their religion.

CHAPTER SIX:
LIFE AT THE CLUB

Shortly after Father left for Hong Kong, Mother decided to down-size our household. She discussed with Grandmother that she needed to sell the house and move us kids to live full-time in the back of the restaurant's compound. Chi-Cam would live with us and keep an eye on us. We would be close to Mother and away from the neighborhood gossip and rumors. Grandmother agreed and moved back to live with my uncle in Nha Trang, where we visited her during school breaks. It was an eight-hour ride on a public bus from Saigon to Nha Trang and a six-hour drive for our chauffeur.

Mother had her carpenter build a residence on the back of the restaurant. The apartment had its own entrance, facing the back of the open field where the airport runways were. The restaurant's entrance was far away from us. When we first moved, she told me not to play in front of the restaurant. She said I had all the land in back of the restaurant to run and play in and I could use the back kitchen stairs to go up to her office. She slept in her office, which was located in the back of the nightclub. I wasn't allowed to wander around the restaurant inside or outside. If I needed to see Mother, I could ask one of the servants to walk me upstairs to her room.

The mansion was located on the right side driving in from the gate and was straight across from the airplane. The entrance had a covered portico so cars could drive up next to the front door. Walking up to it, there were four or five steps at the center and two big white Plumeria trees on each side. The Plumeria trees have thick, strong bark and their flowers are very beautiful and have a strong tropical fragrance. My brothers and I would grab hold of the bark and hang from the tree. We found all kinds and sizes of lizards in these two trees.

The front entrance opened to a large lobby with a high ceiling and a big open area. There were slot machines facing the entrance. The floor had big black and white square tiles and there was a beautiful, massive chandelier hanging from the ceiling. In the back on the left side was a long, curved staircase. On the right was the entrance to the bar. As I recall, the bar was a very dark room with a strong cigarette smell that drifted out of the room when the door swung open.

Walking toward the long curved stairs, I could see the entry to the dining room. The tables were set up in sections. One side had a French style setting and the other side a Chinese motif. The tables on the French side were set with knives, forks, and spoons. Those with Chinese decor were set up with chopsticks and bowls. The color scheme was white and red: West met east. I could see the stairway when walking out of the dining room. The stairs were covered with very thick, red carpet with gold trim tassels on the side. I pretended I was a queen when I went up or down the steps, waving at the crowd of people I imagined standing below in the lobby.

There were five doors on the landing at the top of the stairs. Be-hind four of them were conference rooms. Behind the far left door was a spacious ballroom/night club which had a red and black designed carpet and a grand piano on the stage. The center of the stage was a wooden floor the servants always cleaned with wax during the day. One of them told me that guests danced there at night. She said if they didn't clean it during the day, the manager would be mad because the floor had to be smooth and shiny for dancing. The whole room was very grand and had a high ceiling. All the windows around the room had heavy red curtains, and the center stage was decorated with long black curtains.

Behind the black curtains was a room that controlled the lights and sound. Next to it was a small counter. The servants told me it was a small bar where guests got drinks. There was a short hallway in back of the room and counter which connected to my mother's office, and a stairway that went down to the kitchen. Next to the stairway was a dumbwaiter. The servants explained that the chefs used the dumbwaiter to send food up and down. The stairway had a straight pole and the steps circled around the pole. My brother and I played on the dumbwaiter and the stairs. We went up around the stairway and came down in the dumbwaiter, or the other way around. Mother spanked us whenever she had heard us in the hallway. About two hundred feet across from the restaurant was another building that had a steam room, massage room, and game room. The game room had pool tables and Ping-Pong tables. We were not allowed to play in this area during business hours. To the left of this building was a wine cellar that faced the kitchen. Next to the warehouse was a garage and workshop.

We were not the only children living in the back of the restaurant. There was a family living on the other side of the property, the family of the captain of the guard. They were permitted to live there because he had to be available at all times. He had four children, and his oldest daughter and I were the same age. Her name was Thuy and we became playmates on the property. I still saw my friend Xiao-Wei at school, but I no longer saw Kim-Wei.

The field behind the restaurant was an excellent place to explore. I was always occupied and entertained by all the natural resources in the backyard. I loved to catch grasshoppers and crickets. There were many different plants and wildflowers, each with its own unique smell. One of my favorite grasses was called "shy fern." When touched, it closes its leaves and reopens seconds later if left alone. It grew wild all over the open field, and I could play with it for hours and never get bored.

Life in back of the restaurant was like living on a farm. There were goats, ducks, rabbits, cats, and dogs. Before father left Vietnam, we had German Shepherds. Thuy's English bulldog had puppies shortly after we settled down in our new apartment, and she gave us one of the puppies. Our mama duck also had eight little babies. One day when we came home from school, we noticed that our puppy's stomach was really big. He couldn't move and looked very sick. When a baby duck walked past him, he got up and tried to eat it. He got the whole baby duck in his mouth. We took the baby duck away from him and took him to the doctor. The doctor did an x-ray and told us he had swallowed a baby duck. He said he couldn't do anything for him and sent him home. He was very sick for two days and then died. He was only a little bigger than the duckling he ate. To this day we still call English Bulldogs "duck-dogs."

We had servants who took care of our animals. One of the teenage servants always smelled like the goats. Chi-Cam said he ate and slept with them. His parents were killed during the Tet Offensive and his uncle was one of the chefs. Mother gave him the job of taking care of the goats, so he would have a place to live and be close to his uncle. He ate his meals after the staff in the restaurant kitchen.

The back left side of the restaurant held the employees' quarters. It was like an apartment with individual rooms inside, but the outside of the building looked like a greenhouse for the restaurant. All the night-shift employees had their own rooms because they were not able to go home after closing time due to the curfew. They had to clean up and prepare for the next day. The others slept dormitory style, with male and female quarters.

My favorite thing about living in the restaurant was the food. Our restaurant was known for its steak, and to this day Vietnam veterans I meet tell me they had the best steak of their lives at our restaurant. I know my father made a good steak, but I am sure it seemed a lot better after fighting in the jungle for weeks or months before the fine meal. When we lived in Cho-Lon, Father used to bring us to the restaurant for meals on special occasions as a treat. We learned how to use a fork and knife and European place-settings when we ate French food. But living in the same building, Chi-Cam sometimes brought food to us from the restaurant. Mother joined us for meals and then returned to her office to work. It was there I discovered my favorite dessert.

One day, Thuy and her three younger siblings, my two younger brothers, Stanley and Ken, and I were playing soccer in the field. I noticed a wonderful smell coming from the kitchen. Although the restaurant breathed out tantalizing smells every day, this particular smell was very tempting and pleasing to my senses. I couldn't resist it. It was different from the daily smells I was used to. It smelled like eggs and vanilla and sugar, but not cake. We stopped playing. Thuy told me there must be a big party that night in the restaurant. She said, "I notice every time the restaurant has special guests or a big party, it always smells very good, just like now." I told her, "Let's go see what the smell is." She tried to stop me because she never went near the restaurant. Her parents would not allow it. I told her, "It's okay. My mother is the boss and no one can do anything to me." I had her back. After all, didn't she want to know what that smell was?

Before we got to the restaurant, Thuy backed out and kept her younger siblings from following me. I told her I would come back after I found out what was going on in the kitchen. Stanley and Ken decided to stay with Thuy. I went in the back door of the kitchen where the stairs were and told one of the servants I needed to go upstairs to see my mother. I noticed the chefs on the French team were very busy. When the servant came back to let me know Mother was waiting for me, I told her that since she was very busy with her work, I could walk myself out after talking with Mother so she wouldn't have to come and get me. I went up to Mother's room and came right back down the stairs after stopping in for a hug and a smile. I saw custard cream puffs that had just come out of the oven and I knew the smell was from them. I still can smell it. It was heavenly good; the duck eggs and vanilla called my name.

I couldn't resist the smell or the temptation. I took as many as I could carry in my folded up shirt and ran out of the kitchen. The French chef noticed some were missing, which meant he would have to make more. He was mad, and he screamed and yelled in French. The cream puffs were hot in my hands and my mouth as I ran as fast as I could out of the kitchen. I took only enough to share with Thuy and the rest of the siblings. Of course, Mother heard about it, and later I got a spanking. Would it stop me? No. Some of the peace talks between the northern and southern governments took place in my parent's restaurant and each was just another party for me, another opportunity for cream puffs.

I remember hearing the story about Jane Fonda and her visit to North Vietnam. The word in Saigon was that she betrayed the American and South Vietnamese governments. The TV showed her wearing the North Vietnamese uniform and smiling with the North's soldiers while she stood next to big guns. She laughed and smiled and shook hands with them. I didn't know her name, but I recognized her face years later when she made an exercise video all my junior college friends raved over. Her picture was all over the Saigon news and the politicians spoke of their disappointment with her visit. The Vietnamese government criticized the American government, claiming they betrayed us and their support was simply a means to exploit us for financial gain. They said the Americans were two-faced.

Fear that the Americans might not be on our side after all caused chaos throughout the entire country. News about it increased roadside bombing and bombing in the open market, and suicidal war protestors filled the news reports. I remember a report about a monk who set himself on fire in front of the American embassy to protest the war, not wanting the Americans in our country. For months, we heard about these demonstrations. Slowly the media tired of reporting the rumors, but they continued, nonetheless, by word of mouth. It was a very confusing time; no one knew who was friend or foe.

I thought Jane Fonda must be some kind of American princess because the media made such a big deal out of her visit. Her appearance stirred up so much confusion and violence. How could one skinny young woman cause so much unrest? It even became unsafe for us children to go out without an adult present. We could no longer go to the open market, movie theater, park, zoo, or even church or temple without fear. I began to question whether I was on the side of the good guys or the bad guys. After all, this "American Princess" had visited only the North, not the South. Hadn't the North invaded us? My neighbors were the ones who were being bombed and killed. It was my family who had to go into hiding for months to survive. Didn't we fight alongside the American soldiers? What happened to that friendship?

At Christmastime, I remember seeing Bob Hope and Sammy Davis, Jr. on TV. I didn't know who they were at the time, I only knew they were very important people and I recognized them from seeing them at the restaurant. Mother was always very busy when special events were about to happen. I could tell when someone special was coming because the French chef would be very busy making his signature dessert, the custard cream puffs. I never missed the chance to steal them. We could smell them baking from anywhere in the compound, even before they came out of the ovens.

Mother had always forbidden me to play close to the front gate or the kitchen doors, but the thought of those custard cream puffs was such a strong temptation that I gladly risked the threat of a spanking in order to get them. After the chef realized why his special desserts were not counting up correctly, he would leave out a few imperfect ones for me to steal. Then, any time he saw me, he would pretend to put up a big fuss to scare me away. After sneaking off with pockets full of imperfect cream puffs, I would safely hide in the airplane to enjoy my stolen treasures. Often, because I had refused to share my bounty, my younger brothers or nanny would tell on me, and I endured the dreaded cane-switch spankings I deserved.

CHAPTER SEVEN:

THE LIGHTS OF HONG KONG

After Father successfully arrived in Hong Kong, Mother continued to manage the business. At the same time, she planned for our escape. Since she was still under suspicion of the South Vietnamese government, she couldn't close the business and buy plane tickets for all of us to go to Hong Kong. She had to move strategically. Also, she had to consider the welfare of more than a hundred employees who had worked for our family for many years.

With the help of the Air Force base, she was able to close the business in February, 1974. She told everyone my father had disappeared and left her with the burden of running the restaurant, and it proved to be too much for her. She had decided to divorce him and retire. She sold everything in the restaurant, even the dishes, linens, and gambling tables. She paid all the employees six months' severance pay. She arranged for a small "vacation" after the business closed and took us to two of the most beautiful resort beach towns in Vietnam, Nha Trang and Hue. My grandmother lived with one of my uncles in Nha Trang, and we stayed there for two weeks. The purpose of the trip was for us to say goodbye to them. Then we went to Hue. Mother had two purposes in going there.

First, she heard that Hue was a very beautiful and historic city and she had always wanted to visit it. It was once the capital of Vietnam and was and still is a stop for cruise ships. Second, she had paid a ship's captain to arrange our exit from there. This was our first escape attempt.

Unfortunately, when we arrived in Hue, things didn't go as Mother planned. She was to meet someone who had passage to Singapore, but he never showed up. She had paid a middleman for the arrangement, money she would never recover. We did all the usual "family vacation" things—visited the temples, toured the town, played at the beach, and ate at fun restaurants. Mother even gave money at the temple for the monks to pray for us, but the joy was absent. We missed my father and brothers. We laughed and appeared to enjoy ourselves, but our hearts weren't in it. We longed to be reunited with the rest of our family. After two weeks, we returned to Saigon. Mother thought perhaps losing the money we spent on this attempt would bring us good luck for the next one.

Fortunately, she didn't lose hope. She continued to plan and search for other options. In May of 1974, we took another "vacation," this time to Vung Tau, another beach town in South Vietnam. We stayed in a huge beachfront home with five other families, all single mothers with their children. We were the family with the most children and we were not allowed to play outside. Vung Tau was a well-known beach resort town. There were lots of tourists all year round, even during the war. We didn't want it to be obvious that we were living there temporarily, not just on vacation. The local police would harass us if they thought we didn't fit the tourist mold.

In the past we came to Vung Tau for family vacations. Father took us there with my two older brothers before they left. When we were in the hiding place, we often talked about our last family visit. Mother encouraged us not to give up hope. We would be together again soon and couldn't take any chance of blowing our cover being here during hiding time.

One night, when the weather was warm and not too windy and the moon was just a sliver in the sky, my mother told us to get out of bed quickly and dress with as many clothes as we could. "Quickly! We must go now!" she urgently whispered. She appeared calm but kept hurrying us, grabbing clothes and pulling them over our sleepy heads. "You must be very, very quiet. Not a word! You must do exactly as you are told. Ting-Ting! No disobedience. No whining. If you do, we could be caught and killed. Do you understand?" When I saw how serious she was, I became very excited. This was what we had longed for. I would soon see my father and brothers!

She herded us out the back door and we walked quickly toward the beach. The people in charge of the mission walked ahead of the group, sometimes signaling for us to duck and hide in the bushes. My heart pounded as I hid under those tangles of branches and leaves. I could smell the salt air and taste the brine on my lips. I looked at my little brothers, whose breath came in short quick gasps, and could see they were both as white as the porcelain dolls I had left behind in Saigon. I could see a tiny fishing boat bobbing in the surf. Small groups of people were being signaled to get onto the boat. It only held five people at a time. The boat would disappear with five people on it and reappear empty a few minutes later. Soon it was my family's turn to get onto the boat. My mother wrapped her arms around us as we dashed to the shoreline.

My heart was racing as I stepped into the little skiff. My head was dizzy with excitement and terror. The boat pushed off without a word and we soon arrived at a slightly bigger boat. We were lifted by rough hands into a ship with at least fifty or more people. Who were all these people? How did they get here? I couldn't believe how many had joined us. We were shoved below deck. Everyone was packed in on the top and bottom decks. Mother huddled all of us together on the bottom of the hull, near the engine. The smell of diesel fuel was overwhelming. On the little boat, even though I had been nauseous, I made sure I didn't throw up. But now, with the diesel smell so dense, I could not get a breath of fresh air and I became very sick. I threw up repeatedly during the long trip. Everyone got dizzy and drowsy and soon everyone else was throwing up, the sickening smell of vomit mingling with the diesel fumes.

I fell in and out of consciousness. It seemed like we were on the boat for a very long time when finally it stopped. Again, the rough hands picked me up and shoved me onto yet a bigger boat. We were again told to hurry, that daylight was approaching. This time we were on the open sea. I could only see the boat connected to the ocean and the sky. There was no land in sight. The voyage on this ship was very different from the previous one. This trip was very calm. It almost felt like we were standing still. There were many huge containers stacked on this ship, but I didn't know what was in them. Once again, we huddled together. My mother was grim-faced and stoic, but her family was still intact. Exhausted and filthy, we all fell asleep for a long time.

I woke up to the sound of men laughing. The smell of vomit still hung in the air, but I had grown used to it. I sat up and looked around. It had been very dark when we boarded the ship and now I could see that there were many people on board, mostly men between the ages of sixteen and forty, draft age. There were others, too, such as widowed women with small children. They were Chinese people like us, trying to escape from the racism, corruption, and threat of communism that were swallowing Vietnam.

We were served breakfast and allowed to wash up. We dried our outer clothes in the sun on deck and watched the dolphins swim in the wake and seagulls fly around our ship. The ocean was a deep, dark blue and there was water as far as the eye could see. I could feel the terror begin to lift from my soul. There was enough room on deck for us to run and play, just as we did on dry land. We made up games and played for hours with the other children. We were on this ship for nearly a week.

The sunsets at sea were beautiful. Sometimes, my sister and brothers and I sat listening as the adults told story after story and sang songs with the horizon, the men with wavering voices would quietly sing an old Chinese song called "Sea Gull":

"Sea gull, flying above the blue, blue sea. Not afraid of the storming wind and strong waves. Flapping its wings and looking straight ahead, very focused and not losing its direction. Flying higher and higher, seeing further and further, it is looking for its own destiny. I want to be just like the sea gull, full of strength and courage."

Finally, land appeared in the distance. We knew it was Hong Kong and the excitement on board the ship was visible. Children began to jump and dance. Women hugged each other and smiled a lot. The men stared at the growing rise of land with tears in their eyes.

The captain told us we would be transferred to another boat when the sun went down. I remembered the other boat, the small one that had transferred us to this one, and I began to feel afraid again. As the sun set, I saw a fishing boat approach. I dreaded leaving this beautiful ship with its big, clean decks and the friends I had made. We were lowered into the boat after dark and told that it would get us to Hong Kong by midnight. I felt a lump rising in my throat, hoping my father and brothers would be waiting on the shore with a snack for me.

Again we huddled together on the floor of the bottom deck. We were there for several hours, but this time only a few people got sick. We listened intently, waiting for salvation to come. It was very quiet for a long time. Then, we heard faint noises on deck, and then footsteps. My heart leapt as the hatch was opened and bright lights flooded into the compartment where we were hiding. Father! Hong Kong! We had made it!

Yes, we had made it safely to the calm harbor of Hong Kong, but something was wrong. We sat in the dark for a long time, not knowing what was happening. People began to murmur that something was not right, that we should be getting off the boat quickly. We could hear voices on deck, but no one came for us. Perhaps the organizers of our escape were just waiting for something, making sure that we would not be caught. But the voices we heard were not our friends'. They were the voices of the Hong Kong Royal Harbor Patrol. In the early morning hours of June 2, 1974, after nearly nine days at sea, we had been caught.

We made it past the border alright, but a fight broke out on deck among the organizers. They had become afraid and accusations flew about the money not being divided equally. They abandoned the boat, leaving it to circle aimlessly in the water. That drew the attention of the Royal Hong Kong Harbor Patrol and they boarded the boat to investigate. After finding us below deck, they realized we were being smuggled into the country and handed us over to the Hong Kong police.

Before we left Vietnam, my mother had exchanged a lot of our money for U.S. dollars which were more valuable and less bulky than Vietnamese currency. Before we left Vung Tau, she had rolled hundred dollar bills into balls and hidden them in her clothing and undergarments. Each roll was about $10,000 and she carried five or six rolls. Now, in the pre-dawn hours of June 2, she asked her captors if she could use the bathroom. There, she threw out the rolls of cash, as well as several belts she was wearing. Each belt was hiding seven to eight pounds of solid 24 karat gold bars. Mother said I was too young to wear these belts, but my sister had two and several rolls of hundred dollar bills. She, too, excused herself to the bathroom and fed her valuables to the hungry waters of Hong Kong harbor.

Each of us wore several layers of clothes when we left Vung Tau. My mother had secretly hidden her jewelry in the seams of our clothes and the buttons were all hand made out of precious stones and diamonds and covered with ordinary cloth. When we were caught, she made us take off all but our inner layer of clothing, those which had snaps and not buttons. She rolled them up and hid them in a corner of the ship. Not wanting to appear well off, she denied to officials that those were our clothes. My mother and my sister disposed of cash, gold, and jewelry valued at more than a quarter of a million dollars.

When the refugees were transferred to land, the police did a head count. There were a hundred and nineteen in all: twelve adult females, fifteen male and female children, and ninety-two single adult males. All of the males were of draft age. Most of them were trying to escape the war. I heard of one who jumped off the ship before the coast guard realized what had happened.

The police took our fingerprints and picture, and then strip-searched us. We were very frightened and my younger brothers were crying. I thought we were going to be killed. My mother was frantically trying to keep us all together. They inventoried everything we had and asked questions for hours before finally giving us some food and water. Even though Mother and Anna had disposed of most of the cash and jewelry before the strip-search, she still carried the most jewelry and gold among the group.

They separated us into groups and handcuffed us. I had never been handcuffed and now, ten years old, I was being led away like a criminal in a foreign land. Mother and Anna were taken to the women's prison, Stanley and Ken were sent to the boys' detention hall, and I was sent to the girls' detention hall.

By the time I arrived at juvenile hall, it was past midnight. The facility was closed and all the lights were out. Everything was dark. Shadows danced like demons as we passed through several heavy doors. A lady officer first took me to the showers. A single light bulb hung above the stall. She stripped me naked and told me to get into the shower. I stepped into the lukewarm water and felt like crying but the tears wouldn't come. Within moments, she reached in and turned the water off and handed me a rough towel. She gave me a set of clean clothes: a buttonless shirt and pants with a drawstring waist. I quickly put them on. She then led me down a long hallway and into a very large room.

As we entered, the lady officer flipped on the lights. The room was bare except for a number of narrow beds. Seven of the beds were occupied and the intrusion of the bright lights roused the sleeping girls. "This is our new guest," the lady officer barked. "You are not to be mean or harm her in any way. Do you understand?" Several of the girls looked in my direction. "Do you understand?" she said, raising her voice. The rest of the girls tried to sit upright and mumbled, "Yes, Miss!"

She walked me over to an empty bed. "This is where you will stay. You will address all the female officers as 'Miss' and all the male officers as 'Sir.' You will answer all questions with either 'Yes, Miss' or 'No, Sir' so we know you understand. Do you have any questions?" I nodded my head, not looking at her. "You will answer me with 'Yes, Miss' or 'No, Miss!' Do you understand?" She took my arm and forced me to look at her. I choked out a whispered, "Yes, Miss." At that moment, tears began to silently slip down my cheeks. She sat me on the bed and marched out of the room, flipping the light off as she left and leaving me whimpering in the darkness. I listened as the footsteps receded into the corridor. None of the girls said anything but I could feel their eyes on me in the darkness. Oh, how I wanted my mother to come in and hold me! I wanted to feel my sister grab hold of my hand and whisper for me to be brave, or to shut up, or anything.

I began to shake with chills on both the inside and the outside. My hair was still damp as I lay on the thin pillow. I tried to close my eyes, but sleep would not rescue me. I lay there awake in the darkness for a long time before I finally fell asleep. I was awakened by the sound of a loud bell. I sat up, wondering where I was. Girls were rushing around the room, making beds and getting dressed. I sat partly up on the bed, watching them and trying to remember.

One of the girls came over to me and asked if I understood her. She was speaking Cantonese. I nodded. "You have to get up before Miss comes in. You have to get up and make your bed or you will be punished," she said as she pulled me by the arm. "Hurry," she said. "You will be punished!" I had never made a bed before. My nanny always made my bed. The word "punish" kept going through my head. What would a punishment be like here? Would I miss a meal? Would I get a spanking? Would they kill me? I sat on my bed, paralyzed. Then another girl came over and told the first girl that maybe I didn't understand, maybe she should hit me in the head and that would get me to understand. A third girl then approached us and told the second girl to stop, that if she hit me she would scream for "Miss" to come.

I didn't know what to do. I had never been in this kind of situation before. It felt like a dream, but I knew it was real. Everything was so unfamiliar, but memories from the previous night started coming back. Just then, the sound of keys in the door made everyone scramble back to their own beds. The girls stood bolt upright next to their beds, but all eyes were on me. I was still sitting on my unmade bed.

A lady officer entered followed by a male officer. The lady officer asked if I was the new guest who had arrived last night. I nodded. The girl who had wanted to hit me said that I might be mute or not understand Cantonese. The male officer turned to her and told her to shut up. The lady officer gave me a kind smile and encouraged me to talk just as another lady officer came into the room. I recognized her as the guard from last night. She told the kind lady officer, who must have been her boss, that she had checked me in last night. She turned to the other girls and reminded them to not be mean to me. The kind lady officer's name was Miss Chou, the lady officer who checked me in was Miss Ma, and the male officer was Wong Sir. They told me I was a new guest and would not be punished. I was told if I had any questions, I could ask the other girls and they would fill me in. Then they told me to get ready for breakfast. One by one, the other girls introduced themselves. They told me that Miss Chou was the head officer of the detention center, Miss Ma was the nicest one to ask for favors, and Mr. Wong Sir was the only male officer. The older girls liked his attention.

All of the activities there were strictly scheduled. When I went to the dining hall for breakfast, it felt as if everyone's eyes were on me. There was a TV on, and the reporters were all talking about last night's capture. No one spoke. I heard only the sounds of people walking, plates being moved along the metal countertops, and spoons scraping the insides of bowls.

One of the girls from my room led me to our table. Miss Chou came over and stood next to me. She introduced me, but I don't remember what she said. I do remember that she informed the girls I wasn't one of them. Some of the girls were runaways and some were in for shoplifting or other trouble with the law. They seemed very "street smart," and even though I understood their language, I had no idea what they were talking about most of the time. I could have come from a different planet for all I understood of their slang. I felt stupid and scared around them. I tried to keep to myself and not even look at them. I missed my family so much and cried myself to sleep that night.

During the two weeks I was there my uncle Wen-Caw came to visit me once. He was the only family I saw during my stay. A newspaper reporter came to interview me. They asked what I was most afraid of if I was sent back to Vietnam. They also asked why we came to Hong Kong in the first place. My mother had coached all of us on what to say if we were ever captured. "I came to look for my brothers and my father," I told them. "I'm afraid if we are sent back to Vietnam, they will kill us," I said, choking back tears. It wasn't far from the truth. We would surely be treated as political prisoners and given lifetime sentences in prison. The draft-dodgers would be given a death sentence or a front line opportunity to serve and die for their country.

CHAPTER EIGHT:
WE BECOME POLITICAL PRISONERS

In the early hours of June 17, 1974, I was awakened by Miss Chou and Miss Ma. I wasn't told what was happening, just to get up and come along. The girls in the room woke up and began to ask if I was going home and why was I being taken in the middle of the night. The guards told them to be quiet and go back to sleep. I was led to the bathroom in the front office. There, Miss Ma handed me my clothes and told me to put them on. "Where am I going?" I asked, pulling my blouse on over my head. I was still very sleepy. "Just get dressed," she said. She knelt down and helped me with my stockings and shoes. "Everything will be fine," she said, looking into my face. Her eyes were red and her lips were quivering. She stood up quickly.

"Here are some things for you to take with you, Dinh-Dinh," said Miss Chou, handing me a fabric grocery bag. "There are a few toys, some candy, and a snack for you. Don't share it," she whispered as the door swung open. Several police officers came in. Miss Chou answered a few questions, took my hand, and led me to the door. Outside were more officers. One signed some papers while the other one handcuffed me. I was led to a big van. The door swung open and I was lifted inside. I recognized several people who had been on the boat. Many of them were crying.

Just then, I caught a glimpse of a familiar face. It was my mother! Next to her were Anna and Stanley and Ken. I almost started to cry, I was so happy to see them, but I noticed my mother giving me the look that said, "No. Don't cry. Don't be worried." I held back the tears and rushed over to her, nuzzling into the space between her and my sister. I must have been the last one they picked up because no one else got in our van after that. I had seen two vans in front of ours and several police cars followed us. I quietly asked my mother where we were going. She just turned her head away from me and said she didn't know.

After a while the van began to slow down. I looked out the window and there, along the street, were mobs of people, many waving signs and shouting. "Don't get on the plane!" they yelled, "Don't get on the plane!" Others were crying and screaming, "Give me back my family! Don't send my family back!" "We object to the Hong Kong government sending our families back to die," read one sign in Chinese. "Let our brothers live!" read another. The crying in the van got louder. "They are sending us back," one woman wailed. "We are going to die!" "We should not get out of the van…," one man shouted, "…Fight!"

I couldn't hold back any longer. I started to whimper. My little brothers were crying and my mother hugged us all close to her. "Don't worry," she said, her face stern. "Don't fight. Just do what they tell you. I don't want you to get hurt." Suddenly, the van doors flew open. The police started to grab us and pull us out of the van. People were fighting and screaming. There was so much chaos. Two officers climbed into the van and started to carry people out like sacks of potatoes. They were kicking and hitting. I frantically looked at my mother, but she remained very calm. When it was our turn to get out of the van, she walked in front of Anna, and the police grabbed her arm and helped her out. Then they grabbed me, Anna, Stanley, and Ken each by an arm and walked us out. We didn't have to be carried out because we were not resisting.

The sight outside the van was surreal. It was well past midnight, but there were lights everywhere. There was a chain link fence set up around the van and a pathway that led to a plane. People on the other side of the fence were shouting and screaming and trying to knock the fence down. Arms reached through the holes and people screamed, "Don't get on the plane!" Men shouted obscenities and women wailed. The police maintained the boundary by hitting people with clubs. Cameras flashed as reporters documented the chaos.

I followed Mother to the plane and climbed the steps. The words, "Air Vietnam" were written on the side. People inside the plane were crying and begging, "Please, please don't send us back! We are Chinese! We want to stay! The Vietnamese government will kill us!" But no one paid attention to our cries. As I sat down, I watched another plane in front of us take off. Before our plane took off, a Hong Kong official came in and called one person's name. It seems this man had a birth certificate that verified that he was a Chinese citizen. He was allowed to get off the plane.

After the plane was airborne, people began to calm down. Their wailing became quiet sobbing and some fell asleep. I asked my mother what would become of us, what we should do next. "Everything will be fine," she said. "Whatever will happen will happen! You should go to sleep now. Don't worry. Just do as I tell you, and everything will be fine." I could see the fear in her eyes, but she remained very calm and soothing.

The Hong Kong government deported us back to Vietnam. They considered us trespassers. Even though our heritage, ancestors, and language were Chinese, since we were born in Vietnam we were considered outsiders. We were the first group of refugees ever turned away from Hong Kong. The government received a lot of criticism for deporting us so quickly. Other countries like Taiwan, Poland, and Australia all took an interest in our cause and argued that they would have opened their borders to us. They openly chastised the Hong Kong government for being so hasty in returning us to Vietnam. Because of the political pressure, Hong Kong asked the Vietnamese not to kill us. Our lives may have been spared by that request, but we did not escape unpunished.

At the airport within sight of our old restaurant, we were transferred from the Air Vietnam plane to a military aircraft and flown to an island called Dao Cong Son. This island was infamous for housing criminals serving life sentences, political prisoners, and death row inmates. No one escaped. Prisoners sent there never returned. The South Vietnamese police transferred us by army truck as soon as we arrived. The trip took about an hour, winding through mountainous roads and along the coast. The scenery was breathtaking but no one enjoyed it. People were crying quietly. Those who had fought with the police were contemplating their cuts and bruises. Fear and hopelessness filled the air and settled into our bones.

When we finally arrived at the cellblock, the police put all the female adults and young children into a big, empty, rectangular room. Our building was divided into two cells. Each concrete cell had an entry door made of iron bars, and inside the door was another iron bar wall and door, making a cage inside the cell. Other than the cage, the walls were all concrete blocks. Narrow barred windows along the length of the cell just below the ceiling ventilated the room, as did barred openings along the front wall. We could see out through the doors and the windows in the front facing the prison's courtyard, but the back windows were too high to take in the view of the outside world. They were only there to let daylight in and heat out. Directly across from the front door at the back of the cell was a low, u-shaped concrete wall with a box in the middle. These were our toilets and water reservoir. There were two holes in the floor on opposite sides of the reservoir box, and strategically placed bricks allowed us to squat over the holes. Buckets on the ground outside the cell held our waste. The water reservoir held about five gallons of fresh water, or at least at one time the water had been fresh. Slime and other lower life forms covered every surface of the toilets and water reservoir. Each step and handhold was an adventure.

After we were left in the cell, my mother sat down in one corner and began to cry. I had never seen her cry like that before. During this whole ordeal, Mother had not let out a single tear, but now she was sobbing. She wept so hard it scared us. We all huddled and cried together for a very long time. Through her tears, we learned that she was sure we were all going to die. She blamed herself for not thinking the plan through more thoroughly. She said she should have separated us into groups. That way if one was captured, the whole family wouldn't be caught. She had heard of this island prison, but never in her wildest dreams had she thought we'd end up here. She couldn't believe that now we were all going to die together on this island. She knew that prisoners on this island had been massacred just a year prior. She did not want for her children to die like this. She said she wasn't scared for herself, but for us. We had a long future ahead and now she was afraid we wouldn't live to see it. She cried so hard for so long that I could see she had lost hope, and that took me by surprise.

The noises in the jail outside the cell walls scared me enough, but the howling wind terrified me. The wind blew consistently during the day, but at night it intensified and sounded like someone crying. People said the spirits of prisoners who died there had no place to go since they couldn't go home, so they stayed on the island and cried, especially at night. We believed there is an underworld where people go when they die. If someone dies without proper arrangements for them to live in the underworld, their life will be very poor and they will not be able to be reincarnated. Their spirit would then wander around the place where they died and haunt people. Sometime they would even take a life if it was offensive to them. When we heard about all the spirits that inhabited the island, we were very frightened.

"Don't be scared," Mother told us. "All my life, I've never done evil to anyone on purpose. Those spirits will not bother us." I believed her because I couldn't remember a single time when she had been mean or hurtful to anyone. A central tenet of Buddhism is that what you do in life echoes in eternity and influences your options in the afterlife. If you hurt someone out of spite or are intentionally cruel, it's like asking for eternal punishment; likewise, if you live righteously, you inherit eternal blessing.

One night a mysterious man visited our cell. I could tell it was a man because of his broad shoulders. He wore a white gown and walked the center aisle between the prisoners' feet. The doors were locked at night to prevent us from escaping, and I never heard a door open or close, but I saw him walking slowly, looking at all the sleeping ladies. Every few steps he took he would lean over in one direction or the other, as if he were checking on us. Although he didn't look scary and seemed harmless enough, I was too afraid to speak and, as he passed me, I closed my eyes and pretended to be asleep. I didn't want him to stop and look at me. As far as I knew I was the only one awake at the time, and in the morning I asked why a man dressed in white had come into our cell during the night. Our cellblock and our jailers were all women and children, and no men were allowed.

The ladies said I must have seen a ghost, and if he came back I should ask what he wanted. We could make an offering to him so he wouldn't bother us again. They were very afraid he would harm us because I had ignored him, but he never came back. I had never seen a ghost before. In fact, my grandmother calculated my destiny according to my birth date in the Buddhist tradition. She told me I was born to marry god, not man, and that I would become a Buddhist nun. Because of my high status, I was not supposed to be visited by spirits, but to be protected from evil due to my dedication to serving the gods. I was very frightened that because I had seen a spirit, I might not have the destiny my grandmother had calculated.

Our cell had no bedding or blankets. We slept on the cold, damp concrete floor with just our clothing for pillows. We slept facing the wall on both sides with a narrow walkway down the center for us to get to the door. These cells were very different from an American jail cell. We would consider an American jail to be a five-star hotel compared to them. We were given food and water depending on the guard's mood. Our toilet was a simple bucket and, again depending on the guard's mood, we might be able to empty it each day. Some days the bucket ran out of room.

Worms and maggots shared our living space. Mice and bugs were long-time residents. They were kind enough to share their community with us, but occasionally they bit us to show who was boss and remind us who was there first. I seemed to attract all the worst biting bugs in the jungle. I was constantly swatting and shooing them off my skin, but not always before they feasted on my blood. Before long, I was covered from head to toe with oozing sores that would not heal. Each day, my condition worsened. The bites bled and became badly infected. They not only itched and caused me pain, but my whole body began to swell. My mother constantly scolded me for scratching. Sometimes she spanked me to get me to stop. She knew the more I scratched with my dirty fingernails, the more infected they would become, but I couldn't help it. I was crazy with the itching and scratching.

I looked like a leper and I stank. The stench came from oozing infections and dried blood, and from the fact that bathing was nearly non-existent. Nighttime was the worst, as I woke up throughout the night with bugs and maggots crawling in and out of the sores. I felt like the living dead and must have looked like it, too. Even the guards avoided me, calling me "disgusting" and "hideous." They said I was the ugliest thing they'd ever seen.

Anna was also suffering. There was no medical care in the prison and the facilities were far from clean. Her health had never been good, and in this place it declined ever faster. The stress of our situation made her lose weight and color. Her high cheekbones accented the sunken hollows of her eyes and cheeks, and she developed dark circles under her eyes. While I felt like the living dead, she looked like it. The guards thought she had a ghost living in her. Needless to say, none of them ever touched me or my sister.

Because of the agreement South Vietnam made with Hong Kong,

they were not allowed to kill us, but they were free to torture us enough to cause the fear of pain and death. The guards were not allowed to torture children, but they made us watch and listen to the cries and screams of other prisoners. We were not allowed to make any noise, plead for mercy, or say anything at any time. If we did, we were hit, kicked, and thrown. The guards would shout at us and intensify the beating of the prisoner. I learned to act like I was watching, but my eyes glazed over and I thought about being somewhere else so I wouldn't hear the terrified screams that went on for hours. I later found out that I became what mental health professionals call "disassociated." I just checked out, a body with no soul, it seemed, but my soul was just in hiding.

CHAPTER NINE:
WE BECOME COUNTRY PEASANTS

The South Vietnamese government soon learned who we were and ransacked our homes. They ransacked the homes of friends and relatives as well. They wanted to know who organized the escape attempt and hoped our homes would turn up clues. After being in the island prison for three months, the pressure from Hong Kong and the governments of other countries, along with bribes paid to government officials, persuaded the Vietnamese to free us. We were flown back to Saigon in the same aircraft we came in on. The ninety-two men were conscripted into the South Vietnamese army, and the women and children were allowed to return home. Our whole family was put in the Saigon jail for two days before answering to the judge, and we were finally released. It was October of 1974.

Father's oldest sister, our favorite aunt, picked us up from the courthouse and took us to a hotel. Her eyes darted around as she spoke to us. "Sister, because of what you have done, the officials have caused many problems for us and some of your other family," she whispered to my mother. "What do you mean, problems," my mother asked. "The police have stormed into our brothers' and sisters' houses looking for evidence of your cooperation with the smugglers," she said, her eyebrows knitted together. "We had to pay the police not to destroy our homes when they came with all kinds of questions looking for more treasure. No one feels safe taking you or the children in. Everyone has burned your pictures or anything with your name on it. We're afraid. You and your family are hated by the Vietnamese government and we just can't take the risk." My aunt would not look at my mother, and I could see she felt ashamed.

"I understand," my mother said calmly. "We will be fine. No need to worry," she said as she tried to touch my aunt's hand. My aunt pulled away and reached for the doorknob. She said, "I'm so sorry. You shouldn't have tried to escape. It has made things very bad for everyone. You are bad luck for anyone connected to you." Then she kissed my mother and left without so much as a glance at me or my siblings.

So we were back home, but we were homeless. We stayed at a hotel for a few days, trying to shake off the horror of the last few months. My mother spoke to several relatives, but the stories were all the same. It was too dangerous to take us in. There was still no word from my father in Hong Kong. For all we knew, he was aware of our return to Vietnam, but couldn't do anything. We were "bad luck" indeed. In fact, Father had helplessly watched us being dragged off the van and pushed up the stairs to the returning plane.

A couple of years earlier, while my mother had been running the restaurant, the house of one of the employees (our carpenter) caught fire and was burned to the ground. His family had to live in a makeshift tent on their ruined lot. When Mother found out about it, she gave him money to rebuild without hesitation, and made it clear that he was not to repay the gift. She told him to tell everyone that it was a loan, but she gave without expectation of return. Now, in the hour of our desperation, when we were bad luck to everyone we knew, this carpenter came to us and offered to let us stay with him. He had used the money not only to rebuild his house, but also a small studio apartment addition on the back. It was in this studio, built with my mother's money, that we found sanctuary. The gift she had given years earlier became a gift to us in return.

With the help of Mother's carpenter, we disguised our identities. We became the family of his cousin, a widow and her four children who fled from the country because of the war. We lived this secret life for four months. Whenever we went out in public, we spoke only Vietnamese. If we wanted to speak to my mother in Chinese, we could only do so in hushed voices inside the house. We had to pretend that we were from the country and did not have much education. I was able to act like a wild child, which wasn't much of a stretch.

CHAPTER TEN:

THE EVACUATION AND FALL OF SAIGON
AS SEEN FROM BEHIND THE FENCE

All this time, my mother was plotting our next escape. I knew she must miss my father and brothers. She developed a new plan, one that would keep us from being captured together. She planned to divide us into groups this time. Her thoughts were always about putting us kids first.

The seasons changed and the holidays were fast approaching. Through a marriage broker intermediary, Mother met a man named Mr. Lee, who had come from Singapore to make his fortune in Vietnam. Unfortunately, that never happened. With the help of the middleman, and with the price negotiated, he agreed to marry her, making her eligible to leave the country on her husband's passport. To make the marriage look legitimate, Mother bought a rundown studio apartment in a government housing project. We all moved in shortly after New Year's Day in 1975. Our family shared the bedroom area, and Mr. Lee slept on the couch in the family room. We practiced changing beds in case the police ever came to check on us in the middle of the night.

By February, the government announced that all foreigners had to leave Vietnam by April 15. If they remained after that date, they were on their own. Many people had come to Saigon from outlying areas since the withdrawal of American troops left them vulnerable to attack by any of the armed forces. When the war broke into the south, my aunt and uncle walked from Nha Trang to Saigon. Typically this trip took about eight hours on a bus, but they walked it in about four days.

My youngest aunt and my favorite cousin Mary were now ordered by the government to leave, because they had married citizens of the Philippines. Neighbors, relatives, business persons and their families were granted visas to leave Vietnam by April 15, 1975, based on their national ties to Germany, the Philippines, India, Singapore, the United States, Thailand, Australia, Canada, France, Switzerland, Japan, Malaysia, and Indonesia. All these countries sent ships and planes to pick up their citizens and bring them back to their countries. We were hoping China would come for us like these other countries were doing, but those planes never came.

Emigration out of Vietnam was chaotic, with people leaving every day by plane or ship, but it served my mother's plan well. She paid off a whole line of government officials to make sure her paperwork was in place to leave with Mr. Lee. This became our escape attempt number four. By March of 1975, the paperwork had still not been approved. It seems the government had changed the rules. Anna, Stanley and I were not allowed to leave because we were obviously not Mr. Lee's biological children. Mother was approved to leave, along with my youngest brother, but she would not hear of it. She did not want to leave without us. She cancelled her plan and decided to give her place to another woman and her child.

Anna and I pleaded with her to go along with the plan. We insisted that we could stay with our aunt while she made her escape. She could always come back for us once she had successfully made it out of the country. Then the word came that her exit visa was approved, but not her entry visa. She would not be allowed to leave with Mr. Lee after all. This was a crushing blow, as she had spent most of her money on bribes to get the paperwork approved, and had sold most of her jewelry to pay for our living expenses while she wasn't working. Mr. Lee would have to leave alone.

With April 15th fast approaching, tensions ran high. Soldiers fired their guns into the air for no reason other than to let off steam. We couldn't play outside much because there was so much hostility. We didn't know who we could trust. People were packing their belongings and hauling them through the streets, angry at being forced out of the country. Many of our relatives left, too. Some went to China and some to the Philippines, all looking for places safer than Vietnam.

By now, Mother realized her plan to escape with Mr. Lee was not going to happen. She urged him to return to Singapore while he could. Before he left, he brought my mother several small overnight-type suitcases. Each suitcase was filled with gold that some of his friends who were fleeing the country couldn't take with them. People were afraid of being caught with too much money or jewelry for fear they would not be allowed to leave. Some of Mother's previous employees also left their gold with her when they knew they couldn't take it. Even more valuable was the information they gave us on ways we could escape. The money gave us renewed confidence that Mother could come up with another plan. It was very risky to trust people. Some of the information we were given was accurate, some was not, and some was out and out disinformation. My mother tried her best, but often people lied or circumstances arose where they couldn't keep their promises, and she lost her down payment money.

Nine days before the fall of Saigon, President Nguyen Van Thieu announced on TV that he had resigned his position. It was a very confusing time for us. The government controlled what news was released to the public. I remember my understanding was that the Americans were our friends at first, then became our supplier, since North Vietnam was allied with China and Russia who supplied them. Then the Americans betrayed us and left. Therefore, the President couldn't continue to lead our country in battle. He was going to let the war run its course. I couldn't understand all the details in his speech as a child, but I was old enough to remember the reaction of the people around me. The sense of loss was beyond description. A sense of abandonment and desperation grew heavier in the city by the hour.

The adults' talk became more and more angry. Rumors circulated that the president had left the country. He was granted protection by the United States and had flown to Europe. Saigon now had no leader. According to news reports, which I came across while writing this, Nguyen Van Thieu went to Taiwan and was transferred to England under the protection of the United States. He later moved to the States and died of old age.

I don't blame the soldiers sent to Vietnam to fight for our freedom for what happened to us, but I do blame the leadership of both the United States and South Vietnam at the time. The Vietnamese, the American soldiers, and people like me were victims of their political manipulation and greed. I was too young to understand the politics at the time, but I was old enough to remember life before and after the fall.

The last week of April 1975 was chaos throughout Saigon.

Bicycles or scooters left unattended were stolen. The streets were blocked off with concrete barriers, and there was no public transportation, no taxis, no traffic control, and no rules. Gunshots were heard everywhere in the city as people looted abandoned or unattended shops, or took what they needed by force. People yelled on the street, "The war is over!" Little Paris was in a shambles. We lived in a very poor neighborhood so no one bothered going house to house looking for easy wealth in our neighborhood, but the rich areas were prime targets. Mother kept us inside the house behind a locked gate. The television and radio were fuzzy because no one manned the stations. We heard gunshots day and night, and people crying and screaming in the streets. Some were celebrating the end of the war, and some were protesting having to give up their weapons. Others were crying, "What are we doing to do? Are the North Vietnamese soldiers coming into our city?" Most people on the streets cursed President Nguyen Van Thieu and the Americans for abandoning Saigon.

During the three days of the fall of Saigon, one of Mother's employees came to see us in the midst of the chaos. He told her that planes and army aircraft were evacuating people. He said they were landing in open spaces and on rooftops to pick people up. He encouraged us to go. He said maybe we would have a chance. Mother gathered all our gold and headed us out the door. She took us to the airport, which was the civilian side of the Air Force base, a couple of miles' walk from our home. She thought the airport was close enough to the Air Force base that someone might recognize her and be willing to let her get on a plane or helicopter. When we got to the airport, there were many people camping out in the waiting room. The police were calling names for people to board the plane. They said only those who worked for the government and whose names were on the list were allowed to board.

Mother told us to sit in a corner and she walked around to talk to people. She tried to negotiate with them to see if they would be willing to give us their seat on the plane. She even tried to talk to the person who was in charge of the calling list. He told mother that we had to wait until they were done calling the names of people on the list, then they would let people not on the list get on later. That never happened. We watched planes leaving one by one. Mother decided that we needed to try the next day, and we headed home for the night.

On the second day, we were well prepared. We brought food and water with us and Mother put all the gold in belts on my sister and herself. We went back to the airport with a small shoulder-bag of supplies. We walked past the open areas on the streets, the post office, the Catholic Church, and the zoo. People were lined up waiting for the helicopters to come. We continued walking to the airport. By the time we got there, the waiting room was packed with people who were waiting for their names to be called. The airport was chaotic, the same as the previous day. The pressure and stress on people's faces was more intense than before. Mother continued to talk to people and tried to talk them into letting us on their list. People were smoking heavily. The air in the waiting room made breathing difficult and the atmosphere was hot and humid. Babies were crying and people were very impatient. It was not a pleasant place to wait, but we held onto each other and the small hope that we could get on a plane.

We sat patiently in a corner and spent the entire day watching planes and helicopters leave, wishing we were on each one that took off. Nighttime was approaching and Mother was getting restless after wandering all day asking strangers for information or officials for a flight.

"My husband ran an American restaurant! We served the government and the American officials! Please help me or the communists will kill my family!" This sounded like nonsense to the officials who had heard it all before. We were out of food and water by this time, though none of us felt hungry or thirsty. Mother walked us home and prepared to try again the next day. She didn't know the third day would be our last day to try. She was focused on getting us on one of the planes. Later she told me she was so focused that she didn't have any fear or emotion. She was only frantically trying to get even one of us on a plane.

I don't remember how long we were at the airport, but we saw lots of people fighting to get on the rooftops where the helicopters were landing and on the runways where the planes parked between loads. Many of the men had guns and were grabbing each other to get on and off the planes. The soldiers pushed some people on and pulled others off.

We saw people rushing and running toward the helicopters. By this time, no one listened to the names being called from the lists; everyone was fighting to get on a plane. We watched plane after plane and helicopter after helicopter take off and disappear into the sky. I could see fear on everyone's faces. Mother very much wanted us to get on a plane, but the mobs were getting more and more violent. People were hitting each other to board a plane, and some were injured. There were gunshots, people yelling and crying, and the chaos got worse and worse. They stomped on each other to get on board. Soldiers on the plane were pushing people off. I saw people on the plane punch others to keep them off the plane. Without a gun or a strong man to fight our way to the front of the line, we were just faces in the middle of the crowd. Mother had a hopeless, helpless look on her face.

One plane took off and crashed almost immediately because there were too many people aboard. Mother looked at us and shook her head. Tears fell down her face and fear was written all over her. She was so focused, so strong, so determined that I didn't think she could cry in public. We watched the last helicopter take off as we stood frozen in time in that spot behind the fence. We didn't move for the longest time. It felt like the last helicopter took our souls with it. I watched it disappear in the sky and wondered what it was like to be in it. Mother didn't say a word. She stood still and it seemed like an eternity passed. Other people were standing, too, dazed like we were. The fight to escape was over. Some sat down on the ground holding their head. I could hear people sobbing. Some were yelling, letting out the stress and frustration. Finally, Mother started walking toward the airport exit. We followed her without asking any questions. It was only a couple of miles back to the slum we now called home, but the walk seemed like it took centuries. Our footsteps were heavy and slow.

People were running in all directions, tears and fear written on their faces. We walked past the open space where the helicopters had landed. It looked empty, and people were going through bags others had dropped in their desperate haste. We walked past the open market place. Trash was everywhere and all the market stands were empty. Several people ran past us, some children looked lost, and adults were looking for their loved ones or their belongings. We just kept walking and followed Mother without saying anything. We stopped once or twice to take turns carrying our brother Ken on our backs and then kept walking.

We finally made it back home. Mother sat down on the living room floor, hugged all of us, and started to sob. This was the second time we cried uncontrollably with her. Questions that kept coming to us were: How are we going to leave Vietnam? What should we do next? We heard gunshots and people screaming outside in the neighborhood all night long. Mother finally calmed down and stood up with a fresh resolve. She went to the kitchen and put a pot of soup on the stove. She told us that tomorrow was another day and she was not giving up. She would find a way to get us out of Vietnam, one way or another, and she wanted us to eat and rest for the days to come. Surely in a few days we would find another way out.

CHAPTER ELEVEN:
WHAT FOLLOWED THE FALL

In the late spring and early summer of 1975, Saigon was a pressure cooker. No one knew whether the communists would see us as a cash cow and use our financial success to fund the rest of the country, essentially leaving us alone other than imposing a tax increase, or whether they would come in and kill all of us to make room for Northerners. Some predicted that when the country became one nation under communist control, the political control would change to socialist. Others said the new government would be neutral and there would be forgiveness on all sides. Some said life would stay the same as it was. Some said the North and the South would be more united, but remain different states of the same country. Some said the communist government would "clean out" the city and rebuild.

Mother told us not to listen to speculation or believe what we heard. She only believed what she knew from the past, that the communists would be ruthless because they had won the territory and take what they wanted by overwhelming force. She had to find a way to get all of us out. She didn't know when or how, but she was not going to give up. She was well aware that if our family's true identity was exposed, as soon the communist government took over Saigon we would be executed and our property confiscated "for the good of the new nation." We were minorities, wealthy, educated, and had participated on the American side by running the restaurant on their Air Force Base. We were well known to many government officials. Fortunately, most of the old Republic of Vietnam officials we knew had escaped during the evacuation, and anyone still around and not in hiding who might know us would probably be killed. She could only hope that our secret identities would not be discovered.

Even in our poor neighborhood, we heard AK-47 gunfire outside day and night. The city was not safe for anyone to go out. Looters soon discovered what houses were empty and took everything out of them. Homeless people from the North and the countryside began moving into the vacant homes. It wasn't safe to be out of the house even during the daytime. The markets and outdoor vendors were all closed, and no one knew when they might reopen. We ate whatever food we had left in the house. We heard some rich neighborhoods were badly looted. The remaining occupants had no police protection and were evicted or killed by the looters. No one plundered occupied homes in our poor neighborhood, but we did get some new neighbors. No one in our neighborhood knew us, and the people who did know us didn't come forward to turn us in. Mother had been generous to her employees when she closed the restaurant, and they remembered and protected us when we needed to hide.

Everyone stayed inside and hoped for safety. The television and radio networks were not broadcasting and the whole city stopped functioning for days. Some people took down the old South Vietnam yellow and red striped flag from the pole at the police station. The communist flag was being passed out to the neighborhood. We were told by loudspeaker trucks to come out of our houses to welcome the soldiers from the North in the days to come.

Finally, we watched the soldiers dressed in dark green march into the city. People stood on their sidewalks to cheer. Fireworks were set off all over town. The North Vietnamese flag was hung from the flagpole at the police station, and the mobile loudspeakers announced the soldiers' arrival. We knew we had better look happy, or else.

CHAPTER TWELVE:
COMMUNISTS TAKE OVER

The next day, mobile loudspeakers announced that Saigon was now named Ho Chi Minh City. All households had to register at the police station and were required to answer the census questions. Every business was required to report their available food, such as rice, salt, sugar, coffee, tea, meat, canned and fresh fruits and vegetables, and all dry goods such as clothing, scooters, bicycles, woks, pots and pans, etc., to the new government. All livestock had to be counted. Markets and banks in the city were closed until further notice. All South Vietnamese soldiers had to report and surrender their weapons at the police stations.

A few days later, the banks opened for those who had safe deposit boxes. They had lists of box owners and their box numbers and addresses. People who had a safe deposit box were instructed to go to the bank. The banks were open only for this purpose, and people were not allowed to deposit or withdraw money. They had to stand in line and wait their turn to go into a private room. There they were met by two soldiers, one standing at the entrance to the room with a rifle, and the other sitting at a table with a safe deposit box and a document for them to sign next to it. They were not allowed to open their box until they signed the document.

By signing, they were "volunteering" to turn over all items of value to the government for the purpose of rebuilding the country. Anyone who refused to "volunteer" would be shot in back of the bank, no questions asked. Anyone who failed to come to the bank to open their box would be investigated, and if found would also be shot.

The father of a friend of mine, who was a merchant, had acquired hundreds of one-carat diamonds over the years that he kept in his safe deposit box. When he opened the box in front of the soldiers, there were so many that they formed a small mountain on the table when they spilled out. He also had a lot of paper money, jewelry, and a Rolex watch. He was one of the businessmen who thought nothing would change when the new government came, because the new government would be foolish to destroy the system which created so much wealth.

He went home that night and hanged himself. Later the same night, soldiers came and raided his house, and forced his wife and children to leave. They were taken by truck to the jungle and dropped off. His wife committed suicide as well a couple of weeks later, leaving the children to fend for themselves and find their way back to their old neighborhood, only to find Northern soldiers living in their house.

Before the communists took over the government, many people withdrew large sums of cash from the banks and kept it in their houses. They were not entirely sure the South Vietnamese government would fall to the communists, but they wanted to keep their money safely in their own hands just in case. The communists had already planned for this.

When they took over the government, the communists confiscated all the money people had in the bank in checking and savings accounts and of course their safety deposit boxes. But, in order to truly control the wealth people had in their possession, they changed the currency every three months. When customers came to the banks to change their money, they came in with thousands of dollars, and left with hundreds. The amount of money each family was allowed to have was based not on what they brought in, but on the number of people in the family. The more people in the family, the more money they were allowed to have; the fewer people in the family, the less they were allowed to have. The allowance for minor children was half as much as for adults. The paper the new government printed the currency on was so flimsy that as soon as we took it out of our pocket the moisture on our hands caused it to fall apart. We had to keep it in our purses because it could not stand the moisture in a pocket or wallet. We couldn't even use it for toilet paper after its three-month issue was up.

My mother had no open bank accounts or safety deposit box after we returned from Hong Kong, but she sold the one valuable piece of jewelry she had at the time for money to buy food. During the currency exchange, the money Mother had was just enough for food. She didn't lose her money like some people did during this exchange, but she didn't have anything left to lose. The gold we had was useless in the new economy, and would only get us into trouble if we tried to buy anything with it.

Heads of households were issued vouchers to buy rice, sugar, salt, coffee, and tea based on the number of people in the family. Vouchers were not issued for meat or poultry because these were considered luxury items. If people wanted to buy meat or poultry, they had to pay for it out of their own pockets. Vouchers were not issued for seafood, but seafood was cheaper to buy than meat because there was a good supply of it fresh from the delta.

When vouchers were issued, the government officials determined who received them first. It was based not only on family size, but also on the connection the family had with the new government officials. One of the communist beliefs is "equality." No one is richer than anyone else, or lives better than anyone else. There are no rich people or poor people, all the wealth and quality of life are "equally shared" among the people. This belief in equality was a charade. In reality, the relatives of the government officials received more vouchers than anyone on the street did. Like the pigs in George Orwell's *Animal Farm*, some of our countrymen were more equal than others.

The real purpose of the voucher system was to control how much food the people were given. Some people were so poor that they had to sell the vouchers to anyone who wanted to buy them. Thanks to the voucher system, it became more and more common for food to be sold on the black market in the communities and neighborhoods, and there were more and more beggars on the streets and in the temples.

The communist government promised that all the soldiers of the defeated South would be pardoned if they surrendered voluntarily. They were only required to attend a camp for reeducation. Later we found out that the camps were prison camps. They were just given the very nice name "reeducation camp." The soldiers were pardoned from a death sentence, but they still had to serve time in jail. The time served would be from two years up to how long the government decided, and depended on the rank of the individual soldier or on his family connections. Some were in this "reeducation camp" for over ten years. They were not allowed to have any visits from their families. Only if the family paid gold and bribed the officials were they able to visit their loved ones in the camps.

The communist soldiers came into the city group by group. They took over entire big, wealthy neighborhoods. Some people were still living in their houses, but if the soldiers wanted their house, they had to leave. They didn't have time to pack and were not allowed to take anything with them. They walked out of their houses without any belongings. Some wealthy homeowners were put on big army trucks and taken out to the countryside. They didn't know where they were and the officials didn't care. They were left there with no place to go. Some were sent into the open fields to do hard labor. Others refused to surrender their homes and were executed on the spot.

The government required all schoolteachers and college professors to attend "reeducation classes." However, the "education" was militarily, not academically, based. Some teachers or professors who spoke English, Chinese, or French were considered traitors to the new government and were executed in public. Many teachers, engineers, doctors, and merchants simply disappeared, and were never seen again. Their families knew that when they disappeared, they had been executed. They weren't good candidates for brainwashing reeducation.

All students, kindergarten through twelfth grade, were required to wear a standardized uniform when schools resumed. The communist government ordered all the books that had been used before they took over to be burned. The new curriculum was all about how great the communist government was, how to march, how to pay homage to the communist leaders, learning communist songs and chants about how great communism was. In other words, it was about how to grow up to be a good communist. Many students were required to do forced labor, going into the countryside to repair damage to the rice fields done during the war. Some who were physically unable to do the work or unlucky enough to step on the wrong spot died.

When the communist government took over South Vietnam, they dictated who the doctors would be permitted to treat. There was a shortage of medical professionals after the mass exodus, but the old law of supply and demand did not play out as it would have a few months earlier. They no longer had any say about what patients they could treat, regardless of their medical needs. If a person didn't have a connection to a government official, or wouldn't be productive after they were treated, they were denied medical care. The government officials also debased the doctors by forcing them to clean toilets because they were educated and needed to be humbled. Doctors had to live at the hospital and were not allowed to go home. They could only leave the hospital with permission, and they were escorted to make sure they were not treating patients without authorization.

There was a girl in my neighborhood who had heavy menstrual bleeding, and she went to the emergency room to be treated. She didn't have a connection to any government official and was not allowed to see a doctor. Finally, after three days, she died in the emergency room sitting in a pool of blood.

It was mandatory for each household to send one member of the family into the countryside for one to three days to re-dig trenches for irrigation of the rice paddies. Each neighborhood had a police station, so the government would select a neighborhood and require one person from each household to go to the police station at a certain time and day. A big army truck was there to take us out to the countryside. They told us we would be gone for either one day or three days, so we should bring enough food to last us for the entire time we were gone.

Anna had a weak constitution. She caught cold easily, and generally was more prone to illness than I was. I had been exposed to everything and rarely got sick other than mosquito bites. The insects loved my sweet skin and made a terrible mess of it. Because I was the strong one, I got in the truck each time our neighborhood was called. Stanley and Ken were too young to qualify for the job. When we came to our destination, we didn't know where we were. They sent us out into the fields to begin digging trenches in the rice paddies.

On one of these trips, there was a girl who was younger than everyone in the group riding on our truck. It took about half a day to get to where we were going, so to pass the time she and I played "rock, paper, scissors," sang songs, told secrets, and had fun with the other people in the truck. When we came to where we were going to dig trenches, we got off the truck and began to walk on a path alongside the rice paddies.

I didn't mind working in the fields. It was our only chance to get out of the city and we could gather fruit in the jungle after the day's work was done. I eagerly took the lead in our group of teenagers, and walked fast to get to the field where we would be working. There was another group walking further along the path in the distance. I turned to our group and called, "Hurry up, we need to catch up with the other group." We didn't have to catch them, but it was a chance to meet some new people and have more company.

My new friend started running ahead of me and the rest of the group and called back, "Hurry up you slowpokes!" as she went around a curve in the path. Just then, she stepped on a buried land mine, and we witnessed her violent death.

As we peered around the corner, we saw blood splatter on the trail and foliage at first, then her crumpled body. Her body was grotesquely transformed. Her heart still pumped blood but none returned to it. The blast went high enough to reach her head, so she was not conscious. Her face was unrecognizable. The mines weren't made to kill a man by blowing him up, but to create a big enough explosion for shrapnel to reach vital arteries. Her smaller body was badly torn.

We all stood there in shock at what had happened, afraid to move in case there were more land mines. After about a minute, which the guard took to decide what to do, he got in back of the line and forced us to continue to walk on the path past her body. We had to look at her lying there in the red mud, and avoid stepping in it. Everyone became very quiet, and we didn't talk to each other the rest of the time. On the way home, the guard told us not to say anything to anybody about what happened, or how she died. When we returned to our neighborhood, the guard went to her house and told the family she had died on the trip, but he didn't tell them how she died.

I had nightmares about it for many years. I still feel guilty because I was in front of the group at first. Had she not run ahead of me, I would have stepped on the land mine and died instead. I didn't understand why the other group walked on that same path, and no one else was blown up.

I begged my mother not to make me go on these trips anymore, because if I did I might die. She somehow sensed my distress and agreed to pay one of our previous employees to go in my place ... less money for fish and more rice soup for us.

For the longest time I had a terrible image in my head of a red mist on torn green leaves. I couldn't figure out why it stuck there, and didn't connect it with the girl's death. Eventually, thirty years later, when I remembered the event, in my nightmares and my conscious mind I recalled it as if she had merely evaporated in the pink mist. I didn't remember her bloody body. Only in writing this book did the truth come back to me. Now I understand, and I don't dream of red mist on torn leaves any more.

After the camp trucks brought us or our neighbors back to our neighborhood, they said over the loudspeaker, "Thank you for volunteering to help rebuild the country," which was just propaganda since we hadn't volunteered at all. Executions without a trial were also a very common practice. The communist government sought out those who had been associated with the American soldiers, and they were put on an execution list. Since my mother's business fit squarely into this category, she was targeted for capture and execution.

When I share my story, I am often asked why we had to escape. We had to because had we been discovered, we would surely have been killed. The communist government tried to establish its absolute authority as soon as they entered Saigon. They sought out different groups of people to execute. If anyone was found to have helped the American soldiers, they would not escape being killed. The wealthy, the educated, and the Chinese minorities were prime targets. My mother was not only wealthy, sophisticated, and a Chinese minority, but her business was completely based on providing services to both American and South Vietnamese government officials.

Our name was on the execution list without question. We had to live in hiding and use another name to disguise our identity. The government searched for us and posted a reward for any information leading to my mother's whereabouts. Fortunately, people in our neighborhood believed our story of being refugees from the countryside, and enough time had gone by that we did not arouse their suspicion. In addition, the people who certainly would have recognized us had no idea where we lived. Most people never thought that as wealthy as Mother was, she would ever live a peasant's lifestyle.

Mother was very frugal and humble. She never dressed as a millionaire, even when she was one. She said the only way she could stay out of trouble was to be humble and avoid being a target. She had lived poor before, and she could do it again for as long as it took. After we returned from Hong Kong in 1974, we lived a very isolated and low-key lifestyle. Mother bought the same kind of food most other poor people in our neighborhood ate. She always made sure we had well-balanced meals, and spent most of her currency and vouchers on food. Like the other people in our neighborhood, we used many recycled materials for household supplies, such as newspapers for toilet tissue, old shirts for dish towels, flour-sacks for bath towels, and hard cardboard for dust pans. Our frugal lifestyle reinforced our story of being refugees. No more chauffeured limousines for us.

Since Mother treated her former employees well in the past, they didn't report her. We watched many servants report their employers and former owners to the officials. The rewards for doing so were great, so great that a family's stature and opportunity for advancement in the new society could be assured if the father or mother cooperated in locating a wanted former official. Mother says now that she was afraid a neighborhood official would break down our door some night and execute her. She was prepared if that day ever came, but she worried about us. Would our lives be spared or would we be executed along with her?

One day Mother had an unusual visit from a former employee she had promoted to manager of part of the business. He told her he was actually working underground for the North Vietnamese communist government at the time he worked for her. He watched how she treated her employees and experienced the way she closed her business. He knew how Mother helped the employees who had needs, such as the carpenter. He came to let her know that she would be safe as long as she continued living in this poor neighborhood and kept her current identity. He wasn't dressed like a government official, but came with two companions also dressed in common clothes, not uniforms. Nevertheless, they appeared to be very careful. They looked serious and were cautious when they entered the house and when they left. He didn't tell Mother what his rank was, but said if she ever needed anything, he could help. She never knew what he had done or could do for her, but after his visit she felt she no longer needed to worry about being executed anytime soon. She felt she should continue to focus on her search for a way of escape for us.

In spite of the scary threats and constant worry, I had as normal a childhood as I could under the circumstances. I taught myself to play a guitar by using a two-by-four and six rubber bands. One of my friends in the neighborhood had a guitar, and I watched him play. I went home and practiced where my fingers should be positioned on the wooden block's frets, pretending it was a real guitar. When I visited my friend and got to play his guitar, I asked a lot of questions and learned to pretend with both hands.

After I came to America, my brothers pooled their income and bought me a real guitar from a thrift store and I still enjoy playing it once in a while. I repeated my practice regimen when I took a piano class in junior college. The teacher recommended the second class only for students who had a piano at home, so I colored the keys on another two-by-four and practiced every night with the music in my head. The teacher was amazed when he learned that I didn't really have a piano at home, because I had obviously been practicing. I practiced for my final exam on my homemade keyboard, and got an "A" in the class.

Father, having lost all communication with us while living in Hong Kong after his escape from the South Vietnamese prison, decided to sell one of his two Hong Kong houses and used the funds to immigrate to the United States as a businessman. The other house he held onto and Joe and Henry continued to live there so that we could eventually find them if we got out of Vietnam. This was one of the keys to our success in getting out of Vietnam without all of us being together. We had all memorized that address and knew wherever we ended up, all we had to do was get in touch via that address. Because we had been deported from Hong Kong after having made it out once already, he calculated that we could have a better chance of getting legal immigrant status in the United States than in Hong Kong. He figured that once he got to the States the government would help him get his family out of Vietnam because he had helped the Americans in the war. He was half right. His money bought us legal status, but no help would come.

CHAPTER THIRTEEN:
THE ESCAPE ATTEMPTS

Mother continued her efforts to find a way out of Vietnam. She met with some fishermen in the town of My Tho and made a down payment of two bars of 24 carat gold. I remember her packing gold chains in our toothpaste tubes. We were told to put our bags on the boat a day before we boarded it. Mother was ready for us to leave the next day. She had arranged for my brother, sister, and me to go on this trip. The others must have gone through our bags and left without fetching us, and we lost the down payment and our belongings.

Next, Mother went to Can Tho. This time she paid in borrowed gold to build a boat with some of her former employees. We waited three months for construction to start on the boat. The North Vietnamese government was willing to issue a permit to build boats with a bribe; people just had to know the connection. Mother was not involved in the negotiations because her identity might have been at risk. The group decided that it was better for her to stay behind the scenes. She didn't know they decided to skip the negotiations and build the boat without a permit. They were caught and put in jail, and the government confiscated the boat. They didn't report mother, so she didn't go to jail, but she lost about $30,000 in the process.

Mother later took all of us on a trip into the countryside to Vung Tau, the beach town close to Saigon we left from in 1974 on our ill-fated trip to Hong Kong. The plan was to wait for an opportunity to get on a boat. She calculated that as long as we stayed here, her chances of finding someone willing to take us on a boat were greater than staying in the city. She was willing to take the chance to keep us all together for our next attempt. This time, we stayed at a temple and waited for a chance to escape.

While hiding in the temple, we ate what the monks had on hand, and they were strict vegetarians. If they had started ordering meat from the villagers, someone would have suspected they were hiding us. We craved meat but nothing was available.

Four or five of the boys went down to the village one night and stole a chicken. They came back to the temple and told us about it, but wouldn't allow the girls to follow them to town on their next chicken raid. I decided to get my own group together and steal our own chicken.

I went with three other girls who were older, but I was the biggest. We went down to the foot of the mountain and into the village early in the morning. We played all the first day with the children in the village to see who had what and which house had the most chickens. We planned to steal a chicken from whoever had the most and hope the people couldn't tell it was missing. The second day we played with the village children again during the morning, and then they went to school. The schools and businesses closed for lunch and nap at noon and would reopen at 2:00 p.m. While the whole town was napping, we went to the biggest chicken coop and stole a big, slow old hen.

We knew we couldn't take the chicken to the temple, because

either the boys would take it from us or the monks would get mad. We planned to cook it on our way up to the temple. I didn't know how to kill it, so I went to gather wood for the fire. The oldest girl killed it and the other two cleaned it. By the time it was mostly plucked and gutted, the fire was ready. We put a stick through the corpse and roasted the chicken, taking turns holding the stick and turning the chicken, sweating over the fire. We didn't have any salt or spices, but that chicken really tasted good after a couple of weeks of eating only vegetables. By the time we finished eating, put out the fire, and made our way back to the temple, it was nearly dark.

When we got to the temple, Mother was very worried about me. She hadn't seen me all day and none of my siblings knew where I was. I didn't dare tell them my plans to steal the chicken, because one of them would have extorted a piece of it in exchange for not telling Mother. She would have been even more upset. I told her half the truth: I had been playing with the children in the village. She told me that if I went again, I could be captured by the police, get killed by some stranger, or miss the boat when the smugglers were ready to take us and no one could find me. I could be left behind. There went my plans to go into the village again, and goodbye to the very tasty chicken.

One night we were summoned to the beach to board a boat. We waited all night in the tall grass at the end of the path from the temple to the edge of the sand while our smuggler-guide negotiated our fare on the boat. We could see people getting on skiffs and heading off the beach. She returned at sunrise and told us her negotiations had been unlucky. The boat would not let us on, so we had to go back to the temple to wait for the next one.

We were sorry to have to go back to the temple, but we made the hike back up the hill and settled in with our reluctant hosts for a vegetarian breakfast and a nap. About ten o'clock the next morning, our smuggler-guide, breathless from running, arrived at our temple quarters and told us that we must leave immediately. Many bodies had washed up on the beach and the authorities were arresting strangers and searching the area for other people waiting to board boats. We divided our large group into individual families and left one family at a time so as to not arouse suspicion.

It was about three o'clock when it was our turn to walk down the path to the village and catch a motorcycle-taxi back to Saigon. The five of us crowded in the single seat of the taxi for the two-and-a half hour trip to the city.

After four weeks of hiding in the temple, we returned to our poor house. The bodies washed up on the beach graphically convinced Mother that we would not make any more attempts as a group. We would get out by ones or twos. We had missed the boat, but our lives had been spared. We were cursed and blessed at the same time. We could not tempt fate any further by traveling together.

Several times Mother was taken in by the same scam but different crooks. One time she visited the boat construction site in Vung Tau and saw a boat under construction. She made a down payment and waited, but it was a fraud and she lost her money. Sometimes, the boat builders sold "fifth thirds" of the escape, knowing they had a captive market, and when the boat actually filled up the rest of the paying passengers were just out of luck. Most of these times, we didn't physically leave the city.

One of Father's childhood friends came to see mother seeking a chance to escape. Mr. and Mrs. Moon had three sons and two daughters, and their second child was Father's godson. Mr. Moon's two older sons escaped from Vietnam to Hong Kong in 1970, about the same time as my two older brothers. Now he was trying to get the rest of his family out. Their family and ours had been friends since my grandparents' generation. My father and Mr. Moon were friends since Father was four years old. Mrs. Moon had been Father's friend since he was eight. They were still close when they became adults.

When their second son was born, he was very sick. Father worked with a French doctor at the time. He helped them every way he could, but nothing worked. The Moons were diehard practitioners of Buddhism, not western medicine. When all else failed, they went to the temple to seek wisdom from Buddha for a fee. Mrs. Moon took her son's date of birth to the temple and prayed. The monks did an astrological calculation of his date of birth and found a spiritual conflict. They advised her that his birth was in conflict with his parents and he needed to be adopted by other parents to survive the spiritual conflict. They believed the conflict would lead to his death if it was not resolved.

They didn't object to this advice, and came to Mother and Father for help in searching for the right parents for their son. Mother suggested asking the monks to calculate their own birth dates in comparison to the Moons' second son first. When she told me this story many years later, I thought of the organ donor process, but without the blood. Father and Mother turned out to be the perfect couple for this spiritual match. Ming was spiritually adopted by them and became their godson. Whether by the healing power of time or by divine intervention, the plan worked and Ming thrived. The families became even closer than before and Mr. Moon became Father's spiritual brother.

Mother told us that before this happened Mrs. Moon was very helpful to her. Soon after Father and Mother migrated to Saigon, Mother sewed clothes to sell at Mrs. Moon's booth in the open market. Mrs. Moon didn't charge her a rental fee and she was very grateful for her kindness. After Father began managing the restaurant, their friendship continued. Whenever the Moons had marital or financial problems, they came to Father and Mother for help and moral support.

After the spiritual adoption, they came to visit more often. One time, when both of them came to visit, the adults sent all of us kids out of the living room. Their conversation became heated and we heard Mrs. Moon yelling at her husband. She screamed at him so loud we knew he was having an affair. From that time on, whenever they came to visit, the subject was always the affair. I was too young to understand what an affair was, but I understood that Mrs. Moon was really angry at her husband, and it had to do with another woman. One thing I was not sure of was why passive Mr. Moon always sat quietly while she screamed at him in front of Father and Mother. He appeared very busy drawing on papers. He often drew page after page through the visit. Why was his drawing so important?

Mother explained later that Mrs. Moon was always at their business during the day, and usually went to her sister's for a game of mahjong after work, staying until very late at night. Mahjong is a cross between dominos and poker, is very fast, and requires a high level of concentration. She was rarely home for her family and was exhausted when she was there. Mr. Moon quite often came home to an empty house after work. He was lonely and bored, so he frequented a local bar with his coworkers. Prostitution in Vietnam was not a crime. Mother was not sure whether he was involved with prostitution, but she heard he had a lady-friend at the bar. Mrs. Moon found out about the relationship and took her own frustration out on him. The relationship between Mr. Moon and the lady ended, but Mrs. Moon let him hear about it for years afterward. Mother said he was a good man who made a foolish mistake, and his wife wouldn't forgive him. She needed to make herself feel better for gambling her evenings away and neglecting her family.

When Father was in jail, the Moons were Mother's emotional support. When rumors got out of hand, they stood by her. The friendship had grown strong through the years and when Mr. Moon came to Mother about the chance for escape, she had no questions or doubts. He had found a contact that he believed could be depended on to help us escape, but he didn't have enough gold to make the trip. Because of the long, trusting, strong friendship between Mother and them, she helped them by arranging a loan.

Mother knew of an old neighbor of ours from the rich neighborhood who was going to leave, but wasn't able to take all of her gold with her. She knew Father was very wealthy in Hong Kong and trusted that Mother would not take the gold and disappear. She agreed to loan Mother all the gold she had. It was equivalent to $100,000 U.S. Dollars. The Moons vowed they would return the loan when they got out of Vietnam. Their children were older than us so they could work to help pay off the loan if they made it out. In those days, paper contracts were not a common practice. The word of a friend was as good as gold.

On the day we were to leave, mother took Stanley, Anna, my cousin Angie, and me to the bus station, where we met Mr. and Mrs. Moon and their children. She bought tickets to a small town called Ba Rien, where we were to hide until we could escape from Vietnam. A fifteen-passenger van pulled up with a driver and three other people who would be escorting us. One sat in the front passenger seat, and the other two sat in the back seat of the van. We were told this van would take us to the town we were going to. It was an eight-hour drive, and we stopped for lunch and bathroom breaks along the way. By the time we arrived, it was completely dark and we couldn't see anything. Suddenly, one of our escorts announced that we were under arrest. We had been set up. The van wasn't a ride to our hiding place, it was our ride to prison and the escorts were actually policemen! A motorcycle pulled up alongside the van and escorted us the rest of the way to the prison.

At the prison, we were taken into an administration building and strip-searched, the men by a male guard, and the women by a female guard. After we were searched, we were taken down several steps to an outside courtyard where our cells were located. All the men in our group were put in one cell, and all the women in another cell, along with many other prisoners in the same cell. The prison cells surrounded the outside courtyard. There was a well in the middle of the courtyard, and a brick path went around the well. The sidewalls of the cells were made of brick, and the ceilings were grey stucco. A bare light bulb hung down from a wire in the ceiling in each cell. The door was made of bars like you see on a cage in the zoo. The bars allowed us to see out into the courtyard, and let light into our cells during the day. To this day, when I go to the zoo and see the cages, it reminds me of the doors to those cells. I hate the zoo.

The prisons in America have a routine. In the morning the prisoners are awakened, clean up, and go to the dining hall to eat breakfast. After breakfast they either attend classes or go on a work detail. At noon they go back to the dining hall for lunch. After lunch they go back to their classes or work detail. In the evening, they eat dinner, and then spend time in the recreation room watching TV, playing games, or lifting weights. Then they go to bed, and that is their schedule every day.

Prisoners in America have rights and privileges. The court system must provide legal representation for the prisoner during a court trial or any legal proceedings, even when the prisoner has already been sentenced. The prisoners have rights and privileges such as work detail, visitation with family, and being able to buy food, cigarettes, stamps, soda, and personal items at the canteen. The cells are shared with only one or two people, and they have their own bed, toilet, and sink with running water. Prisoners have clean clothes, bed sheets, and pillows. They also have clean water to drink and a daily schedule to shower. Medical care, mental health care, and dental care are all provided depending on their individual needs. It might not be the most complete or high-tech, but good quality basic care is available.

The prison we were in had no routine at all. When we ate and when we got water all depended on what kind of mood the guards happened to be in that day. If the guard was in a good mood, we were allowed to have food and water. If the day's guard wasn't in a good mood, we went without. We were like cattle in a corral, totally dependent on their owners, unable to escape to the green grass outside the fence. If anything happens to the ranchers, the cattle go hungry. However, ranchers have a profit incentive to keep their cattle alive. Our guards welcomed fewer mouths to feed.

Each cell had one bucket that was used to get water from the well, and each prisoner was given a small bowl to use for both food and water. If the guard was in a good mood, he opened the door to each cell, one at a time, and chose a person from each cell to go out into the courtyard with the bucket to get water from the well. That person had to stay on the brick path that ran around the well while getting water. If their foot slipped off the path, they were beaten. We also had to do it very quickly;

if we weren't fast enough, we didn't get any water. When the bucket was full, they went back to the cell and divided the water among the people in the cell by pouring it into each of their bowls. Any remaining water could be used for washing. There was seldom any water left.

Our food consisted of a small amount of rice. Only certain prisoners were chosen to cook the rice in the courtyard. The bags of rice were spread on the ground and examined for contraband, and then refilled. The cooked rice was polluted with bits of dirt and gravel. When we ate the rice we had to remove dirt and gravel from our mouths with our fingers and set it aside. There was enough to form a small mound from each bowl of rice. We then wet our fingers with spit and used the little mounds of boiled-clean sand to brush our teeth.

The living conditions at the prison were worse than animals living in the zoo. Animals deserve a fine life, and zookeepers are proud of the care they provide. Our keepers felt no such obligation. We slept on a bare damp concrete floor. The toilet was a square cement box in the corner of the cell. Next to it was a five-gallon bucket we used to rinse and clean up. Showers depended on the mood of the guard. When they let us out to get water, they gave us time to fill up the water bucket for the toilet and if we were allowed to have water for showers, we were only given one bucket of water per person. The bucket we used for showers was simply a coffee can with a knife-pierced hole near the bottom so you could shower. Brushing our teeth with toothpaste and a brush and other basic hygiene was out of the question. No menstrual supplies, no clean rags, no medical care, no mental health care, or dental care were available. There was no visitation with families and we were not allowed to write letters.

The second day I was there, I got diarrhea from drinking the contaminated water, which went on nonstop for three days. I became so dehydrated, and my muscles pained me so, that the only parts of my body I could move were my eyelids. The guards wouldn't open the door to our cell to give us any help. They just looked in at me. I heard them telling each other that I was going to die.

Anna risked her life by begging the guards to help me. Prisoners were only allowed to talk with permission. If the guards didn't like the way we looked or didn't think that our attitude was right, they could beat us and make us an example for everyone to see. As I lay on the damp, cool, hard floor, I heard Anna's pleadings and the guards' response. They told her that as soon as I died, they would throw my body over the fence into the jungle. They said my body wasn't worth burying; it was only good for feeding the animals in the jungle. Their opinion was that I was worth less than the animals, because at least animals provided food for humans to eat. I, on the other hand, was a nuisance the government had to feed and shelter.

I wanted to tell Anna not to beg them for medicine. I was ready and happy to die, but I was so weak and in such pain that I wasn't able to say anything. I couldn't move my fingers, only my eyelids, to say goodbye to her, and to the light bulb on the ceiling. Then I closed my eyes and lost consciousness. When I woke up, the first thing I saw was the bare light bulb over my head. Then I saw Anna sitting beside me. When she saw that I was awake, she ran and gave me a small amount of water from her bowl that she had been saving for me since the prior afternoon. As the days went on, I slowly began to feel better, though I was still very weak. Eventually I regained my strength. I couldn't explain how I got well after almost dying.

We were often taken to be interrogated by the guards. We pretended we could only speak limited Vietnamese, and spoke with a heavy Chinese accent so the guards wouldn't be able to understand us very well. We all spoke Chinese in our daily lives, so it was not difficult for us to naturally speak Chinese and not Vietnamese. I was never beaten or abused by the guards, only questioned because I was never able to get really clean after the diarrhea and had so many bug bites I looked like I had leprosy. The other girls were treated much more roughly, but the guards were afraid to touch me.

As time went on, we realized the prison also served as a re-education camp for South Vietnamese soldiers. Their "reeducation" consisted of beatings and torture, and we were forced to watch and listen to their screams of pain. I remember watching one middle-aged man being beaten. The laughing guard was only sixteen years old. He wanted the older man to call him "uncle." The prisoner could have been his grandfather, but he insisted on humiliating him. The guard began to whip the older man very hard, because he refused to do what he was told. After he finished beating him, the guard tied him to a pole, making him stand under the hot sun clad only in his boxer shorts for hours. This happened daily to one soldier or another as the guards seemed to make a sport of it. It was obvious that they really enjoyed beating and torturing the old soldiers. I still wonder how one human being can treat another so cruelly and enjoy it so much.

The guards treated us differently from the soldiers who were prisoners. We were not allowed to come out of the prison cells as much as they were because we were prisoners and they were being "reeducated." Also, when they strip-searched us, they found lots of gold. They didn't report our captivity to the main headquarters; that way they could keep all the gold for themselves. They believed we couldn't speak good Vietnamese like the other prisoners, which was another reason to ignore us.

On a daily basis, the soldiers were made to read aloud the "crimes" they were charged with and what they did wrong in the eyes of the communist government by working with the American soldiers. They had to confess their crimes against the new government in front of the camp and pledge to support the communist government from that time on.

Anna told me that after I got sick the soldiers were very concerned about us. When they were able to come out of their cells, they gave her a tin can with boiled water they saved for me every chance they had. Had the guards known they were doing this, they would have been in deep trouble. Anna spoon-fed the water they gave her to me to keep me as hydrated as she could. When the guards walked past our cells the keys on their belt loops jingled. The soldiers listened for the sound of their keys jingling and alerted us that they were coming by humming a few bars of the communist songs the guards wanted them to sing. When Anna heard them, she knew that was her signal to stop feeding me until the guards had passed.

While we were in prison together, I discovered that Mrs. Moon was not the nice person I thought she was. Before we left Saigon, she promised my mother she would take care of Stanley, Anna, Angie, and me, and look out for us. But whenever we got water from the soldiers, she took the water from the bucket and filled her children's bowls with more than she gave us. She was very jealous that the "reeducated" soldiers showed favor toward Anna, Angie, and me.

When we got to eat, she did the same with the rice by giving her two daughters more than us. To this day, when I watch the Walt Disney movie, "Cinderella," the evil stepmother reminds me of her. The biggest difference in our story was that Mrs. Moon's two daughters were nice to us. They were very afraid of their mother. She often talked very mean to us, especially Anna and Angie. I was the youngest in our cell, so she didn't treat me as badly. I always wondered what happened to the kind Mrs. Moon I used to know. When she was mean to us, I remembered a saying my mother taught us: "True friendship is shown during difficult times."

The only way people like us, those who were arrested for trying to escape Viet Nam, could get out of prison was for their relatives to pay a certain amount of money to the government or the guards to buy their freedom. Relatives were given a few months by the government to raise the required amount of money. If they weren't able to raise it in the time given, another month was added to the prison time and the amount of money increased until the relatives paid the required bribe for their release. Mother had to borrow more money and sell most of the possessions she still had to get the amount needed to get us out of prison. She wasn't able to do it in the amount of time she was given, so we had to spend an extra month in prison. When she finally was able to get the money and pay for our release, we had been in the prison camp for five months. She told us not to tell anyone, or we would be taken back to the prison.

Mother lost a lot of money on this escape attempt; not only the money she paid to gain our freedom, but the loan she got for Mr. and Mrs. Moon. Shortly after Mr. Moon's family escaped from Vietnam and were relocated to France, he died. Mrs. Moon and her five older children refused to acknowledge that she had anything to do with the loan. My family ended up making payments to the neighbor who lent the Moons the money. Even though the loan was made for another family, my parents felt we were obligated to repay it. The loan totaled more than $100,000 and we made payments each month for ten years.

CHAPTER FOURTEEN:
JUMP THE TRAIN

After our release, Mother arranged for me to escape at the end of the year by sending me to live and work with my uncle Si-Jet in Nha Trang as one of the caregivers for his daughter. It is a beautiful beach town and always had been our vacation home during the summer. Grandmother lived with us for six months of the year, and with Si-Jet in Nha Trang for six months before the Tet Offensive.

Living and working for my uncle was my cover. His daughter was three years older than I was. When she was an infant, she developed a high fever. She eventually recovered from the fever, but as she grew older her arms and legs never developed. We found out later it was Agent Orange that disabled her and caused her to be underdeveloped. She couldn't sit up, walk, talk, or do anything for herself. Her arms and legs curled, she had no muscle, and was completely bedridden. Si-Jet hired caregivers 24/7 to care for her. I worked as one of them and was a playmate to her while living with them. I stayed in Nha Trang for six weeks, but the people who organized the escape never showed up to take me. Mother lost her down payment again.

Early in 1977, Mother had the opportunity to reunite with one of her older brothers and her younger sister. They had remained in North Vietnam for over thirty years after Mother migrated to the south and she hadn't seen her side of the family during that time. After the government opened the door for family reunification, Mother's older brother and younger sister came to the south to visit her. They were going to leave Vietnam by walking across the border to China. Mother planned to let Anna go with them, but it didn't work out. They went back to North Vietnam and asked Mother's cousin to help us.

This cousin's husband was a school principal in North Vietnam. Mother planned to use his influence to get Anna into the North Vietnamese school system as a teacher. She was eighteen and qualified by her education to be a teacher. The plan was that she would be a student teacher, visit North Vietnam for training, and eventually find her way across the border, but it was risky. Anna wasn't able to go because she got sick. Mother lost money again because she had to pay her cousin money for bribes and the expenses of the trip, and when Anna wasn't able to go, all of it was lost. I couldn't be her replacement, because I was only fifteen and obviously didn't have enough schooling to be a teacher.

Of us all, Stanley had the toughest time escaping. Mother's older brother knew a friend who was a truck driver and had his own truck, which he used to deliver merchandise from South Vietnam to North Vietnam after the communist government took over. He was taking fish sauce from Saigon to Hanoi, and Mother arranged for Stanley to go with him. She heard the border between Vietnam and China was open to any Chinese who wanted to go back to China, as long as they could speak Chinese. It was still a crime to leave the country, however, so we didn't have a free pass. Mother paid the driver's expenses of the entire trip.

Stanley later told me what happened on the road. When South

Vietnam fell to the North Vietnamese army, many South Vietnamese soldiers were forced to hide in the jungle to keep from being killed or captured. Due to the poor condition of the roads, the fish sauce trip took several days, and they had to stop along the way to sleep. He was dressed like a North Vietnamese delivery truck driver, so each time they stopped along the road, they were shot at or assaulted by former South Vietnamese soldiers who mistook them for Northerners. Imagine being dressed like the enemy, and having your own soldiers attack you. They had to fight back at times, but a few times they were able to convince the Southerners that they were friendly. Because of that experience, he is still afraid of the dark, and he drinks himself to sleep with the lights on every night.

When Stanley finally arrived in Hanoi, he walked across the border to China. When he got to the bridge which served as the border, the guard on the China side asked where he was going. He answered in perfect Chinese that he wanted to go back to his home province of Fujian, China, and they let him cross without any problems. He walked a few miles and found his way to a Chinese refugee camp. He was able to write Joe and Henry in Hong Kong at the address we all had memorized, and a few months later Henry went to China and gave him money through the camp fence to travel to Hong Kong.

Stanley paid to get on a small fishing boat to Hong Kong, and reunited with Joe and Henry. The trip from China to Hong Kong should have taken only three days, but actually took almost a month. Instead of sailing directly to Hong Kong, the captain sailed along the coast of China for several days, then finally turned and sailed toward Hong Kong. He did it that way to look like they were just fishing. He didn't want to call attention to the boat because he had several Vietnamese men hidden below. During the month they were at sea, Stanley was abused by the men. He was the oldest of three teenage boys on the boat and took the brunt of the abuse. They threatened to throw him overboard several times, and wouldn't share their food with him. My brother still mistrusts authority figures.

Stanley's boat arrived in Hong Kong, and went straight to a dock in the harbor set up for Vietnamese refugees. Hong Kong started taking in Vietnamese refugees after the war ended, as it was now politically correct to accept refugees from the new communist regime. He lived in the refugee camp for eight weeks before he was allowed to join our brothers. He turned fifteen in the camp. He lived with Joe and Henry for seven months, and then came to America to attend high school and be with Father.

When Mother heard that Stanley had arrived safely in a Chinese refugee camp by traveling to Hai Phong and walking across the border into China, she decided to have me try to escape by the same route. At first, she arranged the trip for Anna, but she heard from Stanley's smuggler that the trip in the fish sauce truck was very dangerous. She decided that I would try the trip north on the train. If I could make it on my own, Anna and Ken would stay with her for the final escape.

Mother asked around in the market district and found a Vietnamese guide who was willing to accompany me over the border, help me find my way around and through Hanoi, and blend in on the train. The trip cost ten ounces of gold, or about $15,000.00 in today's gold values. The guide received two ounces as a down payment and her family would receive eight more when Mother heard from me that I had met Stanley in the Chinese refugee camp just over the border.

Mother woke me early, a couple of hours before dawn. She had packed a small bag with two sets of clothes and snacks for a couple days. She gave me some money for the trip, but she didn't sew gold chains and diamonds into my clothes as she had on the prior escape attempts. Anna and Ken kissed me goodbye and I walked with Mother to a house in Cho-Lon's market district about a mile and a half from our public housing area. She knocked a secret code, the door opened, and we were quickly ushered inside by the lady of the house.

My guide's name was Lang. She was about my sister's age, and was a niece of the lady who owned the house. When the three of us were left alone in the living room, Mother slipped Lang two ounces of gold. Before she left the house by the back door, she leaned over to me, looked into my eyes, and told me to do exactly what the guide told me, no matter what, without asking any questions. She knew I was a loudmouth and might give away the secret of our destination, so she told me not to say a word when I was on the train. I took her literally.

Mother held back her tears and tried to be strong for me, but a glaze of tears was in her eyes as she turned and walked out the door. She knew if she cried, I would fall apart as well. I couldn't stand to see my mother cry. She turned to the doorway, opened the door with her right hand, and slipped out the half open door. I watched from behind a curtained window as she walked down the alley and disappeared into the marketplace, which by now was noisy, filled with peddlers who were setting up their carts and housekeepers needing food to prepare for breakfast. She didn't even glance back in my direction, and then she was gone. I didn't cry.

I've never been the sort of person who could sit still and be silent for an extended period of time. I loved to run, explore the neighborhood, and share my discoveries with anyone who would listen. I would start a conversation with anybody who seemed interesting. I liked to ask a lot of questions and tended to make comments based on what I observed without thinking ahead. My family always said if they wanted to know something about the neighbors, all they had to do was ask me. I knew everyone on the street, what languages they spoke at home, how many puppies their dog gave birth to, and the time and date of the big event. I had an advanced degree in neighborhood gossip. My too-social disorder was frowned upon and worried about by all the ladies in my extended family. Chinese ladies are not supposed to be so forward. Mother and Grandmother both worried that they might have to pay someone to marry me when I got older, because I was such a fatty bigmouth.

Lang decided that since I was already doing so well, it would be a good plan for us to pretend I was mute and deaf for the entire five-day duration of our train ride. She was afraid my South Vietnamese accent would give us away and blow our cover story of returning to Hanoi from a visit with relatives in Saigon. She didn't know how hard this would be for me, because we weren't that well acquainted yet. She told me to follow her when it was time to get on the road. We took a three-wheeled bicycle taxi five miles from Cho-Long to Saigon's Market District. The ride took about an hour. The train station was very busy and crowded, and I was not allowed to make a sound. I had no hearing and no voice. If I needed food, water, or to visit the toilet, I had to use a notepad or improvised sign language to ask Lang to help me.

As I sat quietly on a bench in the train station, waiting for Lang to buy our tickets, I began to force myself to block out all the noises around me. It was hard at first, but I tried again and again and focused on things far outside of my immediate environment. The faraway items and events eventually drowned out the sounds right around me. I put myself in a sort of trance, and checked out of my immediate environment altogether. When Lang came back, she talked to me without making eye contact and I couldn't hear her. All I heard close by me was an unidentifiable nasal droning, like Charlie Brown's teacher on the Peanuts television specials: "Waw! Waw! Whaw? Whaw! Whaw?" I can still relate to his perception of the teacher's voice, and find myself going to that far-off place from time to time when I am upset or afraid.

When it was time to get on the train, I followed Lang silently. Before we boarded the train, we had to go through a checkpoint where policemen asked people for their IDs and tickets. I looked at Lang and she walked in front of me. She had both of our fake IDs and real tickets in her hands. One of the police asked her something and looked at me. I was not nervous. I had already blocked all noises out of my world. I knew I had no emotion on my face and looked at the police with a dumb blank face. Lang told the policeman: "She is my cousin and she is mute. She can't talk or hear you." One of the policemen came up beside me. He bent down, put his whistle next to my ear, and blew it very loudly. I saw him coming toward me and was well prepared. I didn't blink or move, but continued to look at Lang for instructions. The policeman was satisfied, and let us go through the line. People around me started to move away and reacted with fear when the policeman blew his whistle, but I had become deaf and mute.

Lang chose a seat in the back row of the second to last car and we sat down without a sound. She had questions written all over her face, but I couldn't answer even if I wanted to. I put my head against the window, closed my eyes, and continued to block out the noises around me. The train started to move and soon people settled down. When the conductor came by to check tickets I heard Lang answering his questions. She told him I could not hear or talk because of a fever I had when I was little.

For five days on the train I didn't talk to anyone, including Lang. I slept and only got up to use the restroom. She gave me food from the cafeteria car. I must have been very convincing, because people looked at me with a pitying expression when I walked by. They told jokes and carried on conversations around me, and I had to block them out so I wouldn't laugh or show any reaction. I felt like I was all alone on the train. I missed Mother and my sister and brother very much, so I forced myself in my mind not to be on the train, but at home.

Finally, we arrived in Hai Phong, which is a city north of Hanoi with a large Chinese population. It was just turning dark. I had no idea what time it was, but the streets were very quiet compared to the nightlife of Saigon. I followed Lang to her row house about a mile and a half from the train station. There were a couple dozen people in the house, mostly kids my age or a little older. I didn't realize at the time that Lang's family was running a refugee smuggling operation. I just figured the crowd was actually all her cousins, because she introduced everyone as her cousin.

Once we got in the house, Lang told me I could talk. I looked at the people in the house and took a deep breath. Oh, my God! How much I missed my voice! "How far is it to China from here? When will we be at the refugee camp? Did you see that lady's big funny hat on the train? Did I do a good job of acting deaf and mute? It smells so good in the kitchen. Will we be eating soon? What will we have for dinner? I almost spit out that strong tea on the train. Do you have Coca-Cola in Hai Phong?" She laughed at me and told everyone I had not spoken a word on the train. She almost forgot that I could talk. One of the guys, about nineteen or twenty years old, kept telling me to settle down and rest. He said that tomorrow morning we would have a day's worth of walking north to the border.

We heard footsteps and noise outside the door. As he described the plan for the next day, the door was kicked in and policemen stormed into the house. "Don't move! No one move!" They went around and asked us questions in Vietnamese. Everyone with a Northern accent was separated and placed on one side of the living room. Those with southern accents were rounded up and marched out the door down the street to the police station, which was next door to the train terminal. I have no idea what happened to Lang. I hope she was set free after the policemen separated us, but I doubt it. Most likely, she was put in jail until her family bribed her out. The North Vietnamese soldiers probably would have shot her if they hadn't believed there was a money trail and that someone would pay for her return.

The policemen loaded us onto the same train I had just gotten off of two hours before. All the people on this train had been trying to escape Vietnam like me. Most of us were Chinese. Some had been arrested a few days before, and a few had been on my train headed north. Most of them were traveling with their entire families, some were teenagers with their siblings, and a few kids like me made the trip alone.

We were ordered to find a seat and settle down. An officer told us the train would return back to South Vietnam, nothing more. People were crying but no one dared to speak out. I felt a chill running through my body. I had just been bribed out of jail by Mother six months before after another failed escape attempt, and it had taken five months. The thought of going back to jail made me sick with worry. If the police found out who I was, my mother would certainly be put in jail also. The more I thought of jail, the heavier the weight on my chest became. Although I was no longer a deaf mute, I couldn't make a sound. I went back to my thousand–yard stare. Maybe this was all a bad dream and when I awoke, we would be in Hai Phong.

When we got underway after a few hours, the policemen told us we could go to the bathroom and the dining car while the train was moving, but we had to be back in our seats when it stopped. They began a head count and questioned all the passengers. A man sitting in the row behind me had three small children and I recognized them. They had been on the trip North with me. He handed me a piece of bread and made hand signals for me to eat, and pointed back and forth from my head to his chest. Finally I said, "What?" Startled, he grinned, the only honest smile I had seen for five days. "Listen! When the police come to our car to take our names, pretend that you are one of my kids. Just leave to go to the restroom and hide. Come sit with us again after the police are done with us. They will think they had your information. Understand?"

I nodded and paid attention as the policemen entered our car. When I returned from the restroom, I thanked him for watching out for me. He smiled and said when the police had no information about me, it would be easy for me to get away. He thought I was really a mute, and when he realized I had been pretending the past five days, he felt like a fool. He said someday I would be a famous actress. He told me to call him "Uncle Han."

One of the teenage guys I met at Lang's house came and sat down next to me. He told me he and a few other kids are going to jump off the train the first chance they had. "Are you in?" The thought of going back to jail had haunted me all night, so of course I would join the escape. He told me the plan: as we felt the train slowing before the next town, we would go to the restroom and jump out the window. As the train was coming close to a town for refueling or a break, I did as I had been told. Before I went to the restroom, I said thank you and goodbye to Uncle Han. He told me to be careful and watch for land mines.

On my tiptoes, I looked out the rocking train's window and saw that I would have to jump what seemed about twenty feet down, farther than any house's roof I had ever jumped off of. It was this or jail. I jumped and landed uninjured on the edge of the jungle in a thick-leaved bush a few feet from the tracks. The ground was soft and muddy. The sun had just gone completely behind the horizon. When the train disappeared from view, our little group got together. A quick inventory showed that none of us had a compass or flashlight. We had one pocketknife, some snacks, and a few coins. Well, we didn't need a compass to tell us to go the opposite direction away from the train. We headed into the jungle because one of the boys said the tracks were likely to be patrolled.

As we walked through the jungle, the moon came up and just enough light filtered through the trees for us to see the jungle floor in front of us. There were three girls and four guys in our group. The other girls were sisters and they walked together. I ended up walking by myself. The guys were going as fast as they could ahead of us and we just tried to keep up with them. As we walked through the mucky jungle floor, leeches grabbed on for the ride. We tried to get them off of our legs and ankles as fast as possible. If we let them stay on too long, they would dig in and it would be harder to get them off. A few times I pulled off a little quarter-sized patch of my own skin along with the leech. It stung like a bee sting, but it had to come off.

Finally, our fearless leader told us to stop and climb into the trees to rest. We couldn't sleep on the ground, because the bugs would eat us alive. Bugs in Vietnam are very big. We were exhausted. The tree branches were very big. About ten feet up, they were big enough to prop ourselves up in and go to sleep. The tree right in front of me would work just fine. We all went to sleep hugging our trees.

Before the sun came up, I was awakened by a strange sound. It sounded like someone was walking around under my tree. I tried to move, but felt like my whole body was very heavy. Something or someone held me down. I couldn't move, but I managed to open my eyes and saw the tail of a huge snake. The tail section I saw was about as big around as my thigh. It was moving away from me in my tree, draped across two other big branches and headed off into the jungle. When it slithered away and I couldn't hear anything, I went back to sleep. Or maybe I fainted.

Before dawn, our leader rousted us out of our sleep and told us to get moving. I rubbed my eyes and looked around for the snake that woke me up earlier. I told one of the boys and we decided to go find the monster. We found him stretched out across three branches of three different trees just a few trees from where we had been sleeping. I wasn't afraid at the time, but I wanted to get out of the jungle as fast as I could. We just kept walking and walking. I don't know how long we walked, but the sun was hot when we came to the train tracks again.

Along the way, we picked our breakfast of fresh-fallen fruit from the jungle floor. At lunchtime, the boys found a tall jackfruit tree full of monkeys. None of the spiky watermelon-sized fruit had fallen so we could eat it, but we knew it was ripe if the monkeys were in the tree. We picked up some other fruit from the ground and started throwing it at the monkeys. The monkeys became very upset. They screamed, jumping from limb to limb. They picked the jackfruit and threw it down at us. We had to duck because the heavy fruit had sharp spikes protecting the sweet meat around the seeds. When each fruit fell, we swooped in, picked up the broken pieces, and ate the sweet, slimy yellow meat with our hands. I think the monkeys figured out what we were up to, but they just screamed louder in frustration and threw more jackfruit.

After lunch, we walked along the train tracks for a while to get some relief from the jungle floor. In about an hour, we saw a train stopped on the tracks. The engine was headed north, back towards Hanoi. We were very excited. It was close to sunset. We waited until dark and snuck onto the train. We walked up one car from the one we had gotten on. I saw an empty seat and headed for it. As I was sitting down, a man said: "Hey, little one, didn't you get off the train yesterday?" It was Uncle Han. IT WAS THE SAME TRAIN!!

It turned out that the train was broken down and had been sitting all night just around the bend from where we got off. It was almost like this train was waiting for us to come back. About ten minutes after we had gotten back on, the train began to move, SOUTH. We couldn't muster the energy to jump again. As the train got underway, the thought that I had nearly been eaten by a jungle snake gave me chills again. Except for bathroom breaks, I sat in the same seat the rest of the trip. The thought of jail no longer worried me. I almost looked forward to it. There weren't so many bugs and snakes in jail.

The train pulled into the Saigon station about four o'clock in the morning. I was afraid I would be followed if I went home when the streets were nearly empty, like they had been in Hai Phong. If that happened, everyone in my house would be put in jail. I wandered around in the Saigon marketplace all day like one of the homeless children. I watched people buy snacks from the street vendors and wished I hadn't spent my snack money. I kept looking over my shoulder for a familiar face to see if someone might be following me.

Some of the homeless kids were very mean. They walked the streets in groups of five or six. When they saw me walking by myself, they threw rocks at me and told me to get out of their territory. I wandered all day without food or water. Because I hadn't washed for over ten days I smelled bad, and my clothes were in rags, filthy from the jungle floor, the trees, and the sticky jackfruit. I lost the bag Mother gave me for the trip when the police came to Lang's house, so I had been wearing these clothes the whole trip.

When I was too tired to walk, I sat down on a corner and closed my eyes. It was dangerous because a group of homeless kids might see me and beat me up, but I was beyond caring. Today, when I see a homeless person in an alley or on a street corner with legs folded up to his bowed head, I smell that street corner. I know how he feels. Fear gives way to apathy when hope is gone.

The moon was at its highest point overhead when I walked home and whispered for my mother at my front door. Mother heard my whispers almost immediately and opened the door. I passed out into her arms. I was home in bed for two weeks with a high fever and hallucinations. Anna said I was burning up and screaming at a ghost and a snake in my sleep. Mother couldn't take me to the hospital for two reasons: Father had been a doctor's assistant so someone was bound to recognize us, and the communist government controlled who received medical care. She didn't have connections with any high officials in the new government, and couldn't risk the chance of our identities being exposed.

She took care of me the best she could, using all the herbal remedies she could think of for what might be wrong with me. She wasn't sure I would survive the fever … what would she do with my body? We were in hiding. She had no way to mark my grave, and she would not leave me in the street. She watched me day and night without rest, checking my pulse and making sure I was still breathing. When my screams were too loud, she smothered me with a towel so as to not alert the neighbors.

Slowly, I began to come to myself again. I cried to Mother that I was willing to die in Vietnam; I no longer wanted to escape. I gave up because I just couldn't do it anymore. I told her to leave me, and I would be okay on my own here. She cried and refused to give up on me. She told me if I wanted to stay in Vietnam, she would stay with me. She would let Sister take the baby with her. Finally, I realized it would not be fair to allow Mother to stay with me. My brothers and sister and father needed her. She promised I would not have to make the next attempt alone. We would try again, and this time I would be free.

CHAPTER FIFTEEN:
WHY BOATS SCARE ME

Mother arranged a trip for Anna and me. The communist government had a "half open" gate for people who wanted to leave. You might wonder what "half open" meant. It meant we paid the government gold to get on a boat. They organized the day and location for us to leave. If they were asked to confirm this, they would disavow that such a thing ever happened.

The going rate for passage out of the country was fifteen one-ounce bars of gold for Anna and twelve for me according to our age and gender. Males cost more than females because they risked the draft and carried on the family name. Mother didn't have enough gold left to pay for one child, let alone two. She used her nightclub manager's skills to get us on the boat; she promoted the trip to earn our passage.

She dealt with the captain, who was a distant cousin (which meant he had our last name and that was all we knew), but we were not close. He knew mother's story through rumors and was warned not to do business with her. Our reputation was "bad luck" by this time. We had tried to escape more than fourteen times, been put in jail three times, and lost everything we had. Even my own uncles and aunts would not include us in any of their families' plans. They announced to us that we were on our own. When Mother heard of this chance and told my uncles and aunts about it, they refused to be a part of it. They told the captain that if he let her be a part of this deal, it would fail because we brought bad luck.

The captain had a good business head, and he knew Mother's reputation. He knew she would not give up. He looked at this from a business standpoint and was willing to take the challenge and the risk. He dealt with her the same way he dealt with other businessmen on the boat. He asked for one piece of gold for a down payment, to cover the costs of fuel, food, and official bribes. In exchange for her promise to fill additional space with paying passengers, Mother was able to get Anna's passage reduced to two-thirds of the full price and I was half price. She also earned one piece of gold for each passenger she recruited. She didn't plan to come with us this trip because she would be the Captain's contact in case we didn't make it through, and she kept my little brother with her.

Mother wasn't able to raise enough money by recruiting new passengers to pay for both Anna's and my passage. Only one of us could go. Mother had promised me that I would not have to travel alone anymore after the train disaster, so Anna would have to travel alone on this trip.

The evening before Anna was scheduled to leave, Mother felt very depressed that she was unable to pay for my passage and I would have to stay with her and Ken. Mother was out of gold and out of friends to borrow from. She would have to try the deadly walk across the Cambodian border with us instead of taking a boat.

Suddenly, there was a knock at the door. A friend of Mr. Lee,

Mother's "husband" from Singapore, came in quickly with a small bag. He explained that Mr. Lee had given him our address and perhaps Mother would be able to use this small amount of gold if she needed a loan. It was like a gift from heaven. I could go with Anna, and she would have enough gold left to live for a few months and pay for the next trip for her and Ken.

Mother's mood went from despair to joy in less than a second as the coins tumbled out of the bag onto the tabletop. She didn't know when or how the money would be paid back, but there it was, and she could not believe her good luck. The gods must be smiling on her again. I was meant to get on the boat with Anna after all.

Mother recruited two of our neighbors, Mr. and Mrs. Foong, to travel with us. Mr. Foong had two wives and two sons. The wives weren't friends, but they tolerated each other. He was a happy-go-lucky husband and father. His favorite phrase was, "No problem!" with a big gap-toothed grin on his face. The two sons were spoiled by their mother. They could do no wrong. Mrs. Foong Number Two, who must have been barely seventeen, was like their playmate. She was good at getting them in trouble with other people, who blamed the boys for her mischief. Mr. Foong held her in great affection and blamed the boys for every little thing, whether they deserved it or not. Their mother made up for it by coddling them, which made Number Two jealous, and her rebellious reactions kept up their dysfunctional cycle.

The second family to come with us was an elderly mother and daughter, Mama Chu and Chu-Jei. In age, Chu-Jei was between Anna and me. Mama Chu was a "country" lady. She had a very round face and a big belly like Buddha. She had been a widow for a long time. She raised pigs in her back yard for a living and had been a single mother to her son and daughter since they were toddlers. Her teenage son fought his way onto one of the planes and left Vietnam during the evacuation in 1975. She and her daughter were leaving now, hoping to reunite with him in America.

A day before we were to leave on our trip, Mother put out the clothes we were going to wear, just our regular everyday clothes. She had no more jewelry to hide in our clothing. She had only a gold band Father gave her for her birthday a long time ago, which she gave to my sister along with twenty American dollars. She gave me a gold chain and a red ruby-topped gold ring Grandmother gave her when she came back from a trip to Taiwan. These last trinkets would be our dowries if we made it out safely, and might save our lives if things got rough in the meantime.

We went to my uncle's house to say goodbye to my grandmother. One of my uncles said we would return again, so why did we need to say goodbye? Grandmother gave me a silver-plated bracelet. She told me she was going to wear this bracelet when she passed away, but now she was giving it to me for safekeeping. She also took her jade earrings off and put them on me. She told me she had them when she left China, and she gave them to me for luck on the trip. Deep inside our hearts, we knew we might not see each other again, but she was very sure we would leave this time, despite what my uncle said. It was no secret that Grandmother had favorite grandsons, but I was her secret favorite granddaughter. I wished she could come with us, but the trip would be too hard on her with her crippled feet. She once said to me that she had been on trips like this too many times in her lifetime. It was my turn to make the trip for my own freedom. She would wait for us to come back someday for her, or her ashes, after we made it out of Vietnam.

The next day, Mother took us to the bus station. She wanted us to obey Mr. and Mrs. Foong. He promised Mother he would look after us like his own kids. We left the city and headed for a small beach town called Rach Gia. There was a lot to say, but Mother just held her chin in one hand and waved with the other one as we disappeared from view. We held back our tears and didn't say anything. We sat in the back of the bus, and I looked out the back window through the cloud of exhaust fumes and dust as we left Mother further and further behind.

Several hours later, we arrived at the gathering place, a big house packed full of people. The guide instructed us to settle down and choose a corner to sleep in. We were told that we would be in this house for a few days before the big day. While we tried to adjust, we made new friends. Anna and I were single teens, and there were plenty of others like us making the trip. Some traveled alone and some were siblings like my sister and me. The captain's children were the same ages we were and we became friends. Some families had small children and some had kids our age, all in the same house with us.

One family caught the attention of just about everyone in the house. The grandmother appeared very strong and powerful. She had three sons, their wives, and their children with her. She often gave orders to her sons and their wives. "Get my sweater!" "Bring me some hot tea!" "Why are you so slow?" She was extremely demanding and critical toward them. It was clear that she was very rich and her children were afraid of her. She wore lots of jewelry from head to toe. When she walked up and down the stairs of the two-story house, we could hear her jewelry jingling. We would have thought she was a queen if she had an announcer to sweep the path in front of her and call out her name as she passed by.

On the big day, very early in the morning, before dawn, we were told to go out to the dock to get on the boat. We had been scammed so many times, we didn't know if this was our time to be carried away, shot, arrested, or whether we would really get on a boat. Trying to figure out what would happen next, each second seemed like an eternity. Lots of people were lined up. The boat was twenty-four meters (about seventy-eight feet) long. It was built originally with only two decks, but the owners had added another platform between the bottom and top decks. People were packed in from bow to stern, from the bottom to the top. Anna and I were in the last group to get on, so we were put on the top deck in the open air. We sat with our knees folded up to our chests, shoulder to shoulder, feet to hips, row by row without any open aisles or personal space. We were packed in tighter than sardines in a can with no room to stretch our arms or legs. Five hundred fifty-six people crowded into our seventy-eight foot boat.

Watching the TV show, *The Love Boat*, when I eventually got to America, leaving port was always a celebration. People said goodbye and they were all waving and smiling. But I had mixed feelings when our boat pulled out to sea. I was sad and worried, wondering how, when, and where I would see Mother and Ken again; yet at the same time I was in disbelief that I was actually on a boat again. It felt like being in a dream where everything that happened around me was outside of my control. We had dreamt about this moment for so long. I wondered if I would make it to the other side of the world. Would I see my father and my three brothers? I wasn't worried about our safety on the boat, but I didn't know anything about draft or hydraulics. I probably should have anticipated a few problems with all of us crammed together so tightly.

Within a few minutes of leaving the dock, people started to throw up. It didn't take long to decide not to try and toss our breakfast over the rail, as it made problems for everyone sitting around us to try and make room for people to get by, and they were all sick too. Some people couldn't make it to the rail and upchucked as soon as they stood up, all over the people around them. It got really gross really fast. As the boat headed toward the open ocean, nearly everyone else was sea-sick and vomited in their laps. We either tried to sleep or disassociated from our surroundings to avoid going crazy. After all, everyone was in the same boat and getting upset would only get us thrown overboard.

The first day at sea, we didn't have anything to eat or drink. That was the intent of the captain, I am sure, to stop the seasickness. The sun became hotter and hotter as the day went on. We could feel the skin on our arms and faces burning. Anna and I, as most of the other passengers, were wearing our luggage, and we started to strip off layers and use the extras for pillows or umbrellas. I took off five layers of clothes and sat on them. The boards on the deck got harder and harder to sit on over the long period of time. I have darker skin than Anna so the sun wasn't burning me too badly, but she had light skin and began to get blisters on her face and lips. We used my big red jacket for an umbrella to shield our bodies from the burning heat. Close to sunset the first day out, we heard that an elderly lady had died on the lower deck. The captain ordered her body to be thrown overboard because the boat had no room for live people to stretch out, let alone the dead.

It was the powerful grandmother who had died. Before they threw her body overboard, her children stripped off her jewelry like vultures tearing meat. They put her nearly naked, very undignified body on an old, dirty, tattered bamboo mat which barely held up under her weight. They tied it up with ribbons and dropped her off the side of the boat.

Now, when I see vultures on TV or at the movies, I always remember what happened to this lady. Her children didn't show any grief or tears. Watching what happened, I thought that all her orders and her wealth made no difference when she died. She was mean to her children, and they treated her with no respect after she was gone. I absorbed into my own philosophy, by watching firsthand, that we do indeed come into this world with nothing and will leave with nothing. We need to be kind to others, leaving behind a good legacy, not just possessions. Life is too fragile to be mean. Relationships are more important than material possessions. When my own family members have died since then, I have avoided their personal property altogether, not because I didn't want anything to remind me of them, but because I still saw those vultures in my mind's eye.-

When darkness came, we were cold and hungry. The wind was harsh and the engines were loud all day. During the day, because the sun was very hot, we didn't notice how cool the wind was. Now we put all the layers of clothes back on, and still felt the chill of the wind. We slept off and on with our knees still folded up to our chests. I had no feeling from my waist down by this time. I couldn't wiggle my toes or legs, and my lips were dry and chapped. I was worried about Anna. Her health was poor and she always got sick easily. When I asked how she was doing, she nodded her head, leaned over on my shoulder, and went back to sleep. We only had each other to lean on now. I didn't know what I would do without her. I missed my mother and Ken, still in Vietnam. I wondered where this boat would take us and how the journey would end. With the smell of salt air, the motion of the boat up and down, and the steady hum of the engine, it was easy to go back to sleep.

I woke several times during the night, but didn't know what time it was because of the darkness. The light on top of the captain's bridge was bright, but it was the only light to be seen. I tried to look out to sea, but it was dark, like our old dining room with no lights on. I tried to force myself to go back to sleep and not to let my hunger and dry mouth bother me too much. I watched the dawn light up the sky, and then the sun slowly rose. The sky and the sea connected unbroken in one line around us as far as I could see in every direction, except where our boat broke my view. I was glad the sun was up, but I hated it as well, because soon enough it got too hot. The rain did come to tease us, and we all held our faces up to the sky with our mouths stretched open like little chicks in a nest waiting for their provider, but the storms passed quickly and the sun dried us out again in just a few minutes.

At one point, someone passed a water bottle around for everybody to drink; we used the bottle cap for a cup. The bottle was only big enough for everyone to have one capful of water per day. We tried to ration water to last us for as long as we could. We had no food on the second day at sea. The small children were too hungry to cry. I had been hungry for days before, and I was used to dealing with it. I dreamed of any food I could think of, the way it smelled and looked, the texture, the taste, and a selection of different kinds of food. The key was not to think of only one kind of food, but lots of different kinds, so I would be satisfied with the variety and distracted from being hungry. I focused on the details of food instead of how hungry I was. Somehow it worked and my hunger pangs subsided.

People seemed to be getting accustomed to seasickness, paying more attention to the fish jumping and the movement around us. They moved around more and got up to use the back of the boat for the "bathroom" more often. It was an excuse to stretch and be able to get up.

To use the "bathroom" on the back of the boat, they had to step over people as they walked. Otherwise, they had to hang on to the rope rail and walk along the outside edge of the boat to get to the back. The "bathroom" was just an open area. It had no cover or tank system set up. It was just made out of a square wooden box with two boards to stand on or squat down. The ocean was underneath and the frame hung out of the boat. If one was not careful, it would be very easy to fall out and down into the sea. Men used it the most. Women avoided using it until absolutely necessary.

The captain told us if the weather continued to hold, we should arrive in Singapore by the next night as planned. We might be hungry, dirty, hot, uncomfortable, sometimes cold and wet due to the rain, but we were hopeful. He knew where we were and how long it would take us to reach Singapore. The sun slowly disappeared and darkness began to surround our boat. We made it through the second day at sea without any problems.

The third day, after we all drank our one cap of water for the day, we saw boats in the far distance. Everyone was very excited that we might be getting some help. We were so hopeful until we heard the captain yell "Pirates!" Then another voice yelled, "Look! More Pirates over here on the right, three of them!" We looked to the right and saw three boats coming fast in our direction. Then the captain yelled again, "There are four on our left! Everybody sit still! Don't move and be quiet! We need to outrun them!" He throttled the engines to full speed. I held onto my sister with one hand and the rope rail around the outside edge of the boat with the other. I could feel the wind whipping harder on my face and clothing. We all held our breath and no one made a sound. Going fast, we could smell the smoke coming from the engines below the boat's bottom deck.

We watched the pirate boats slowly fade away in the distance and then disappear. The captain began to slow the engines down, and the smell of smoke slowly dissipated. The engines died down and didn't make the humming noise as before. We didn't see any boats around us and were back to being surrounded by the sky and the ocean, all alone in the big sea again. We were so happy that we all let out a loud cheer at the same time.

We quickly realized that we were slowing down to a crawl and the engines weren't making any noise. Everybody got very quiet and looked up to the captain's bridge. He told us he had tried to restart the engines, but they wouldn't start. Now we had to rely on the wind to take us wherever it blew. We might not be able to get to Singapore as planned. He told us to sit down and be quiet.-

People began to whisper to each other that the pirates might still come after us, and what would we do? They looked terrified and some were crying out. "OH! OH! GOD OF MERCY! ANY GOD THAT CAN HEAR US! COME AND SAVE US! PLEASE DON'T LET THE PIRATES GET US! SEND US HELP BEFORE THE PIRATES GET TO US!" They were getting panicky, but no one could go anywhere or stand up, so all they did was pray, cry, and shout. Some were crying to themselves. Other people hugged their family members and cried.

The captain yelled out and tried to calm the people. He told them, "We will cross that bridge when we get to it! No point for us to panic now." They slowly quieted and calmed down. I wondered where they got the energy for their excitement. Anna and I hugged each other tight and tried to go back to sleep. We could hear the wind blowing and the waves lapping at the side of the boat, and we could feel the boat go up and down, up and down, since the engines were not running.

The boat bobbed on the sea for a long time. No one knew if it was moving or standing still. The sun slowly went down, disappeared, and darkness came. I was too hungry to think or to stay awake. At one point the rain woke us up. I used my jacket for cover, but I got soaked after a while. We were too tired to keep ourselves covered. Anna and I sat close to each other and held each other tightly to keep warm. She didn't say much and I wondered what was on her mind. She is the thinker and the quiet one in the family. I was more worried about her health than anything else. I was afraid to think about whether we would live through this. I only knew that sixty minutes breaks down into a minute at a time, then a second at a time, and then a breath at a time … and that is manageable. Several seconds could pass before taking another breath, and time passed quicker when I thought about the breaths instead of the seconds.

I was awakened by the hot sun the next day. Anna's head was leaning on my shoulder, so still I checked to make sure she was still breathing. She opened her eyes and said, "I am OK! Don't plug my nose!" She sounded weak, but reassured me that she was all right. She put her head back down on my shoulder and closed her eyes. I looked around and still saw only the sky and the ocean connected around us. The boat was still going up and down, up and down on the sea with nothing in sight. It seemed the world did not exist except for us. The sun got hotter by the hour. We didn't know what time it was, but I knew it was our fourth day at sea. At one point, I wondered when we would be on land. I closed my eyes and tried to go back to sleep. I could hear my stomach growling, and it hurt. I told myself not to let it bother me.

The wind blew stronger and stronger as the sun slowly went down.

I couldn't tell whether the boat was moving or still. Shortly after darkness surrounded us, the rain came down. Then it stopped and came again. The boat continued going up and down, up and down in the dark. I closed my eyes and wished we were moving. I don't know how long I slept, but we were all awakened by a loud voice calling out:

"LOOK! LIGHTS! LAND! We are close to LAND! LIGHTS!"

By this time everyone was awake and looking at where the lights were. We couldn't see very well in the dark, but we saw a long line of lights. Everyone was very excited. No one seemed to notice the wind getting stronger. The rain had stopped, but the waves were hitting hard against our boat. The line of lights slowly became closer and closer, and clearer to see. We began to see trees and buildings. We knew our boat was going in the right direction. We were more and more excited that we would be on land soon. We didn't mind the wind and waves rocking the boat.

SUDDENLY, WE HEARD GUNSHOTS. We might be close to land, but we were not welcome.

The captain ordered four baskets passed around to collect jewelry. He said that we should send some young men with the jewelry to give to the guards on land. The captain asked for four young men to volunteer to swim to land with the baskets. Later they said that as they were swimming to land, the Malaysian guards shot at them and were very mean to them when they did get ashore. They whipped them with a leather whip and yelled, "Get out! You are not welcome here!" These young men knew a little English and understood what the guards said. They got on their knees, held the baskets of jewelry over their heads, and begged the guards to let our boat land. They continued beating them at first, but finally gave up because the jewelry held strong power to convince them to let us land. Perhaps there was more treasure on board.

In the meantime, the wind became stronger and stronger. It rocked our boat up and down, and side to side, and the waves got higher and higher. We felt a big bump; it felt like an earthquake. The boat drove itself deep into the sand, and then stopped moving. The waves hit the boat so hard; it rocked side to side, but didn't move up and down in the surf any more.

The people down in the bottom of the boat yelled up to us on the top, "Water is coming into the boat! Help! We need buckets to get the water out! HURRY!" We were not in any better condition being on the top deck. The waves hit us so hard that we couldn't sit still. We fell from side to side as the boat rocked. I was very worried that our boat was going to flip over on the beach side, where we were standing. When the waves came in, we went down lower than the other side. One time, when the water pushed me off balance I fell right on top of an old man; I got up quickly and apologized to him. He said with a trembling voice: "Oh God! Are we going to die? Oh, God!" He was so terrified that he didn't even notice me in his lap.

The captain ordered those who could swim to jump off the boat. He also secretly told some young men to go down to the bottom of the boat and destroy the hull. He knew that if our boat was in good condition, the Malaysian guards would not let us land. By this time, the waves were already doing a good job of destroying the boat. All the people on the bottom and second decks of the boat came rushing up to the top deck. Most of the young people jumped off the boat. All of the people still left on the boat were old folks, children, and women that didn't know how to swim. People were panicking and yelling, "HELP! HELP! HELP!"

I heard the captain shout: "The boat is destroyed! We are sinking! Everybody must jump off the boat!" I saw pieces of the wooden hull floating around us. People were climbing and running back and forth on the deck from the low side to the high side as the boat rocked. They were crying and yelling, and my ears rang from the chaos. I realized we had no choice. No one was coming to help us, and we had to jump off the boat by ourselves. I knew how to swim, but not very well. I could only dog-paddle in my clothes. Anna didn't know how to swim at all. I wasn't sure I could make it to land by myself. I hadn't been able to feel my legs for a couple of days due to lack of blood circulation on the cramped deck, and I didn't know if I could get Anna safely to land.

I looked at her. She was smiling and eating something in her hands. I tried to talk to her about what we were about to do and how to get on land. She didn't seem interested in what I said to her. She was holding a cabbage in her hands. I thought she must be so scared it had affected her mind. I yelled at her, "Did you hear what I said? What are you eating? How can you eat at a time like this?" She didn't answer me, just handed me the cabbage and said, "Nay! Take a bite! I found it on the floor! It is good! Eat it! You will feel better!"

I looked at her and she still had a big smile on her face. Suddenly a big wave came down on us. I held onto her tightly, and we were knocked to our knees. After the water washed out, I stood and grabbed her hand again. She was still smiling and holding onto the cabbage. I took a bite, but it was salty and mushy. I spit it out and said "There! I ate it; can you listen to me now?" She didn't say anything but continued to smile and nod her head.

The Foongs came to us and asked if we were going to jump. I told them I was ready, but didn't know how I was going to get my sister on land because she couldn't swim. They offered to help her. They were both better swimmers than I was and said they would hold onto Anna between them and jump with her. We walked toward the edge of the boat and Mr. Foong wanted to push me off first. He said, "Don't be afraid! Show your sister how brave you are." I pushed him away and said: "No! Don't push me! I can jump on my own." I turned and saw Anna still smiling and eating her cabbage. Mr. and Mrs. Foong were on each side holding her arms. I said, "Sis, I am going to jump first. I will see you on the beach. Don't be scared! The Foongs will help you get to land. Watch! I am jumping off first, NOW!" She just looked at me and smiled again without saying anything.

I turned and looked down at the ocean one last time and saw a big wave coming behind us. I took a big deep breath and jumped. The water was very deep and I hurried to pull myself up above the wave. The saltwater stung my eyes. I finally got to the surface and started dog-paddling to shore. After a couple hundred yards, I felt the ocean sand against my feet. I stood up and walked as quickly as I could with several wet layers of clothing. I was still not able to feel my legs or toes, and I tripped several times, but I told my legs to keep walking. I finally got beyond the water lapping at the shore and looked for Anna and Mr. and Mrs. Foong. People were lying all over the beach. I stood there, not wanting to walk for fear I'd fall, but not wanting to sit for fear of missing my sister.

Anna found me and we helped each other walk away from the water's edge. The Malaysian guards were very mean to us. They whipped us, yelling, "Sit down!" Not many people understood English, so no one paid attention to them. Everybody was busy looking for their families and belongings. When a guard approached us, Anna pulled me to sit down since she understood some English. As we sat down, the guard whipped our backs. It wasn't very hard, but hurt enough that I felt the sting through my wet clothing.

Daylight came slowly as we tried to settle down. It felt so good to have land under our feet. As our re-stretched limbs warmed, the feeling came back. All of a sudden, the rain came pouring down on us. We heard a voice yell out "Everybody! Open your mouth for water from the rain. It is God's blessing to us! God knows we are thirsty! He sent us rain for water! Drink the water of freedom, the water of being on land!" We all opened our mouths at the same time for the water, like little birds in the nest again. Some people caught the water in their hands and smiled. I looked at my sister and asked "Sis, are we dreaming? We made it out of Vietnam? Tell me this is real! If this is a dream please, don't wake me up!" Anna looked at me with the biggest smile and hugged me. We were crying and laughing out loud at the same time.

The guards told us to sit down and wait for the Red Cross to come. We learned that this island's name was "Kelantan." My best friend, who was born in Malaysia, told me twenty-five years later that this island is a resort area. The Red Cross agents and nurses gave us water and food. They did a head count and finger-printed us. We were all vaccinated for whatever diseases they were afraid we might have or carry before we were allowed to be taken to the refugee camp. When we reported to the refugee camp, we found out we had five hundred fifty-five survivors from our boat. Everyone except the sour grandmother had made it.

While we were waiting in line, our boat lay halfway above the sand. The ocean pushed broken wood, clothing, and other objects all over the beach. I realized that I was wearing all the clothes I had, which was two shirts and two pants. I started the trip with five layers. I asked

Anna how many clothes she was wearing. She told me the same as I had. I went to the beach and looked for the clothes we boarded the boat wearing. Anna and I each had several shirts and pants and a jacket that we wore, because we couldn't bring anything on board but ourselves.

I had put some family pictures in the breast pocket of my jacket. We all wandered on the beach and tried to find our belongings. The Malaysian soldiers left us alone because the Red Cross workers were with us and lots of vacationers were taking our pictures. They didn't want to be too obvious and have to deal with newspaper headlines about their cruelty.

I found Anna's jacket first. I couldn't find our clothes, but eventually found my rose-colored jacket quite a ways down the beach. I checked the pocket for the pictures, but they had been destroyed by the salt water. I was sad that I had no pictures of my family but glad I got my jacket back. The jacket had a long story behind it. It was my favorite aunt's jacket. She was my father's oldest and favorite sister. She had worn this jacket when she was in her teens leaving China with her parents. When I said goodbye to her before leaving home, she gave it to me to keep warm. I still have it, although it's worn and faded by the sun and sea.

Anna and I sat on the beach watching the sunset and waited for an army truck to come for us. Although we had watched many sunsets together in our lifetime, we noticed that this time it was much more beautiful than in the past. We hugged each other tightly, crying and laughing at the same time.

She looked at me with tears in her eyes and said, "This is our first sunset on land without Mother and any of our brothers, yet it is our first sunset with freedom. I hope to God we will enjoy sunsets together with

Father, Joe, and Henry soon!" Risking another beating, I jumped up and shouted across the ocean with all my strength, my fists raised in the air over my head:

"MAMMA! MAMMA! SISTER AND I ARE FREE NOW! WE MADE IT! CAN YOU HEAR ME? MAMMA! WE ARE FREE! MAMMA! THANK YOU!"

CHAPTER SIXTEEN:
REFUGEE CAMP

The Malaysian government used big army trucks to take us to the refugee camp. It was dark and hard to see where we were going. When we got close to the camp, we saw the grounds were well lit and had a high fence topped with razor wire and a guard tower at the entry. Guards were standing in the tower and at the front metal gate. There were bright lights all around the fence. It looked like a prison. The truck took us through the front gate into a courtyard. The courtyard surrounded the guards' quarters, the checkpoint, and office rooms and picnic tables set up for interviews. No one was allowed to enter this section of the camp without permission. There was a second gate, and we saw a lot of people standing behind the gate and the fenced area, looking out at us. The guards yelled at them to go back inside and stay away from the gated.

We were told to get off the trucks quickly and form lines. One of the guards started to give us instructions and camp rules. He looked big and mean. I couldn't understand what he was saying, but his body language was very loud and powerful. He was speaking English, but he could have been speaking German for all I knew. He had a leather whip in his hands and paced up and down, back and forth as he was talking.

When he was in a brightly lit area, he looked big and dark. He had a very full head of black hair and a long thick moustache. A translator relayed what he said:

"You all came to our country without permission. You are not welcome guests. We have no choice but to provide you a place to stay. We want you to follow these rules. If you do not follow these rules, we will send you back where you came from. They are very easy and reasonable to follow:-

-

Rule #1: No buying anything through the fence.

Rule #2: No communication with people outside the fence.

Rule #3: You may enter the front section of the camp only with permission.

Rule #4: No loud activities after 10:00 p.m.

Rule #5: No TV after midnight.

Rule #6: Mail is only picked up and delivered on Red Cross visit dates.

Rule #7: Food is only given out once a week.

Rule #8: Keep the camp clean. You must sign up for chores.

Rule #9: You must sign a request form for an interview with a representative from another country. If you are rejected by a country, you must try another one. The Malaysian government is not interested in keeping you.

Rule #10: Avoid fighting at all costs.

We were all so hungry and tired, I'm not sure how much we remembered afterward, but we eventually learned the rules. He finally finished his speech. We did another head count and at last entered the residential part of the camp through the second metal gate. We had to stand in line to get rice soup for dinner. Anna and I had nothing to hold the soup, so we had to wait for Mr. and Mrs. Foong's sons to finish eating. Then we borrowed the rusty metal tuna fish cans they were using and got in line for soup. It was cooked very simply without salt or vegetables or meat, just water and white rice, but it tasted heavenly.

We looked worse than beggars on the street due to wearing several layers of clothing for many days, and we smelled worse. After four days of seasick people throwing up all around us, starving for food and water, swimming to shore, hunting for our lost items on the beach, and riding to the camp in army trucks without seats, we probably resembled really sick cats.

We were told to find any unoccupied place and try to sleep for the night. By the time we arrived, it was too dark and late for the camp leaders to assign us living space. We had to wait until daylight. Anna and I found a corner inside one of the big residence halls. It looked clean and dry. We sat down, curled up, and leaned on each other, using our jackets for blankets, and tried to sleep. I was now officially a refugee. The tin roof was my shelter, the hot sandy floor was my bed, and the stars were my light. But I knew I was free, and we had survived. Life would surely get better soon.

Mr. Foong found us in the morning. He told us we should stay with him and his family until my brothers sent us supplies. Mrs. Foong did not voice her disagreement, but was not very happy with the suggestion. She went along with Mr. Foong to avoid an argument. She also knew our brothers would be sending us supplies, and hoped to take advantage of that. Another incentive for her to go along with the arrangement was that Anna and I helped her with chores and kept peace

between her and the second wife. She was not pleased that her husband
brought her along. The two wives were not getting along. They hardly
talked to each other on the boat, and Anna and I became their mediators.
Since Anna spoke some English, she was also valuable as a translator
with people outside the fence.

The camp had ten big buildings in two rows of five. Each one was
made of wood and looked like a big warehouse, with four windows
framed along each side and door frames flanking the windows. There
were just the window and doorframes. The windows had no glass and
there were no doors.

Inside each building was a dirt floor. A wooden deck went all
around the inside perimeter of the building, interrupted by the four
doorways on the sides. A narrow sand walkway separated the perimeter
platforms from the one large deck in the center of the building. It was
one step up from the dirt floor onto the deck. If a person walked in one of
the side doors, he could walk past the perimeter platform on both sides of
the door, turn left or right and proceed on the sand path around the center
deck to another door exactly opposite the door he entered by. The
walkway was the only thing that broke up the platforms. These platforms
were where the families in the camp lived and slept. There were no beds,
and no tables or chairs, just platforms. The families had to sit on the
platform when they were awake, and lay on it side by side when they
slept. Mosquito netting set on poles was all that separated the families
from each other.

Opposite the administration area, there were five buildings on the
left and five on the right, with a large open area between. There was a
small TV mounted under a wooden roof on a tall pole in the center of
this open area. Facing this, we could see the entrance gate to the camp on

the left and a big tree on the right. I was told that we sometimes had camp meetings in this big courtyard. Nine of the buildings were for living and one was the community kitchen. The camp was built to house about ninety families, or at most about a thousand people. It's no wonder the Malaysians didn't want us, because our camp held more than three thousand people.

There were ten cooking stoves assigned to each building, so there were ninety cooking stoves in the community kitchen in building ten. The stoves, made out of clay, were about two feet high, and looked like large flowerpots. Each stove had a hole in the side for air to feed the fire, under a clay grate which held charcoal for fuel. We made our own charcoal from burnt wood. There was a ledge a few inches wide built into the top rim of the stove and we placed our cooking pots on top of the ledge. The stoves sat on a long table with enough space between to prepare meals. We ate in our sleeping accommodations or standing outside.

All the stoves were assigned to the families living inside the buildings. They had seniority, and the families who lived outside had to wait until they were done with their cooking. When Anna and I wanted to use a stove, we had to wait and ask permission, because we were latecomers who lived outside. The camp was designed to hold only the people who could fit inside the buildings, and we who had the bad luck to arrive late got the leftovers and had to make do without facilities. Another building or two could have fit in the camp, or another camp could have been built, but it was not a good investment. We were made very aware that we were unwanted guests who drained the local economy, and our Malaysian hosts had to put up with us in order to maintain a good face before the outside world.

At the far end of the camp just past Building #5 were the toilets and showers. There was no septic system. The toilet area had two low metal tanks with two 2x4s placed across them to straddle when you squatted down. The smell was foul, maggots thrived in and around the tanks, and the 2x4s were slimy. As I write this, I am trying to hold my dinner just thinking about it … the smell, the slime, the rot. If you were not careful, it was very easy to fall into the tank. We saw one young man slip and fall in. After he climbed out, he threw away his clothes, took more than three showers to clean himself, and still got very sick.

There were two shallow water pumps the camp used to pump water for drinking and showering. We located the pumps in temporary wells on each side of a building until the shallow ground water was depleted after several days. The pumps were never set at or past Building #5, because the water after that point was poisoned due to the toilets. The pumps were used to bring water to the surface by boring a fence-post size hole to about a meter (three or four feet) deep and running the pump's hose down the hole.

The men and children stood in their underwear or naked and took showers by the pump. The women had to carry buckets of water from the pump and stand in line to take showers in a stall. The mobile shower stalls were just three-sided plastic-draped 2x4 walls with plastic sheets hung in front for privacy. There was always a line for the shower stalls, so we had to change outside. When we changed clothes, we changed under a big sheet that covered us from head to toe.

The showers doubled as laundry facilities which is very difficult to put into words, but every woman can imagine what I am about to describe. When it was our time of the month, there were no options for feminine products. We only had old rags to use. It was our custom never to hang underwear, or anything related, on the clothesline to be seen. When I took a shower, I soaped up with all my clothes on, then placed the rag I used under my feet, trying to clean it the best I could without anyone noticing. I then pinned the rag under my shirt and stood with my arms outstretched in the sun to dry my clothes, the rag, and me. It wasn't exactly comfortable, especially when things didn't quite dry in the humidity. You can imagine that a few months seemed like a lifetime as we waited to leave the camp.

The camp leaders decided the living space in the buildings was only for families with elderly and/or young children. As more of them came, all the young adults and teenagers had to sleep outdoors. The refugees who arrived first had seniority to live inside and in the best spots outside the buildings. There was a waiting list for moving inside. Some had plastic sheets and built themselves a tent outside wherever space was available.

Since we were on the latest boat to arrive, we got the leftovers. Anna and I were teenagers, so we were expected to take care of ourselves. Since Mr. Foong had offered for us to stay with him, and Mrs. Foong did not object, Anna made an agreement with him for us to stay with them in exchange for English lessons. We heard that girls in the camp had been raped. We wanted the protection of a family, rather than having to be by ourselves.

So began our life in the refugee camp. Mr. Foong inquired around the camp and found out we had to buy our own household supplies such as pots, pans, bowls, cups, soap, toothbrushes, salt, sugar, plastic sheets, etc. The Red Cross provided rice, canned tuna and sardines, and wood for cooking every Wednesday. Mr. Foong told Anna that our two families should each pool together $100 for all these needed items. This did not seem fair to my sister; because there were only the two of us. We should spend less for our household supplies than they would spend for a family of five. She thought it would be better if we each bought our own items. So Anna told Mr. Foong that our funds were very limited and we couldn't pay out that much money. He appeared to be a very reasonable man, but Mrs. Foong was not easy to talk to when it came to money. He was thinking ahead and said, "No problem. We'll lend it to you, and when your brothers send you money, you can return what you borrowed from us! Besides, we promised your mother that we would look out for you girls."

Anna later found out that Mr. Foong was not a very honest man. When she went with him to buy the household supplies from the people who sold them over the fence, as she was busy negotiating with the sellers, he took the items. Some he paid for, some he took without paying for. When Anna asked him about it, he played dumb and forgetful. She felt bad about buying things over the fence since it was against the camp rules, but this was easily justified because we needed these things to survive. She felt worse about being a part of Mr. Foong's stealing from people. He rationalized it by saying that the outsiders overcharged us for the items. He was just trying to make it even.

Even though the Malaysian guards told us we were not allowed to buy things over the fence, they didn't provide any basic household supplies for our daily needs. Knowing prison life as I do, my guess is that the Red Cross provided the things we would need, the guards sold them on the black market, and we bought them from the buyers. We ended up with the same things we would have gotten from the Red Cross, so no suspicions were raised by official visitors to the camp, and the guards and their families and friends made a profit. We had no choice but to break the rules. When we were caught, the guards were cruel. They didn't care whether the offender was man, woman, adult, or child. They whipped whoever they caught. We watched them with fear, but could do nothing to stop the abuse. Anna hated going to the fence with Mr. Foong.

Mr. Foong used his charm with the people in Building #2 to let us build our tent outside their building, and we put the tarp up on the third day. Mrs. Foong assigned chores for Anna and me to do daily. When we got up in the morning, we waited in line for water from the pump, did the laundry, and hung the clothes on the line to dry. I learned a quick, hard lesson never to let my eyes off the laundry. Once, when I took the clothes off the line at the end of the day, I discovered that someone had stolen my pants. Since I only had two pairs to begin with, I wore one and washed the other in a nice rotation. After my pants were stolen, I wore my one and only pair for nine months without taking them off to wash. I even showered with them, because if I left them outside the shower, and they got stolen, I might have to humiliate myself even more by begging for pants in my underwear.

We had to get in line for just about everything we did, such as getting water for cooking, drinking, showering, and the toilet. The Foongs used us as their mules, and then as their line-place holders when we couldn't get things for them from a particular line.

I had never learned how to cook and had never even boiled water. When we were rich, Mother had servants to wait on us. When we were in hiding, she did all the cooking. I never had to lift a finger. Life in the camp was a lot different from being at home with Mother.

One day when Mrs. Foong was cooking, she told me to watch the water, because she had to step out for something. I stood by the clay stove watching the water sitting in the pot, thinking it would be no problem. The water looked very calm and still. I looked away to check out the big community kitchen. Lots of people were in and out of the kitchen. It was close to the end of suppertime and people were cleaning up their tables and platforms.

When I looked back at the pot, the water inside was jumping and forming bubbles, I didn't know what it meant. I started to yell and jump with the water. "The water is jumping out of the pot! Water is jumping, water jumping!" You would think a girl my age would know how to boil water. A young lady standing next to me couldn't stop laughing at me. Between trying to catch her breath from laughing so hard, she said: "No! Take the pot off of the stove. It's okay. The water is boiling and it's ready to take off." She helped me take the pot off of the stove. A new friendship had begun. Her name was Anh.

Anh had a very large family. Her boat had come to camp a few months before ours, and she came with them, a total of twenty-one members. Her family consisted of her mother, father, two younger sisters, Lang and Mary, and three older brothers. Her two oldest brothers had their own families and kids. The youngest member in their extended family was only a few months old. To this day, Mary is still my best friend. Anh and I lost an emotional connection after we married. She took on the role of housewife and mother right away and I went to school. Mary and I somehow kept our common spirit and stuck together.

A month went by and Mrs. Foong saw that our brothers had not sent us any supplies or money, so she told us to move out. By this time, Anna and I were glad to leave and stop running her errands. We waited for the Red Cross to come to record the identities of the people who arrived on our boat, but they kept delaying their visitation date. Mrs.

Foong had become very abusive toward us. Her two teenage boys did nothing all day. They spent their days playing soccer and basketball with the other kids in the camp. Anna and I often watched her give money to her boys to buy treats. Some people who came to the camp earlier had family members on the outside who sent them food and treats that they turned around and sold to people in the camp who weren't so for

Anna and I were doing all the chores and standing in line all day for different things. The boys were thirteen and fifteen, but Mrs. Foong treated them like they were younger than ten. During mealtime, we had to listen to her complain about how hard it was for her to cook. Anna and I washed the dishes after meals, and she scolded me if I didn't get water fast enough. She didn't yell for other people to hear, but under her breath, just enough to make me feel worthless. Anna and I were her personal maids. Anna knew what Mrs. Foong was doing to us a long time before she kicked us out. She told Anna I had a bad attitude and she thought it was best for us to live on our own. Thank God I had such a bad attitude; it saved me from being her slave.

When we lived with Mr. Foong, people were very envious of him. They thought he was the luckiest man on earth. He should have gotten an award for being a great actor. To those around us, he appeared very happy and was "mister nice guy." His two wives didn't fight and they didn't give him any problems. Little did they know that Anna and I were the peacekeepers and the scapegoats. We were blamed when anything went wrong, but I usually got the worst of it because I wasn't the English teacher.

When we moved, Mr. Foong cut us a tattered end of his stolen plastic sheet big enough for a pup tent for two. The thin plastic sheet painters use to cover and protect carpet during painting and then throw away is better quality than the sheet we used for shelter. Mrs. Foong later charged Anna for it. The camp was very full by this time and it was hard to find space to build our tent. Initially, Anna and I found a space to nail up our plastic tarp under a window against one of the buildings. That space was available because there was no room to stand up. The window sash was only four feet off the ground. We had to get permission from the people living further down the wall, because our tarp blocked their view of the courtyard and television. When it rained, water ran down the wall and off the window sash right into our living space, and water falling from the eaves flooded our floor. We had to find another, drier place to stay.

We began to move nightly from one building to another, even outside building nine by the toilets, depending on whether the people were willing to let us sleep under their windows. We had to get up and leave their window as soon as daylight came the next morning. Anna and I had the plastic sheet for cover, but the eaves of the buildings poured water right into our "house" when it rained hard. At those times, we would stand against the wall, covered by the sheet, and wait until the morning sun dried us out.

Malaysia was very hot during the day, and cold at night when the rains came. Out of curiosity, I poured a bucket of water on the ground around ten o'clock because I wanted to know how hot the daytime could be. I timed it. I watched the water steam up and within ten minutes the ground was just as dry as before the bucket of water was poured on it. By nightfall, the ground hadn't cooled down much, and we often had to sleep on very hot dirt. Our backs would be hot, but the wind was cold on our chests and faces. The rain didn't fall a few friendly drops at a time. It came down in a deluge. When we were awakened by the rain, we had to sit up quickly or we were drenched. We could have drowned under the eaves if we hadn't sat up.

Anna and I were well aware how vulnerable we were away from Mr. Foong's family. We tried our best to stay together wherever we went. We made friends with other single girls in the camp, formed a group, and did our daily activities together.

Anna and I never said anything bad about Mr. Foong's family. People often asked us why we moved out, and we always said, "Oh! It is time for us to be independent." We continued polite and open communication with Mr. and Mrs. Foong. Everyone in the camp knew everyone else's business because we all lived in such close quarters. Fights between the two Mrs. Foongs began as soon as Anna and I moved out. Mr. Foong's "dirty laundry" began to be aired. Their fighting became the daily live entertainment of the camp, and the highlight of everyone's day. People heard and understood why we moved out, and what happened to us while we were living with the Foongs. We didn't have to justify moving out.

After the move, our life was much simpler ... hard, but happy. I didn't have to hear about all the mistakes I made or wash and clean anyone else's dirty laundry or dishes, only Anna's and mine. I was no longer responsible for water, and I didn't have to get in line at shower time for other people, only Anna and me. We had lots of free time as soon as chores were done for the day. Our chores for the camp were to clean the toilet steps and shower stalls once a week, rake the leaves on the ground, and gather the trash daily. The chores for our personal living area were to keep it clean and organized, cook the meals, boil water for drinking, and wash clothes. After these were done, we got together with our friends and sang songs, told stories, and cried and laughed together.

The hard part was that we ran out of money after two weeks while we were living with Mr. Foong's family. When we first arrived at the camp, Anna sold a gold ring for us to live on. Anna said that the money she got for the ring would keep us until our brothers in Hong Kong sent us money for support. Mr. Foong kept asking her for a dollar here or five dollars there while Anna was helping him buy supplies at the fence. He always said he was short or didn't have enough. He would promise to pay her back, but afterward, he would act forgetful or like it never happened. If Anna asked him for the money, he would act dumb or say he did not have enough change to pay her then, but would pay her back later. Later turned to never.

Since we were moving out we needed to get our own supplies. We needed a pot for cooking, a bucket for water, containers for storing drinking water, soap, toothpaste, and one more set of bowls and cups for meals, etc. The elder Mrs. Foong played "know-nothing." She would charge us for anything we took with us such as a toothbrush or the bowl that we used for meals, and the plastic sheet. If Anna said that she already paid for it, Mrs. Foong would ask Mr. Foong to clarify it, and he would play dumb and say he did not remember, or he could not be found. The camp may have been small, but it was hard to find him.

Anna decided she should tutor young kids in the camp in English to earn some money, since she no longer needed to be in charge of me or do chores every morning. I'd do the household chores and cooking, since I had no other skills to earn money. We didn't have many household chores since we didn't have a place to stay. I had only one set of clothes to wear for months, so there were not many clothes to wash. I did have to learn how to cook.

The Red Cross gave us very limited food each week. The rice we got only allowed us to eat two meals per day. I had to stretch it out by cooking three days of solid rice and four days of rice soup so it would last us seven days until the next rations came. Anh said that I was an excellent rice burner. She said that other people usually burned one or two layers of their rice. I ruined all four layers. The four layers would be divided into the top layer, half cooked and half raw, the second layer which would be raw, the third layer which would be cooked, and the bottom layer which would be burned. My poor sister had to eat whatever and however I cooked. Anh sometimes felt so bad for me that she would give me some of her rice to make up for the burned rice that we couldn't eat. She could have gotten in trouble with her family for giving me her rice. She was also a very patient teacher. It took me two weeks to master rice cooking.

When we were living with Mr. Foong, we met a medical doctor. Dr. Dung came to the camp with his wife, Co-Hanh, and his little sister, Co-Thuy, and her husband, Chu-Cuong, several months before we arrived. They lived at the end of the platform inside Building #2. When Dr. Dung saw that Anna and I were not living with Mr. Foong's family, he asked us why. We didn't say anything bad about Mr. Foong, but he had heard the fights between the two wives, so he understood what happened to us. He took pity on us and was concerned about our safety. He used his influence with the camp leadership to assign us a place to live as soon as space could be arranged.

Just before Dr. Dung could set us up with a place to live, Anna got sick. She had a high fever and I didn't know what to do. We had no medication available. I sat and watched over her weak, skinny body lying there and wished it was me. My worst fear was that she was going to die and I would be left all alone. I went to Dr. Dung for help and asked if he could sell me some medication on credit. He not only gave me medication for free, he also moved us in to live next door to his platform that night. It happened that five families in Building #2 had just been given permission to leave for Canada. Anna and I were officially assigned the corner end of the center platform near him, due to her sickness. The leader of Building #2 had to move people around and made a few adjustments to fit us in.

Anna got better and stronger each day. We no longer were beaten up by the weather, heard swearing and harsh words in response to asking permission to build our tent for the night under people's windows, or had to be scared of being raped or robbed at night. Things began to look better for us after living in the camp as vagrants for three months. Sometimes reaching the bottom is what has to happen in order to get the help you need. Things got better for us each day after Anna got sick.

A few days after we moved into Building #2, we received a big box, which our brothers in Hong Kong had sent. The box had been opened and re-taped already and was far too big for the small amount of items it held. We received one set of clothing each, a sewing kit with a few items amounting to a few colored rolls of thread and a needle, a single package of sanitary napkins, two bras and two panties, a plastic cup and bowl, one notepad, one pen, one pencil, a roll of toilet paper, a comb, and a bar of soap.

Anna wrote to Joe and asked why he only sent so little in a big box. He replied with an inventory of what he had sent: a dozen this, half a dozen that, a full sewing kit with ruler and scissors, blankets, jackets, canned fish and dried fruit, and six boxes of sanitary napkins. Our next letter just said, "Don't send any more packages; they will never get to us." We were happy to get the items we did, but really mad that so much had been stolen by the camp officials or customs agents.

Two weeks after we moved and settled into Building #2, I found a wooden box after the Red Cross finished passing out food. I asked the Red Cross workers if I could have it, and they gave it to me. Anna was getting ready to leave the building for her teaching job. She asked what I was going to do with the box. I told her I didn't know for now, but I'd give her a surprise when she returned. I borrowed a hammer from Anh's second oldest brother, Long. He was very curious about what I was going to do with his hammer. He asked if I had ever used a hammer before. I said: "No! But I am going to learn how." He was hesitant at first, but let me have it. He knew if I didn't get it from him, Anh would loan it to me later.

I hammered away on my wooden box. It was about the same size and construction as wine cases you see at the store. I took the box apart and saved all the nails that were in it. I straightened up the nails by pounding them on a flat rock with the hammer and put all the pieces of wood together. Not all the boards were the same length, so I let them run wild on one end of my new table. My table had very short legs, only as tall as the end boards of the box had been. At least the table didn't wobble because the sideboards were the same length. The tabletop was rather droopy and uneven at the edges, but I managed to create a nightstand-sized dinner table. Anna could use it to write on for her English lessons, and we could have something besides our laps to hold our cup and rice bowls. It was a success, a masterpiece, and a Ting-Ting Number One original.

Long watched me the whole time I had his hammer from too far away for me to ask him for help. He was afraid I would give up and throw his only hammer and someone else would pick it up. I must have impressed him, because he told Anh that he was surprised by my determination and my creation. Several years later, after we had not seen each other for years, he was still talking about my masterpiece to his children. When Anna returned from work and saw the low, uneven table, she was very proud of me. We used it for the rest of the time we were in the refugee camp. She used it for writing in her diary, and when she wrote poems. We used it for meals and all the single girls we knew gathered around it for tea, trying to be as sophisticated as we could under the circumstances.

Mrs. Foong Number One was very curious about how we got moved into Building #2 so soon after we moved out on our own. Her family was still living in a tent. She often asked us if our brothers sent us anything. She always ended our conversation by saying: "Maybe your brothers don't have the money or don't know what to send you girls!" She burned with envy when she saw all the good things that were happening to us one after another. She was even jealous of my short-legged table.

In late March 1979, I was sixteen. We finally got Father's letter from America. It was in a plain white envelope, addressed in English, but handwritten in Chinese. Anna and I cried uncontrollably as we read his letter written on blue, lined paper. We had not seen or heard from Father since he left in February 1972, when I was nine and a half years old. I can't describe the feelings as we read his letter. All we could do was cry and let our heartfelt relief pour out. Everybody that lived near us didn't understand what our problem was. They thought we were crazy.

There were four major events that made people very excited, and were the highlights of living in the refugee camp: mail, international delegations, new boat arrivals, and hearing our names called to leave. A priest from a nearby Catholic church was our unofficial mailman. He often brought us mail, donations, and newspapers from the outside world. He was able to come to the camp about once a month. When his church donated enough money to buy stamps and postage for our outgoing mail, he would send it out and then ask the camp's guards for permission to come visit us again. Anna and I had none of our own money for stamps, so we relied on his congregation to send out our mail to Joe and Henry in Hong Kong. They sent letters back to us through him as well.

In February, the priest gave us some donated clothes. It was time for me to get something besides my one and only pair of pants. Anna tried to patch them over and over but the patches began to fail little by little. When we were standing in line for some donated clothes, the priest even commented about how pitiful my patched-up outfit looked. The clothes I received did not fit. They were "XXL" shirts and skirts and I wore a small. Anna used her teaching money to buy the missing items we needed for our sewing kit. She borrowed scissors from the people who came before us. Then she took the skirts apart and sewed the material back together into shorts by hand. All the shorts were long and went past my knees, though much shorter shorts were in style. She used all the material and didn't waste anything. When I see ladies wearing long shorts during nice weather in the summertime in America, I feel like a fashion pioneer.

When we put in our requests for interviews, we never knew when an international delegation was coming, or what country they represented. We also didn't know when they would decide to process our paperwork and set dates for our interviews. We were encouraged that when we put in our requests, we had to put down more than one country

we wished to be accepted by. We couldn't choose Malaysia. If we were
rejected, we had to try again. They told us that if all else failed, the
United States would eventually take us. The process of being accepted
for entry into the United States took longer than any other country. If we
had to wait for acceptance by the United States, we could count on being
in the camp for over a year.

Before we received Father's letter, Anna and I planned to go to
Australia, since the majority of the single friends in our group were
going there. She said Father and Mother's original plan was to send us to
Canada. We agreed that no matter where we went, we would have to
start life over again, so we would go to any country that wanted us. We
were still young, ready to work, and ready to rebuild our lives. We could
go anywhere. The sky was the limit for us. Having heard that other
countries took refugees faster than the United States, we put in our
requests for Australia as our priority, Canada second, the UK, France,
and Germany as third, fourth, and fifth, and the United States last,
because we didn't want to stay in the camp for another year.

There is an old Chinese saying, "One's plan is not always God's
plan." Australia came to interview us first. They agreed to take us on the
spot and we were excited. All the other countries we had applied to were
to be notified that we were accepted by Australia. We were told that no
later than three months after our interview, we would leave the camp and
be flown to Australia.

We counted the days with excitement. We had to wait for the
official departure date to leave. The camp's group departure date
depended on the number of people who were leaving and how many
countries were involved. The United States often took the longest time,
but the people they accepted were the largest group to leave. The U.S.

usually sent a chartered plane to take the refugees so they wouldn't have to be mixed in with others.

A week before our three months was up and we would be going to Australia, the United States representatives called us to their table. They told us our relocation to Australia had been canceled and we were to go to America to be with Father. We would not go as refugees, but as immigrants. There had been a delay of two months after our arrival in the refugee camp before my father received the telegram from our brothers in Hong Kong informing him that we were in Malaysia. As soon as he got the telegram, Father set the wheels in motion for us to be sent to the United States. His immigration attorney, Margaret Redmond, had already laid the groundwork and helped him get the paperwork processed for us based on his immigration status as an investor, which meant we automatically qualified for immigrant status and not temporary refugee status. He had already lost his money in business, but we would all be able to stay in the United States.

When we had arrived at the camp, we had to report to the Red Cross any family members living in any other part of the world, so they could help us reconnect with them. Before Anna and I left Vietnam, we heard a rumor that Father had left Hong Kong for the United States in 1975 after the fall of Saigon, but we were not sure if it was true or just a rumor. When we reported to the Red Cross, we put down only what we knew. Anna wrote the report: mother and one youngest brother in Vietnam, second younger brother in a Chinese refugee camp, two older brothers in Hong Kong, and father unknown.

The United States representative said: "Girls, we found your father and you are going to the United States! You are not going to Australia!" Of course, we were happy we would be reunited with Father, but we had to start the countdown to our departure from the camp all over again. Since all the paperwork and official plans had to be changed, we were stuck in the camp for another three months.

Everyone hoped to see family members, relatives, friends, or distant acquaintances show up in each new convoy of boat people which arrived. When we knew a new boat had arrived at our camp, we were all very impatient to see if we could find anyone we knew. Anna and I always hoped and wished that our mother and Ken could be two of the new arrivals. The guards had forbidden us to get too close to the front gate. When new boats came, I always volunteered to help welcome them by cooking and serving food. This way I got to see and meet the new people without the chance of getting beaten by the guards for being too close to the front gate.

Everyone in this camp had a story to tell. Some were luckier than others. For example, Anh's family escaped only one time and the whole family of twenty-one members made it out to freedom. Anna and I made more than fifteen escape attempts and were put in jail three times during these attempts, but we were also lucky. We made it out of Vietnam to this camp free and alive without being robbed, raped, or getting blown up. I was the luckiest one because I still had Anna to escape with me. Some of the single girls in our group were not as lucky. The reason they had to escape alone was because they lost their family for one reason or another.

Li-Chu was one of our new friends in the camp. Her family was murdered after being loaded onto a boat leaving Vietnam. Li-Chu said her parents and brothers were the last group to get on the boat. She didn't go with them, because she was going with her grandparents. The boat was full, over four hundred people. Shortly after they stepped onto the deck, the boat exploded and sank. She later found out that communist officials had put dynamite under the boat's bottom deck. This boat was only for people who were rich enough to leave Vietnam. All of them died because they were rich. Her grandparents could not bear the news. They decided Li-Chu was better off taking her chances by escaping alone. They did not want her bad luck rubbing off on them.

Another girl in our group, Yieng-Hao, shared her story. Her boat had about three hundred Chinese and Vietnamese people on board. They made it to Malaysian waters and were stopped by a Malaysian Navy ship. The Navy captain asked for payment in gold for the number of people on board. The refugee boat's captain could not comply, and the Navy boat towed the refugees' boat further out into the ocean. The Navy boat was much lighter and stronger built than the fishing boat, which was much more heavily loaded, and the fishing boat began to break apart from being pulled too fast.

As it broke apart, people began to fall into the ocean and drown. The captain got a movie camera and taped the whole incident. They saved some women and children, but all the men on her boat drowned. Fewer than a hundred people were saved. Yieng-Hao and her aunt were the only members of her family to survive. Later, the naval captain laughed and bragged that this tape would help him make lots of money and bring him fame. He would be the hero who rescued these poor drowning refugees at sea, as though the Navy had just come upon them by accident.

Thirty-one years later, my dear friend Peng, whose family lives in Malaysia, took me back for a visit. While I was there, her high school classmates came to visit us and I shared the story with them. Of course the ladies were mortified. I didn't know it at the time, but the husband of one of the women was in the Malaysian Navy at the time this happened, and he confirmed that it did indeed happen. He said the rumor of this sinking spread, but the Malaysian government chose to ignore it. However, someone in the United Nations found out about it, and they put so much pressure on Malaysia that the Malaysian government was forced to discharge the captain and all the sailors who took part in it. I also found out that, in an ironic twist of fate, several years later the captain was in a terrible car accident and almost died. His life was saved by several Chinese people.

In Chinese culture, boys and girls are counted separately. If the first-born is a girl, and the second child is a boy, he would be counted as the first-born child in the family because he was male. Also, if the parents were absent for any reason, the oldest siblings assume the parents' responsibilities for the care of their younger siblings.

Tu-Jian came to the camp with her oldest brother's family. She was the oldest girl in her family. Her parents had decided to split up the family to escape. They took two younger siblings with them, leaving Tu-Jian with her oldest brother, who was married and had three small children. They needed her help with the kids. She did not know how her parents and two siblings died, but she heard their boat was captured by pirates. They simply vanished into the deep blue sea. It took her two years to accept this bad news. She had planned to stay in Vietnam, but her brother talked her into escaping with him. She didn't get along with her sister-in-law after she came to our camp, so she hung out with our group after dinner every night.

One day, the camp leader announced to our group of girls that we had to help cook for a new boatload of fifty-seven people, as they would soon arrive at our camp. We busied ourselves getting the food ready.

Anna had to teach that day, so she didn't get to welcome the newcomers. Anh had taught me some very good cooking skills by this time, and I was happy to help. Before these people came into camp, everyone was busy talking about the new boat, wondering what their story was, and how horrible that this boat held over two hundred people, but had only fifty-seven survivors.

I walked in and out giving food to these people and listened to the newcomers telling their story. I didn't get the whole story, just a little here and there. This boat had been caught by pirates. I hadn't had time to process the story about what happened to them, when I noticed a young girl sitting by the big tree, all alone. She had been served with the others, and they were mostly already finished, but her food was getting cold. I went to her and said, "You haven't eaten your food and it's cold! Would you like me to get you some more that is hot?" There was no response or reaction to my questions. It was like she hadn't even heard me. She was in her own little world. I tried a second time and shook her shoulder to get her attention. Again, she had no reaction. Anh came to pull me away. She told me this girl had been raped seven times. She was in major shock and was unable to talk to anyone. I looked at her one more time. She was looking straight ahead, but had no emotion. Her eyes looked empty like there was no soul inside her. I know the look now. It's mine, too, sometimes.

I looked at Anh and said, "It's okay! I'm going to get another hot soup for her. She doesn't need to respond to me." I walked toward the kitchen and passed a young man. He looked at me as I walked by and called out my name. When he first called, he was not sure it was me. I looked back, turned around, and walked toward him. He did look familiar. He called my name a second time. This time he was very sure it was me. When I got closer to him, I was very excited as I recognized who he was. He was my best friend Xiao-Wei's older brother, Da-Minh. I quickly asked, "Where is Xiao-Wei?" as I looked around for her. When he didn't answer my question, I looked back at him. He held his head down and took a deep breath before he spoke. My heart dropped deep inside me.

He gathered his courage and his breath, and still choked on his sobbing as he replied: "She didn't make it! The last I remember was my mother handing my baby sister to me. We were in the bottom of the boat and it was a stormy night. The boat was rocking hard. We were all very scared. My other little brother was crying. My mother told me to hold my baby sister, so she could attend to my little brother. As soon as I held my baby sister and wrapped her in my arms, I heard the water push through the side of the boat. The next thing I knew, I was on the beach and my baby sister was still in my arms. I don't remember how we got to the beach. I can't find my other family members. There were fourteen of us that got on the boat." We cried together as I listened to his story. I felt the weight of the world sitting on my shoulders and my heart was heavy. Then questions came to me that I was not able to ask him. I felt a cold chill come over me. I thought of the story of the girl that was raped seven times. She looked about thirteen or fourteen years old. What happened to Xiao-Wei? He hadn't told me she was on the boat when it sank.

I suddenly remembered that I was on my way to get another bowl of soup for the girl under the tree. As I walked with the soup, I talked to myself in anger. I knew Xiao-Wei knew and loved her God. She had talked me into joining the youth choir at her church. Why did God not save her? What kind of god was it that would let her and her family die this way when she loved him so much?

I laid the soup next to the still-silent girl who now had tears in her eyes. She would not reach for it. As I walked back to Da-Minh, a lady came toward him holding a baby girl. Da-Minh told me this was his baby sister. She was just eight or nine months old and looked just like the baby-pictures I had seen of Xiao-Wei that sat on a table in their home. Da-Minh told me he didn't know how to take care of his sister. All his life he had prepared to take on a man's role, and now he had to care for his baby sister. It was a foreign concept to him. She was crying and refused to eat anything. I dared not ask if she had still been breastfed, because that was not an option now. She was going to have to get used to rice soup and canned tuna. Some of the ladies in the camp volunteered to watch her for him. She probably reminded them of children they had lost. The camp leaders assigned the two of them a living spot inside one of the buildings.

The camp loudspeakers blared that the new boat people should line up to go to the beach to identify bodies that had washed up on the beach. They needed people to go and see if they could recognize the bodies. Da-Minh asked if I could go with him. I was not sure the guards would let me go. He agreed to let me know if he found his family. I didn't know which building he was assigned to, but I saw him standing in line for water the next day. I asked if he had any news. He told me that when he got back to the beach, the bodies were washed up by the waves and dropped on the beach like so much driftwood when the tide receded. They all looked like big purple balloons. He could only tell whether the body was an adult or a child by the size, and male or female by their clothing, but he couldn't recognize their different characteristics. I still remember his descriptions as if I saw the bodies myself. Maybe I did go with him.

I asked how his night went. He said he felt like he was still in a very bad dream. He just wished he would wake up and this nightmare would go away. He wanted his family back. He had no more tears for that day. I agreed. You can only grieve so much in a day in refugee camp, or you can't find the strength to fetch water. Looking at him and talking to him, playing with his sister, I could see Xiao-Wei's smile.

I learned from Da-Minh that Xiao-Wei's boat left Vietnam a few days after mine. Three days out to sea, their boat was caught by seven pirate boats. Seven pirate boats. How many groups of seven pirate boats do you think there were in the seas off Thailand and Vietnam? Seven pirate boats had chased my boat. If they had caught us, maybe Xiao-Wei would still be alive. Seven pirate boats. Seven pirate boats. Seven pirate boats.

I knew in my heart these were the same seven pirate boats that our boat had outrun. My chest tightened so that I had to work hard to breathe, as if the beach had landed on me. My worst fears and questions about Xiao-Wei were already answered. She had been caught in the trap that was laid for me. I knew that, like the girl under the tree, Xiao-Wei and Xiao-Yiang had been raped many times by many different pirates, but they hadn't made it to the tree.

Da-Minh had to get his story out. For some reason, it was going to be me he told it to first. He told the story with great animation and emotion as we stood in the water line together, in our own world, speaking a dialect we knew no one around us could understand. Reliving it, he told me the painful details. Here they are in his own words as best as I can remember them:

"The seven pirate boats took turns taking all the women on our boat to their boats. The youngest girl was eight, and she stayed with all of us men. We had to strip down to our underwear. The men and babies were forced to stay in the lowest deck of the boat. The pirates took all our jewelry, gold, food, and water. They guarded us as prisoners on our own boat. The seven pirate boats took all the teenage girls, wives, mothers, and grandmothers. Some of the boats were gone for days. One by one each boat returned and traded women and loot with another boat, and that boat would take over, and be gone for days. Some women were lucky and were left on the refugee boat until the next boat decided to take them again. Each time a boat brought the women back, some would be missing. If the husband, father, brother, or son asked where their loved one was, the pirates would beat them or shoot them right on the spot and throw them to the sharks, dead or alive.

"We were given very little food and water as we waited. All the small children were too hungry and tired to cry for food. They slept all day and all night. The ones who stopped breathing were thrown overboard. When my mother and two younger sisters finally returned, we could not ask them any questions. Xiao-Wei and Xiao-Yiang did not return to us. I did see them going from one pirate boat to another pirate boat four or five times. After the fishermen-pirates grew bored with their catch, they let all the remaining ladies return to us. They gave us some food and water, but kept all our gold and fuel, and left our boat drifting at sea. We didn't know where we were, and our boat was not able to go anywhere. We were at sea for days. I can't remember how many days went by, and the rest of the story you already know."

That was the last time I talked to him at the water pump. I didn't know him very well in school in Vietnam. We had seen each other once or twice when I visited Xiao-Wei at her home. He was the "big man on campus" basketball star at school and I was the ugly, fat girl playing with his little sister. This was the longest conversation we ever had. Now, he had to focus on taking care of his baby sister. I saw him from time to time in the kitchen line or the mail line. We just acknowledged each other and moved on. In my culture, males and females have very clear boundaries. Socialization between boys and girls is very limited, unless they are dating or spoken for in marriage. I did find out that he was accepted by Canada, but never heard what province he ended up in. I left the camp before he did.

Another reason I didn't keep in touch was that I couldn't handle thinking about Xiao-Wei and Xiao-Yiang. When we talked, I couldn't help but cry. I can't put into words how badly it hurt deep inside me to know what happened to them. Living in the refugee camp I learned that there were many other stories about people who had died like Xiao-Wei and Xiao-Yiang, as well as the families of the other girls in our group. Over half a million boat people died at sea.

Many of these pirates were not real pirates at all; they were poor fishermen from Thailand, and also the Malaysian Navy. Thai fishermen should have been fishing for fish at sea, but instead they fished for boat people like us. They raped, robbed, killed, and got away with their crimes and treasures. I'm sure all these pirates had family members at home. How they faced their families after committing such barbarism I'll never know. When they spent the blood-money they got from selling the gold and jewelry they stole, how did they face their wives? I am still beyond angry and disgusted. Where is their sense of humanity? I remember that Buddha and other gods teach us to be kind and merciful. Isn't Thailand a country with a strong Buddhist religion, and strong Buddhist practices? Where are their consciences? Didn't they learn that because of their sin against their fellow human beings, they are going to be sent to the lowest, eighteenth level of hell? Didn't they hear the cries of their victims?

The Buddhist religion teaches that humans or animals that practice mercy and kindness toward other life forms can become gods. For example, Buddha was a man, but practiced mercy and kindness toward other humans, and taught this to other people, so he became a god.

A well-known legend in Buddhism tells the story of a princess who was the youngest daughter of a mean and heartless emperor. She was the emperor's favorite daughter. Her two older sisters were mean and heartless just like their father. She often heard reports from the servants that the people of the kingdom were happy and had plenty to eat. She wondered if all these reports were true.

One day, to see for herself, she snuck out of the palace. What she saw was exactly the opposite of the reports she had been given. There was sickness and poverty throughout the kingdom. When she returned to her father and told him what she had seen, he told her not to worry about it, but to look at all the wealth that she had. He told her he was also going to give her everything he had and would arrange for a rich prince to marry her just like her two older sisters. She refused, went against the emperor's wishes, and left the palace. She lived among the sick and the poor and was so compassionate and caring to the people that she became known as the goddess of mercy.

According to the Buddhist faith I grew up with, even if an animal like a fox or a snake did not kill or eat other animals, but ate only fruits and vegetables, meditated, and received energy from the moon, the animals could also become gods. Buddhists also believe in hell. Hell is controlled by the god of death. This god is a judge. When a person dies, he or she has to answer to the god of death who decides whether the life they led on earth entitles them to go to heaven or condemns them to hell. For example, if the person was mean to an animal while on earth, the god of death can turn the person into that animal and send them back to earth if he decides this is the appropriate punishment.

The god of death can also decide to send the person to hell. Hell has eighteen levels. Each level is worse than the last, depending on the kind of sins the person committed while on earth. For example, if the person lied, the god of death can send them to the level of hell where demons will cut out their tongue and send them back to earth to be born without a tongue. If the person stole, the god of death can send them to the level of hell where the demons will cut off their arms and send them back to earth to be born without arms. If the person used their eyes to look at pornography, the god of death can send them to the level of hell where demons will cut out their eyes, and return them to earth to be born blind. The eighteenth level of hell is the absolute lowest and worst level a person can be condemned to. That person has no chance of returning to earth but will be condemned to stay in hell for all eternity.

Whenever I hear the words "Thailand", "fishermen", "pirates", "Malaysia", "prison", or "guards", I still think of the eighteen levels of hell. I used to pray that the god of death would do the right thing and send them to the eighteenth level of hell. When I missed Xiao-Wei, I would curse those men that raped and killed her. I sometimes felt guilty for thinking this way, but I couldn't help myself. I struggled between my thinking and my guilt for wishing this on those people. My soul hated them so, that I secretly rejoiced when the Tsunami washed so many of their families and fishing boats out to sea.

Of course, the guilt of my rejoicing drowns me as well.

I felt terrible that Xiao-Wei's boat was caught instead of mine. Part of me felt guilty that our boat got away from them and her boat didn't. I knew if our boat had been caught by the pirates, what happened to Xiao-Wei would have happened to me. I was angry that she had to die this way. I understood that we all have to die at some time, but not that way. Nothing made any sense or lightened the burden of my guilt for being alive. She had a beautiful soul and a kind heart. I missed her smile, and it hurt that I couldn't see her again. I wondered what it would have been like to grow old together. Who would she have married? What would her children have looked like? Our kids could have been best friends.

I am still envious when some of my friends here in America show me their childhood friends' pictures or introduce me to their best friends. I even felt jealous of Peng and her friends in Malaysia. I wondered why they got to live such happy lives together when their people or their government kept us captive in the camps or hunted us at sea. Now that I am older, I don't have my childhood best friends beside me, or on Facebook, or a phone call or plane ticket away. Xiao-Wei's God took them from me. Why didn't he take me? Did he leave me on this earth to suffer for my whole life?

CHAPTER SEVENTEEN:
GOODBYE ASIA

We had to stay in the refugee camp at Kelantan waiting for plane tickets. We watched our friends leave one by one for the countries accepting them. Finally, it was our turn. After eight months in the Kelantan camp, we were transferred to a holding camp in Kuala Lumpur. Anna requested that our brothers send us clothing as soon as we reconnected with them after being transferred to the new camp. They did send them, but things were missing as usual. By the fourth try, we finally built up a set of nice outfits, underwear, duffel bag, and female products. We saved the nice outfits for leaving Malaysia so we wouldn't look so much like we just got out of a refugee camp.

When we were transferred to the holding camp, the food was much better. We were given prepared food and didn't have to cook it ourselves. It wasn't like eating in a restaurant, but it was much better than we got at the refugee camp. We still had to get our own water and stand in line for food, but it was a first-class hotel compared to the camp we had been in.

We found out that our first camp was once considered a model camp, but was the worst of all the camps. What made it a "model camp" was the ten buildings it had, but it had a reputation for the worst food of all the camps. Other camps had freedom to buy food and received services from the Red Cross, but residents had to build their own houses from lumber they collected in the jungle. They were given freedom to walk around the islands and didn't have to deal with guards. Our camp was supported by the Red Cross, but managed by the Malaysian guards. They controlled when and what to give us. By the time food got to our camp, the guards had exchanged the value of the food. For example, the Red Cross budgeted four U.S. dollars per person per week for food. The guards exchanged the money for the equivalent of four Malaysian dollars, which were worth only a small fraction of American dollars. Our food was down to only rice and canned sardines or tuna; no vegetables or fruit, and we didn't have enough to last the week.

We had news from Joe a week after we arrived at the holding camp. He told us he had a letter from our grandmother saying that Mother and Ken had left Vietnam by boat. Our father had immediately planned to go to sea to look for her. Joe wanted us to try to talk him out of the trip. Knowing my father, and that he had not seen or heard from Mother and us for over seven years, it would be a very difficult task to persuade him not to go. We could only hope he would be delayed until we got to America, and would change his mind once he saw us.

A week before our call came to leave Malaysia, we got a letter from Father saying he was leaving America to go to sea and look for Mother. He wanted us to stay with Uncle Wen-Caw in Orange County, California, when we arrived. He gave us his address and telephone number. By the time we got the letter, it was too late to talk Father out of leaving. He was already aboard the World Vision missionary ship.

Finally, Anna and I were called to leave Malaysia. We were in the two Malaysian refugee camps for a total of nine months. The United States loaned us the money for our plane tickets to America, but we had to sign a promissory note that we would repay the loan to the United States government before we got on the plane. The United States chartered a 747 plane to come to Malaysia and bring a big group of us to America. The plane was very big and all the people on board were refugees except the diplomats, pilot, co-pilot, flight attendants, and the two of us.

I was excited and so ready to leave Malaysia. My heart was broken and dead for Asia after my experiences in Vietnam, Hong Kong, Malaysia, and with the Thai pirates. I felt empty, angry, and rejected after everything that happened to my family. Asia had nothing left for me. She was the place of my roots, my birth, and my youth. I would always long for her, but at the same time, I was done with her.

When I stepped off the portable ladder-stairs onto the threshold of the plane, I turned and looked at Asia for the last time, said goodbye to her, and waved farewell to no one. I vowed to myself that I would never return to Asia again as long as I lived.

I had been on an airplane once before, when I was deported from Hong Kong back to Vietnam. I felt hopeless and horrified then. This was something new. I felt excited and hopeful and determined. The old Ting-Ting stepped off the ladder, and the new Ting-Ting stepped onto the plane. This chapter of my life was closed forever.

I walked in and down the long aisle until I found Anna. The plane was full of excitement. People were smiling and helping one another with their seatbelts and handbags. Some people were busy telling which cities or states they were heading to, or where they knew they had relatives, and where the big Vietnamese settlements were: "I'm going to

Houston." "I'm going to Minneapolis, but they say it's really cold." "I want to go to San Jose or San Francisco." The flight attendants were busy getting everyone to settle down so the plane could take off. I looked at Anna to make sure she was okay. She wrapped her arm around my arm and said, "This is it! We are going to see Father in America! This is not a dream!" No, not a dream! I knew exactly what she was thinking. We were worried about Mother and our youngest brother, but we were excited that we were going to see Father in America, and soon our brothers, too.

We thought America would welcome us with open arms and lots of opportunities. We were ready to rebuild our lives, family, home, and future. The flight attendants gave us a lesson in emergency survival before the plane took off. Anna quietly translated for me and added at the end, "We have to be on this plane for twenty-four hours before we land in America. We waited for so long and only twenty-four hours left to go!" We watched as the door of the plane was locked, felt the thrust of the engines push us back in our seats as the plane started to build speed going down the runway, and lifted off into the air. We felt the wheels leave the ground and the plane going up, and up, and up. We were finally off of Asian soil. CALIFORNIA, HERE WE COME!

CHAPTER EIGHTEEN:
JOHN WAYNE AIRPORT AND THE PINK HAND

The plane finally arrived at San Francisco International Airport. Before we got off, the flight attendants took pictures with the refugees, and a government official came onto the plane. He began to call names and instruct us what to do after leaving the plane. He also handed papers to the people whose names he called. When he called Anna's and my names, he gave us a large, thick, yellow envelope with a big red seal in the middle. He told us not to open it until we saw the immigration officials. We were told that we had to catch another plane to our final destination. He rushed us out, pointed across the asphalt in the direction of our next plane, and said we had to hurry.

Anna understood about thirty percent of what he said, and told me to run after her to catch the other plane. We didn't have time to talk, just run. I followed her without asking any questions. When we boarded the second plane, she told me the big envelope meant we were no longer refugees. We were officially immigrants, and our father was our sponsor. He had to pick us up when we arrived at the airport. Other refugees had church groups or organizations pick them up and make arrangements for them. Of course, Father was in the Indian Ocean looking for Mother, and we were on our own from that day forward.

We were on a plane headed south from San Francisco to Santa
Ana. A few of the refugees from our long flight were with us. This time
we were on a plane with business travelers and tourists, not just
Vietnamese refugees. Our group was not assigned seats together, and
Anna and I were given separate seats. I sat two rows in front of her. She
tried to let me know what I was supposed to do and tell me what the
flight attendant said. We could have been going to the North Pole, for all
I knew. I just followed whatever Anna said. I couldn't understand
anything that was said around me. The people on the plane, the
buildings, the rolling hills without jungle below, and even the clouds
looked gigantic and vastly different from anything I had ever
experienced. Before the plane took off, Anna told me that the "ghost"
(foreigner) sitting next to her agreed to change seats with me after the
pilot let us get up out of our seats.

Finally, we arrived at John Wayne Airport. When we left the gate,
we were met by Mr. Wang. Maybe his first name was John, too. Mr.
Wang was the refugee coordinator from a local church. He spoke
Chinese and gave gifts to all the refugees. Everyone got a shirt and a
jacket. Anna and I didn't get them, because we were not on the refugee
list. Mr. Wang also made sure everybody was picked up by their sponsors. One by one, the refugees were picked up. He saw that no one was
coming to pick us up, so he offered to help until someone came. Anna
told me to sit and watch our one and only duffel bag. She went with Mr.
Wang to make a phone call to our uncle. After they walked away to find
a phone, I finally got a chance to take a look around.

I sat quietly on my duffel bag and looked at the people in the
airport coming and going. I suddenly realized that all these people were

enormously big and tall. I felt very out of place. People walked past me; some were busy talking and others just gave me a strange look. I felt the newness around me, and felt new myself. I was wearing new clothes that my brother sent me, clean new clothes from underwear out for the first time in years. The smell of the new air, the sight of the new environment, and the sound of the new language reminded me that I was definitely out of Asia.

I saw a big group of tall, mostly black men walking my way. They wore brightly colored uniforms and some of them carried basketballs. People were taking pictures of them. They seemed to attract lots of attention as they walked toward where I was sitting. The man closest to me had a basketball in his hands; or rather he held it with one hand, which was nearly as big as the ball. He held that basketball like I would hold a softball. His hand was very shiny, silky dark on one side, and very pink on the other side. The line between the two colors was clear and distinct.

I had seen big, black American men in Vietnam, but never this close. He was smiling from ear to ear, and his teeth were very white like the toothpaste commercials on the billboards in the streets of Vietnam. His dark pink lips were very distinctive next to his huge white teeth which looked like the Chiclets chewing gum treat I loved. They all lined up very nicely in his mouth. I must have been staring because, before I realized it, he walked right up to me. He looked down, said "Hi!" and waved at me with one huge hand. I was taken by surprise that he was so super-sized and so close. As I tried to get up and move back at the same time, I tripped over the duffel bag and landed on my hands. He tried to help me, but I recoiled and crab-crawled sideways away from him. I rolled off my hands onto my knees and stood up, still shocked by the encounter. He walked away, caught up with his group, and I heard them laughing, but I couldn't understand what they were saying. I didn't know it at the time, but I had encountered an American professional basketball team.

When the group was far enough down the hall for my comfort, I walked back to my duffel bag and sat down. After about five minutes, Anna and Mr. Wang came back from the phone booth. She saw the shocked look on my face and asked, "What's wrong?" I asked, "Did we land in the right country? This is a country of giants! Remember the story you told me a long time ago? There was a man who traveled on his adventures by boat. He landed in a place with very small people, and later in a giant's land where the people were giants. We are definitely in the giant's land!" My sister smiled at my *Gulliver's Travels* reference, but I noticed she, too, had a worried look in her eyes. This time it was my turn to ask, "What's wrong?"

She didn't answer, but Mr. Wang told me he talked with our uncle, and he should be there any time to pick us up. He said he would stay with us until our uncle came. I sat back down on our duffel bag and looked at the clock on the wall across the terminal. It was 4:00 p.m. At least I could still tell time in America. I hoped our uncle would get there soon. I was hungry and tired. They fed us on the plane that morning, but now we were on our own. I asked Anna if she had money to buy dinner. She said, "I have forty American dollars that Joe sent before we left, but we have to be careful and not use it up too fast. We still have a long road ahead of us. I don't want to ask our brothers for more because they work too hard for their money. Let's not think of food now, but think of what we are going to do tomorrow."

Five o'clock came, then six, then seven. Our uncle still had not come for us. Mr. Wang and Anna went to call him almost every hour on the hour, but they kept coming back with the same answer: he should be there any time now. I had been sitting on the duffel bag for a long time. Since we had to wait and didn't know when Uncle would come, I decided to walk past the food court. I didn't know how to order food in English, and didn't have money anyway. I had seen twenty and hundred dollar bills, but none of the other bills. In the past I was able to eat anything that was available, even rice with dirt in it. Now I was hungry, not because food was unavailable, but because I couldn't tell anyone what I wanted. I walked up and down the food court a few times, looking for something familiar, then went back to sit with my sister.

I hoped walking past the food court and smelling the food would help me not to think about being hungry. The smells and appearance of the food were very strange. I never thought food could look so different. I looked at the menu boards as I walked the entire food court, but I couldn't read them. For the first time I experienced how plentiful food was, but didn't have the money to buy it, or know how to eat it. My past experiences were opposite from this. After the war, food wasn't available, though I carried enough gold and jewelry on me to buy anything I wanted, had there been anything to buy. This was okay, because the greasy smell of the unfamiliar food made me lose my appetite.

At first Mr. Wang was very upset that our uncle was taking so long to come for us, but he was over it by this time. He appeared to give up on calling our uncle, and just sat in the corner across from Anna. She told me Mr. Wang didn't have to stay with us. His responsibility was to make sure all the refugees were picked up by their sponsors. We were not his responsibility but, true to his word, he stayed with us. Finally our uncle came to get us at a half hour before midnight. Before we left, Mr. Wang gave us his phone number and told us to call him if we needed his help in the future. He didn't make any small talk with our uncle, but told us to take care.

When we arrived at Uncle's three-bedroom apartment in Orange, it was after midnight. Again, the smells and everything around me were very different from what I was familiar with. Uncle Wen-Caw pointed us toward our father's room down the hallway. Anna opened the door and we looked at each other and slowly walked into the room. There was an air of melancholy there, in sharp contrast to our father's cheerful personality I remembered. We stood by the bed, just a thin twin-sized mattress on the floor. It didn't have a frame or box spring. The white sheets lay crumpled and dusty in the middle of the mattress.

We looked around the room and the closet. There was a small TV sitting on a wooden board supported by two cement blocks on the floor along the outside wall. He had a few Chinese language newspapers, an *Orange County Register* newspaper, a few Chinese books, and *Reader's Digest* magazines in a pile by the bed. There were no pictures on the walls. A dirty, white, restaurant-style coffee mug, Father's black-rimmed reading glasses, a black ashtray, and some pens and pencils were on the floor on the other side of the bed. This was my father's sad life … a mattress, a TV, some pens and pencils, a mug, and an ashtray. He lived like a prisoner.

We found a few shirts, a heavy jacket, and a coat hanging on the rod inside the closet. He also had a small overnight bag sitting on the closet floor. There were a few old pillowcases and a set of bed sheets on the shelf above the rod. Behind them I found a small revolver in a plastic bag, wrapped in a Chinese language newspaper, on top of a shoebox. I opened the shoebox and it had two heavy boxes of bullets inside. I looked at Anna and put the shoebox and pistol back where I found it. She quietly wiped a tear from her cheek. As we made the bed, we didn't exchange words, but we each knew what the other was thinking. We knew he was thinking about committing suicide. He had bought the two boxes of bullets to save face at the sporting goods store. I could feel the coldness, loneliness, hopelessness, and sadness in his room. After we shook out the sheets and made the bed, we stopped looking around, sat down on the floor, and leaned against the wall. We were still dizzy from our travels, but it seemed like the world had stopped turning.

Uncle Wen-Caw had come to the airport from his restaurant after closing and cleaning up. His oldest daughter, Xien-Yi, called us out of our room to help with dinner. She was the same age as my brother, thirteen years old, and was in the eighth grade. Years later, my father told us she often acted mean and disrespectful toward him, and Uncle did nothing to stop her. He was supportive and encouraging of her bad behavior around my father. Uncle Wen-Caw had brought his oldest daughter with him when he came to America with my father in late 1975. He left his two younger daughters and his wife in Hong Kong, and they arrived a few weeks after we did.

Wen Caw's second child, Xien-Ching, was eight years old. She was developmentally challenged, and a slow learner. His youngest child, Xien-Chee, a girl, was six years old. She was still developing her own personality and character. However, she listened to her oldest sister, followed her around, and mimicked her bad attitude. It was just a matter of time before she became just like her oldest sister, because she was the smartest of the three and a quick learner.

Eventually, Father would tell us his story of coming to America.

He decided to move to America in May of 1975 after the fall of Saigon. He said it would have been very difficult for him to find all of us and Mother if he stayed in Hong Kong. He felt he had a better chance to find us if he came to the United States. He was going to apply to the United States for refugee status so he could come to America, but the process took too long. In order to apply for refugee status, he would have had to check himself into a refugee camp and wait for the paperwork to be completed. He didn't know how long this whole process would keep him in Hong Kong.

Father was not a very patient man. He applied for immigrant status, but this process would also take too long. He finally settled for business investor status in the United States. He had more than enough money to qualify, even after losing millions in Hong Kong business development deals. After he came to the United States with a tourist visa, he opened a Chinese restaurant and applied for immigrant status before his visa expired. He lost a lot of money between 1976 and 1977 by hiring the wrong attorneys to help him apply for immigrant status. He paid them thousands of dollars, but nothing was done. His new business also lost a lot of money. His heart was not in America nor in the business. The language and the way a business was managed in the U.S. were very different from Asia. He just couldn't endure the emotional pain and guilt he felt because the rest of his family was still missing. He had no way of knowing what happened to us and to Mother. Were we alive or dead? For years, he drowned himself with alcohol to help him sleep at night and release his emotional pain.

His money was running low and his immigration status was still not resolved. He met Margaret Redmond, an immigration attorney, at the end of 1977. She helped him get Green Cards for his family and made sure to follow through with Father and the Immigration and Naturalization Service with any needed information or clarification. She went beyond the call of duty, and became a dear friend of our family.

I forgot how hungry and tired I was after we had been in my father's room. Anna told me to go and help with dinner, and that she was going to clean the room, so I went down to the kitchen to help. Uncle looked at me and said with a very gentle voice, "Wow! Everything is all done cooking! If I had to wait for you to help, we would not be eating until morning. Why don't you wait 'til cleanup time to help?" I apologized for not helping and said I would do the cleanup after dinner. Xien-Yi gave me a look that said, "Yeah, you will!"

For some reason I wasn't comfortable with his calm, gentle voice. I had met this uncle, my mother's younger brother, only two times before I came to the United States. The first time was when he came to Vietnam for a visit in 1969. He must have taken Mother's jewelry and cash back to Hong Kong on that trip.

The second time was when he came to the jail to visit me in Hong Kong in 1974. The two times I saw him, he appeared polite, but cold and distant. There was something about him that I was not able to describe. Now I had the opportunity to learn more about him by living with him.

Anna got a rash on her hands the second day after we arrived. She had never had any skin problems before. Uncle Wen-Caw became very anxious because he was afraid he would have to pay for her medical care. He told Anna to call Mr. Wang for help and insisted that she needed to find a job as soon as possible. He said a job would allow her to get insurance for her medical needs. He was not going to pay the costs if she needed medical care for her allergy problems. Uncle said that by law she had to work and support herself.

Anna called Mr. Wang, but not only because my uncle had insisted. She hoped it would give her a chance to find out how to become independent of our uncle. Mr. Wang, familiar with the sponsored refugee system, asked why Uncle Wen-Caw was not helping her since we were living with him. Anna let him know that if she had been able to get help from our uncle she would not have needed to call him.

Mr. Wang reluctantly agreed to help and arranged for a volunteer from his church to teach Anna how to take the bus to work. The volunteer was a kind, older gentleman named Mr. Johnson. While she was learning how to catch the bus, she also learned how to eat a hot dog, hamburger, and French fries. Mr. Wang was able to get her a job as a seamstress in a sewing factory making clothes for toy clowns. Anna had to get up at four in the morning to catch the first of two different public transit buses to get to work from our uncle's apartment. Her starting wage was $2.75 per hour, which was California's minimum wage at the time.

Anna later told me that when the weather turned from summer to fall, it was very cold standing at the bus stop every morning waiting for the bus without a jacket. She only had short-sleeved shirts and light-weight clothes that she brought from Malaysia. During her conversation with my uncle's wife about how the weather had turned so cold in the morning, Uncle responded that Anna complained too much about the cold. His wife couldn't stand his unconcerned attitude and said to him, "You have been standing near the oven all day in the restaurant, so you don't notice how cold the weather has turned. She stands outside waiting for the bus without a jacket; she is bound to notice the weather has turned cold." He ignored them altogether and never offered to buy Anna a jacket. She saved enough money to buy herself a jacket at the Salvation

Army two paychecks later.

My uncle said that I was seventeen and still under legal age, so the law required me to go to school. I was expected to work part-time after school at the restaurant to earn my free rent in the apartment my father had paid for. Mr. Wang realized that we were not refugees, but we had no resources of our own. He arranged for medical benefits for me, and applied for food stamps. My uncle took me to shop for food with my food stamps as soon as I received them. I never saw any dollars. The food stamps looked like play money, yet they could pay for food. It reminded me of the money we used when Saigon became Ho Chi Minh City after the fall, when the communists printed new money every three months during the currency exchange.

The market smelled very nice, was clean, and was all under the cover of a big building. It was nothing like the open markets in Vietnam. All the food was neatly displayed and well packaged. All items were displayed in aisles of shelves with many types of products to choose from. It was overwhelming and amazing. When we were in the meat section, my uncle picked the most expensive cuts. I never saw meat packaged this way and didn't understand what cuts were more expensive and which were cheaper. I just understood the number behind the dollar sign on the label was higher than the others, so it must cost more to pay for it. I asked my uncle why he picked the most expensive ones. He looked at me and said, "The American government wants you to eat good food, or they wouldn't give you the food stamps. Trust me! I would not teach you wrong!"

He also put lots of items in the cart that I had never seen before. I didn't know what all these items were. The half-liter bottles were white, yellow, and red. He calculated my allotment and told me to buy several bottles of each one. Now I know they were mayonnaise, mustard, and ketchup. When we went to the cashier, my uncle stood at a distance to assist me. He said I needed to learn how to pay for my food myself. I noticed the cashier's attitude was not very nice when I used the food stamp money to pay for the condiments and steaks. I couldn't understand what the cashiers were saying to each other, but I knew something was not right. I felt like a lamb being led to slaughter, unknowingly buying steak and restaurant supplies with my welfare benefits.

Anna canceled the food stamps and medical benefits after just a month. She was very aware that we needed the benefits, and we did eat the steak my uncle brought from the restaurant in stir-fry or with noodles at home, but she suspected the government would not let our mother and youngest brother come to the United States if I received government assistance. Her instincts were right, because Mrs. Redmond told us later that one of the requirements for investor status was that we were not likely to become public charges relying on welfare to survive.

My uncle's voice may have been gentle, quiet, and calm, but the words that came out of his mouth were mocking and sarcastic. When he spoke to me, his words were meant to hurt and tear me down, not build me up. When he spoke about my mother, he made me feel depressed, because he would discourage me rather than try to make me feel better. His words hurt much more than any of the beatings I endured, or the words that were spoken to me while I was in the prison camps in Vietnam. He was my uncle and was supposed to care for me and love me. I wished he would beat me like I was beaten by the prison guards rather than speak to me sarcastically.

When he talked about Mother, his own sister, he spoke in a very condescending tone and would say, "You girls shouldn't get your hopes up about your mother making it out of Vietnam alive. If she makes it on a boat, she will probably wind up being shark food." When he said "your mother" I was always tempted to ask him, "Is mother your sister, or isn't she?" When he cursed my mother by saying she would die in the ocean, I wondered why he said it, and what made him so hateful toward her that he condemned her that way. I would not wish on my worst enemies the things he predicted for my mother.

Somehow he managed to say mean things around the dinner table. He cursed my family by saying we would never see each other. He said mean things about my father and brothers. He called my father a bad drunk and my brothers useless gangsters. He said our father didn't love us. He told us, "Your father only cares about himself and his alcohol. He raised all his boys to be gangsters, good-for-nothings, and bad for society. You girls are better off without him." I had to wait until after ten o'clock to have my only meal for the day, and take his verbal assaults while I ate. Anna would sometimes kick me under the table when I was about to say something back to him. I had to swallow my words with the food.

He wouldn't give me a key to his apartment, so when I got out of school, I had to walk two miles from the bus stop to the restaurant and wait there until it was time for him to close and go home, at ten in the evening. I couldn't speak English so I couldn't work at the front counter. I wasn't able to read the orders, and I didn't know how to operate the stove, so I couldn't cook. I had to sit at a table in the far back corner of the kitchen away from the staff and customers and do my homework while I waited. When he saw me trying to learn the English alphabet, he would say, "I don't know why you are bothering to study that, you are never going to learn English. You are too old and stupid to learn in school like a child. The only thing you're going to be able to do is stand on a street corner waiting for someone to pick you up." Or, "Xien-Yi speaks very good English, some day she will be a doctor. Xien-Chee is still young, but she will learn English faster than you and catch-up with her older sister, because she is the smartest one of the three. Xien-Ching is a slow learner, but she will speak English before you because she is younger than you."

Uncle Wen-Caw told us that we could eat any of the food we wanted in the refrigerator and in the pantry in the apartment. He sounded very generous, but when we opened the refrigerator and pantry, they were empty. I got up in the morning to go to school with no lunch and an empty stomach. There was no food in the house. He stored all the food at the restaurant. I often went to school hungry. I watched other kids eat and throw their food away in the trash at lunchtime. Some of my new friends at school participated in the free lunch program because they were refugees. I got nothing because I was not qualified for this program. I didn't understand the system well enough to ask for it. I couldn't tell the teachers or the school officials what I was going through because I couldn't speak the language. I used to look at all the food in the trashcan and wish I could eat it. One time, I was very tempted to grab a perfectly good apple that one of the students had thrown away into the trashcan right in front of me, as I stood staring into it. The only thing that stopped me was the class bell ringing, signaling that it was time to go back to class.

I often wondered why so much food was being thrown away when there were so many hungry people that could eat it. I really wasn't looking for an answer. It was just a way to kill time by thinking about my miserable life.

By the time I got to Uncle's restaurant after school I was hungry, because I hadn't eaten all day. He would say, "If you're hungry, there is food in the refrigerator you can eat." But when I went to get something, he would say to his daughters, who also came to the restaurant after school, "don't eat too much or you'll spoil your dinner." Although he was speaking to his daughters, I knew he was actually speaking to me, so this stopped me from wanting to eat anything. If I ignored what he said and continued making something to eat, he would look at me with a smile and say with a gentle voice while I was eating, "I see you are eating a lot! The food must be very good, and you are very good at eating, but not very good at working!" I wished he would just yell at me.

When his two younger daughters got to the restaurant, his wife would fix French fries or fry some fish for them as a snack. They never finished it all, but she would throw out what they didn't eat in front of me rather than let me eat it. If I asked if I could have it, she would respond with a very disgusted expression on her face, and in a very patronizing voice just like her husband's, say, "I don't think it's a good idea for you to eat food from the trash! But if you must! You need to think about dinner time. It's getting close and you might want to wait." Sometimes I wanted to yell back at her, "Dinner is about six hours from now, witch!" But I bit my tongue and said nothing. Anna said that if I didn't control my tongue, our uncle would use this to blame our mother for not teaching us respect and good manners.

I cleaned the restaurant six days a week without pay and had only one day off. Every Saturday I had to wash and wax the car. Uncle would inspect it to make sure I did the job to his satisfaction; if not, I would have to do it all over again. I often had to wash and wax his car twice. Years later, I watched the *Karate Kid* movie on television. The old master told the young student: "Wax on; wax off." It reminded me of washing and waxing my uncle's car. The only difference between the boy and me was that he was learning something, and he got the car at the end. Uncle Wen-Caw would tell me, "You should thank me for having you do this because I am teaching you a skill that will keep you from having to stand on street corners."

My favorite day was Sunday because I didn't have to work at the restaurant. I stayed at home with Anna. We did our laundry, went to the supermarket to buy food, and cooked the food we loved to eat. I noticed that ever since I used the food stamps at the local super market, the cashiers there were not friendly to me. One time Xien-Yi wanted me to go to the supermarket with her to shop. She wanted me to come so I could push the cart and carry the groceries. A lady started to yell at me as I stood next to the produce. I didn't understand what she said, but looking at her face, I knew she was very unhappy and hostile toward me. I wasn't sure what I did wrong. I looked around for Xien-Yi, and saw everyone's eyes on me and the lady. The employees looked at me, but said nothing. Xien-Yi finally came to my rescue.

She yelled at the lady and pulled me out of the store. I asked, "What was that lady's problem?" Xien-Yi said I was standing in front of something she wanted to get to, and wouldn't move when she asked me to. But of course I didn't move because I didn't understand the language. She told me the lady was telling me to go back where I came from. Xien-Yi said my clothes were out of date and poor looking, and that created the problem. I looked at my clothes. I had only five thrift-store blouses and two pairs of pants as my entire wardrobe. Anna worked very hard and made so little money that we couldn't afford to buy new ones. Uncle finally took us to the Salvation Army thrift store for clothes, but it was still very expensive for us. Uncle wouldn't spend a dime on us. Anna was trying to save money for us to move to an apartment of our own, so I couldn't ask her to buy me clothes.

Father had sent us a letter when we were in the refugee camp, saying that he made some new friends at church a few years ago. He told us he couldn't wait for us to meet them. We did meet Steve and Christy. They were very nice to us, but I couldn't communicate with them. Christy was pregnant with their first child. She also worked at my uncle's restaurant part-time when Xien-Yi and I were in school in the morning. She never knew how bad my uncle treated me. She couldn't believe it when I told her thirty years later how awful he was to us. She said, "He appeared to be very kind and gentle toward you girls. He always talked to you with a very kind and soft voice. I always wondered what he was saying to you in Chinese. It was very interesting to listen to you all talking, but I didn't understand a word!"

Father told us years later how he met Steve and Christy. He was working at the fish and chips restaurant with my uncle. Although Uncle owned and managed the restaurant, the money he used to buy it was my parents' money that Mother sent him years ago. Steve and Christy came to eat after church one Sunday afternoon. They were dating at the time. After they ordered their food, they were looking for a table. Father was sitting in a dark corner by himself. He'd had a few drinks, but he wasn't quite drunk. He noticed that they came his way and sat down at the table next to him. They struck up a conversation, and he started to share his story with them. It was very out of character for him to share the sad story of his life with people he didn't know very well. He said he felt like he was going to lose his mind, and in his melancholy state, he poured his heart out to them.

He told them he hadn't seen his wife and the rest of his children for more than six years, and didn't know whether we were alive or dead. He had tried everything he could to find us, but nothing worked.

Steve and Christy offered to pray for him. He looked at them, smiled, and told them he had lost his belief in religion. He had tried for years and given lots of money to the local temples and monks to pray for his family. The years passed, and no one could tell him any news about whether his family was dead or alive. He said he was done with gods, that if there was a God, He must have forgotten August Chan.

Steve and Christy told him it was okay for him not to believe that their God is real. They just wanted to pray for him. Father saw the sincerity in both of them, and couldn't say no, so he agreed to let them pray. While they were praying, Father listened and thought to himself: "If you are a real God, let me find out if my family is still alive or dead! I want to know about my wife and the rest of my kids. What happened to them, and where are they now? If you can tell me, I'll believe in you."

After Steve and Christy prayed for Father, they continued to visit him. They came to the restaurant with a group of friends after church. They invited Father to go to church with them, and continued to build a good friendship with him. He admitted that their friendship was more appealing to him than going to church. He wasn't very interested in religion, but he went a few times to be respectful of their friendship and to practice his English.

Within three months, Father received a telegram from Joe and Henry in Hong Kong saying that Mother and Ken were still alive in Vietnam getting ready for another escape attempt. Anna and I were living in a Malaysian refugee camp. Stanley was alive and living in a refugee camp in China. Everyone was accounted for, everyone was alive, and his prayer was fully answered.

Father kept his word to God and became a Christian believer after receiving the telegram. It was actually very unusual that my father would become a Christian. He had never been very religious and was the last person I would ever have thought would convert. When we got his letter in refugee camp telling us that he had become a Christian, we were very surprised. How could this be possible? He didn't share the whole story, so he left us to wonder whether everyone in America had to be a Christian.

Christy took Anna and me to the immigration office to fill out paperwork. Mr. Wang told my uncle before he left the airport that we should report to the immigration office as soon as we arrived, but my uncle kept saying he did not know where the immigration office was. A month later, Christy quit working for my uncle because her baby's due date was getting close. Actually, knowing my uncle, I think he didn't want to pay her while she wasn't able to do much physical labor. He used the excuse that customers were spreading rumors about him and Christy. He said they thought she was his wife and he made her work too hard as pregnant as she was.

I hadn't seen my father in almost eight years, and didn't know what he would look like. Would he look the same as he did in his picture, or had he changed? After nine months of living with my uncle, I wasn't just missing my father and mother. I also missed having a place to call home. I hated every minute of being in America. I often wondered what I would be doing if I were living in Australia with my friends from the refugee camp. I thought life would be better once I came to America, but I didn't feel welcome here. People were mean to me at the market and at school. My own relatives treated me like a stranger. I would rather have been a house servant with strangers in Australia or Canada than here. I was desperate for my father to return. Things will get better when Father returns and takes us away from this new American nightmare.

One Saturday night, Anna and I were invited to Steve and Christy's house for dinner. She had just given birth to their first baby the week before, a girl. It was our first time to visit their home. While we talked and made dinner in the kitchen, the phone rang. My English was very poor, but Anna was able to understand enough to follow Steve's half of the conversation. Steve hung up the phone and came back to the kitchen. He looked at all of us with big round brown eyes. He was excited and said "Girls, it was your dad on the phone. He just arrived and he is at the airport right now. I need to go get him; who wants to come with me? I didn't tell him you are here." Anna told me as quickly as she could translate what Steve was saying. My heart was pounding as fast as the words came out of her mouth. I watched her eyes get bigger and bigger as she talked. By the time she finished telling me what Steve had said, her eyes were as big as a bug-eyed goldfish. I felt the house spinning around us. Anna and I looked at each other, and we both knew what the other was thinking: Now we could leave our evil uncle's home.

Finally Anna gave in to my cajoling and told me to go with Steve. On our way to the airport, I had so much on my mind, so many emotions. I just couldn't process what I was feeling. The drive to the airport from the house was only thirty minutes, but I felt like it would never end. Finally, I found myself walking inside the airport. I followed Steve blindly. There were lots of people coming and going past us. I looked at the people passing by, and I was not sure that I would recognize Father's face. Then I saw a short Asian man in a light brown nylon jacket standing in the middle of the walkway looking around. I looked hard into his face as I slowed my pace. My heart was pounding faster than before, my throat tightened, and I knew this was the face I was looking for. He looked much older than I remembered him, and appeared dark and thin.

As I walked closer toward him, he gave me a tired glance then turned his head and looked the other way. My face was wet with tears as I heard Steve's voice calling him, "Hi there, August!" My father didn't know me. How could he not recognize his youngest daughter? I felt my feet start to run, and I heard my own voice calling, "Papa! Papa!" I was calling from the bottom of my heart, but I don't know if I made a sound. He looked at Steve and then me blankly again for a second, then with a surprised smile opened his arms and hugged me tightly. We were embracing and crying at the same time. He said, "Oh! Shame on me for not recognizing you! I thought I would never see you again!" He couldn't believe it was me. He asked again and again, "Is it you? Is it really you, my little girl? You have changed so much and are all grown up! You're not so fat. " Steve stood behind me, his eyes red and full of tears. Finally, I was home.

CHAPTER NINETEEN:
THE REUNION

1980 was our big year. One by one, our family members arrived. In January, we received news from the immigration department that our mother and younger brother, Ken, would arrive in the United States by the end of March. In early March, we moved to a one-bedroom apartment in the same complex. We had lived with our uncle for nine months.

Mother told us later about her escape from Vietnam.

After she got the news that Anna and I had successfully left Vietnam, she began to plan their escape. She made two more connections with smugglers, but they both failed. One of her old employees came to visit her one day. He told her he had a permit to build a boat and it was getting close to being completed. He would let mother join him if she helped him pay for it to be finished and if she was still interested in leaving.

The communist government issued unofficial permits for people to build boats if they paid enough gold to bribe the officials. After the boat was completed and ready to leave, the officials would gather together people who paid them bribes. The people who built the boat would also have their own group of people to take as well. By the time the boat was ready to be boarded, it would be packed way over the limit with people who paid bribes to the government directly and those who paid the captain of the boat. The captain had to pay the government for his people to get on the boat. Mother's boat was no different from the boat Anna and I were on, or any other boat permitted to leave by the government. That is why the boats which made it to land in countries like Thailand, Malaysia, Taiwan, and Hong Kong, had so many people in such small boats. Because of the overcrowding, the number of people who died at sea was very high. The overloaded, untested boats couldn't outrun the pirates or overcome the waves during storms.

Mother told her former employee that she had no more gold for a down payment. Would he be willing to take her word that she would pay him after they escaped Vietnam? He knew Mother had connections and good credit. He agreed to let her come with him, but she had to help him gather enough other interested people to join them, or she would still have to pay her fare.

Mother found three families of six and ten people, headed by single women, to join her. She earned enough commission not only to pay her down payment, but enough to pay the entire fee for her and Ken. Even though she worked to recruit passengers, her fare was still considered a loan. The loan was to be repaid after she reunited with us in America. They began their journey in late May, 1979.

Their boat was nearly lost at sea because the captain wasn't sure of his way. She said he was her best electrician, but he knew much more about electricity than he did navigation. In order to escape, he had to become captain of the boat, even though he knew nothing about being a captain or the sea. He just sailed the boat out to sea, pointed it toward

Malaysia, and hoped for the best. They were at sea for nine days without food and they ran out of water on the eighth day. She began to lose hope by the ninth day, and then they saw land. They landed at one of the Malaysian islands called Kuantan, which was a resort area and had many tourists.

Luckily, tourists saw their boat and notified the Red Cross for help. The Red Cross came to their rescue before the Malaysian police came. Had it been the other way around, the boat would not have been allowed to land. The Malaysian government would have towed them back out to sea. Mother said before they left Vietnam, there was news that the Malaysian government was closing its borders and refusing to accept any more boat people. When she was settled at the refugee camp, some of the other boat people shared their horror stories about how the Malaysian government refused permission for their boat to land and towed them back out to sea. She was very glad the tourists had saved them.

They lived on the beach on Kuantan for a few weeks, and then the Malaysian government trucked them to a nearby area called Cherating. This area was near the jungle and Mother had to build their shelter. The holding area was full of refugees from Vietnam. She was free to roam around the island to get wood from the jungle to build their place.

Mother and Ken lived on this island for eight months, and then were transferred to a holding camp in Kuala Lumpur where they lived for about two months. They finally left Malaysia and came to the United States in late March.

After Father returned to Orange County, Uncle Wen-Caw no longer voiced what he thought about my family. In January, 1980, when we got the news that Mother and Ken would soon be coming to the

United States, he told us we would have to move, because it would be too crowded in his apartment to have all of us living there along with his own family. I am sure he was nervous about what we would tell mother and about the accounting he would have to produce. A few months later, his guilt drove him to move to Reno, Nevada, hundreds of miles away from us.

Within a few days of the big news about Mother and Ken, we also received notification from the U.S. Immigration and Naturalization Service that Stanley would be coming to the United States in April. After he arrived, Henry called to let us know he had quit his job with the Hong Kong Tourism Board and would arrive in June. Joe was the last one to come. He left his bank job and arrived at the end of August.

In early March, after nine miserable months with my uncle, and while we were waiting for Mother, Ken, and Stanley, we moved into a one-bedroom apartment in the same complex. Father had made friends with the manager, so we didn't have to worry about an application or hunting for another place in an unfamiliar neighborhood. Mother, Anna, and I shared the bedroom. Father, then Ken, then all my brothers as they arrived, slept on the living room couch and floor. Father was the only one who could drive, and we bought an economy car in our budget, a used Ford Pinto. If you don't remember the Pinto, it was Ford's smallest hatchback, with an unsafe gas tank and seatbelts for four.

We tried to look for a house to buy, but Anna was the only one working full-time, and she had just one year of work history. It would be impossible for us to get credit from a bank to buy a house. Fortunately, Joe sold our parents' last remaining asset, our home in Hong Kong, and brought the money to the United States. It was enough for a substantial payment on our debt and a small down payment on a "distressed property" in West Garden Grove, with a seller's loan on the side and a regular mortgage for which Anna's meager income could qualify.

Our family's new home was in the lower-middle class neighborhood of West Garden Grove. The houses were put up in a hurry after the Second World War to accommodate the booming Southern California population. It was a four-bedroom, two-bath Hawaiian-style bungalow with a small living room and kitchen and an attached two-car garage. The former owners were an older white couple. We made an offer in late October, and the bank approved our loan in late November. We finalized the sale two weeks before Christmas. Our real estate agent told us he was very surprised that we got the house so fast. He said he had never sold a house in California and closed that quickly before. Of course, we didn't know any differently.

The house needed some fixing up, like new carpet, paint, and minor cosmetic repairs. We had no money to change the pet-stained carpet, so we cleaned it as best we could. It still stank of cat urine. Steve had his own painting business, so we bought paint on his commercial paint store account and he helped us paint it inside and out without charging us. We fixed all the little things that needed to be fixed as best we could with what we found at garage sales and the Salvation Army thrift store.

We moved into our new home just two days before Christmas. Our moving boxes were left over from Joe's and Henry's trips from Hong Kong. We had no money left for anything else. We all slept on the floor the night we moved into the house. We had just a few pieces of furniture Steve and Christy and other friends from their church had given us when we lived in the single bedroom apartment. We didn't have enough chairs to seat all of us, or a dining table. We did have a portable black and white TV, a refrigerator, and a toaster given to us by our church friends. Of course, being Chinese, we didn't eat much bread, so the toaster didn't get much use.

Christmas morning, someone from church came to our home and gave us a dining table without a pedestal. Father, Joe, and Henry cut some old 2x4s that were stacked in the woodpile in the yard and built a stand for the table. Mother, Anna, and I tried to unpack some of our boxes. When Father finished setting up the table, he looked around and said, "It is good to have our home back!" We looked around our new home... it was missing something. Mother asked Father, "This is our first Christmas together! How should we celebrate?" Joe said, "We don't have any cash left, and it is late afternoon. Are the stores still open for shopping?"

Father checked his pockets and pulled out a five-dollar bill and some change. He put it in the small basket we would be using to store oranges fallen or picked on our side of the fence from our neighbor's tree. Henry called us all together and ordered, "Let's see how much change we all have in our pockets!" We did as he said and put all our money together in the basket. Anna counted it and said, "We have $29.30, total."

Father told us, "I know Fed-Mart is still open until six o'clock today. Let's go and get a Christmas tree. Who wants to come with me?" We all answered at the same time. We all wanted to go. Mother looked at us, smiled, and told all of us kids to go. She still had things to do and it was getting close to dinnertime. She wanted to make dinner for us when we returned. The seven of us piled into our four-seater Pinto. Seatbelts were not required at that time, so we sat on each other's laps and bent into the cargo area of the tiny hatchback.

Last-minute shoppers filled the store. We tried not to lose each other as we joined the crowd. We went to look for a tree first. The cheapest plastic tree would cost us $15.00. We found some decorative lights for the tree for $5.00. Anna reminded us that we only had about $9.30 left for ornaments and sales tax. We couldn't buy ornaments that cost more than a quarter each. We were on a mission. We looked through all the ornaments that were marked down to a dime because they were missing hooks or were cracked or broken. Anna established an assembly line around the shallow display table, in which we combined the good parts, and assembled enough good ornaments from the ten-cent bin to fill our little tree. We got in line and paid for everything. Anna calculated our spending and tax down to the last ornament and only had to put a couple back once the tax was added, and then had only a few cents left over. We tied our miniature plastic tree to the top of the Pinto and drove home singing Christmas carols in Chinese. Years later, Fed-Mart changed ownership and became Target. I still shop at Target at Christmastime, for the good deals and also for the memories.

When we arrived home and got out of the car, we could smell the dinner Mother had been preparing for us. She hadn't put her change in the basket, and she had walked to the grocery store while we were gone.

We hurried to set up the tree in our little living room and strung the lights on it. The lights and ornaments overwhelmed the little tree. Joe turned on Anna's alarm clock radio for some music. "Silent Night" came on; just the melody without lyrics. We all jumped in and sang along with the music in Chinese. We were short of chairs for our new dining table. Father had built a bench from the used 2x4s in our yard, which we covered with brown paper grocery bags so we were all able to sit around the table at the same time. We didn't have any presents under the tree, but we had each other. It was the best Christmas we ever had or will ever have, after ten years of being apart. Anna still uses that same Christmas tree and most of its original ornaments in the same living room more than thirty years later.

CHAPTER TWENTY:
THE NEW WORLD

Life in America was not as we had pictured it when we were in the refugee camp. We imagined we would all live happily ever after like in the storybooks. Rather than a storybook ending, we had to work hard to build a new beginning. We had to learn a new language and culture. We had been separated for over eight years, and had to get to know each other as who we had become rather than who we had been.

Of course, there were a few stories we told about each other over and over again, like when baby Ken fed soap flakes to the fish in Joe's pond, or when I told Mother at breakfast about the neighbor's puppies born just the night before. But there were stories we could not tell each other as well, because we had hidden them away in the back of our minds. Unfortunately, we were even making a few of those memories in America. We tried to interact normally in our new surroundings, and do what we had to in order to make our American dream come true. We later figured out that the frequent fights, outbursts, and nightmares our family members now experienced were our memories trying to escape.

When Mother had been in the United States less than a week, she went to visit her friend, who owned a sewing factory. The friend had arrived as a refugee but had gotten a fair amount of money out of Vietnam beforehand, enough to start her own factory employing other refugees sewing clothes for fancy department stores. The labels read "Made in America," and the labor was cheap. She paid a nickel or dime or a quarter an item, and the seamstresses could work at her shop or their homes. Mother went to visit and to see whether there was any piecework she could do at home to earn money to help repay our debts. She owed this friend money, as well. She came home in a really good mood and got to work, but not on her sewing.

We came home from school and work as usual, throughout the evening. The house smelled especially good, with the smoke of pan-fried steak, stir-fried seafood, and fish sauce coming from the kitchen. When we all sat down together for dinner, we realized that every dish on the table was one of Father's favorites. We asked Mother, "Did we miss Father's birthday?" Mother didn't say much. She only looked at Father differently and smiled. She kept serving him during the meal, refilling his tea and replenishing his bowl as if he were the last Emperor of China. We all noticed and kept guessing at what the special occasion might be. As she peeled an apple for desert, around and around the apple she went without breaking the peel, and she finally began to tell us her story.

"I met a very interesting woman at my friend's factory today," she began. Father turned as white as the neighbors, wondering what she was up to, and whether this had just been his last meal.

"While I was talking to my friend in the back office, a very fancy special white and gold Cadillac pulled up, blocking the window and entrance to the factory. The driver who got out of the car was a Vietnamese woman about my age. She looked very well dressed and very rich. Her clothes were made of high quality material, bright and loud in color. Her perfume was so strong it announced her presence to people within before she set a foot inside the entrance. Her makeup was thick and bright. She wore a lot of jewelry on her arms and around her neck and ankles that made a jangling noise as she walked in the shop and down the aisles between the suddenly-silent sewing machines. As she walked into the back office, all eyes were on her, and she interrupted my conversation with my old friend. She began speaking with my friend, and didn't seem to notice me sitting behind the door she had just left open.

"My friend came around her desk, shut the door, and introduced me to her new visitor. 'Mrs. Le, this is my old friend, Wana. She just arrived from Vietnam to join her husband, who is a local businessman.' Suddenly, this lady put down her purse as if she was going to stay. She turned, looked at me and asked, 'Are you the wife of August Chan? You must be his wife, aren't you?' I answered with a smile and nodded my head. She pulled up a chair, sat down right next to me, blocking the door, and said, 'I want to know your secret, why your husband not only loves you so much, but is also so very devoted to you? I offered him my money, my cars, my house, my business, and even my body, but he turned me down flat without hesitation or a second thought! He didn't even know whether you were still alive or dead, yet he said he would still rather wait for you!'"

Mother ended the story at this point and kept smiling at Father. She didn't tell us how she ended her conversation with this woman. Father's face turned from white to red and he smiled his huge grin and laughed out loud as only he could; "Khii-Khii-Khii, Ha, Cheee, Ha! He poured himself a drink from an expensive-looking bottle, and went off to their room in relief.

We all knew many families who had been separated by the war or during the great exodus. It didn't matter whether the spouses had been together for many years and had several children, or were newlyweds when the war broke out, they still were torn apart by circumstances. Many spouses remarried and started another family. When they finally reunited with the family they left behind or who had abandoned them, the relationships were very complicated. We knew husbands who had totally abandoned their first families and later tried to support both families. Some families even tried to live together as one big family, like the old times back in our grandparents' day, when it was socially accept-able for men to have more than one wife if they could afford to support them and all their children.

After Mother visited her friend's shop, she wanted to be able to earn money to rebuild our family and start making payments on the debt we owed from our escapes, as well as the money we owed the United States government for our plane fares from refugee camp. Mother had also signed a promissory note to the United States government for her and Ken's plane tickets to the United States. We could have chosen not to pay back the promissory notes, but we didn't want to be the cause of other refugees being unable to come to the United States because we didn't pay back the money we owed. Mother also still owed the person she borrowed money from to give to Mr. and Mrs. Moon in 1976. Altogether, we still owed around $200,000.

Mother's friend agreed to give her some sewing to do at home, but first she had to have a commercial sewing machine. She had to come up with money for the machine. Father was looking for work, but no one would hire a fifty-five year old man who spoke minimal English and had limited useful skills. Father's medical and translation skills were not valuable in the United States, because their professional practices were so different compared to Asia. He was not a registered physician's assistant or nurse, so his skills were not transferable.

Anna was the only one in the family working full-time. Her minimum wage factory salary had been barely enough to pay our rent, food, and electricity bills. We couldn't afford to buy anything, even in the secondhand stores, and we could not afford a car. I wasn't able to work full-time due to being under age and going to school. I found a part-time job after school at a local Carl's Junior hamburger restaurant, shortly before we moved out of Uncle's apartment.

I needed to learn and understand five words to keep my Carl's Junior job: ketchup, napkins, straw, salt, and pepper. Please and thank you, and welcome, Anna had already taught me.

When Mother arrived in the States, she never asked Uncle about the money she sent to Hong Kong. He found out through Henry that she needed money for a sewing machine. He told her he returned all the money to Father. He said Father squandered the money she sent over the years. He claimed father spent the money on gambling, women, and alcohol. He showed Mother pictures he had taken over the last few years in Las Vegas and Reno, Nevada, casinos. They showed Father standing by gambling tables with different women on his arm and alcohol in his hand. The women were dressed in low-cut, fancy dresses and Father looked happy with his trophies. Uncle's stories were very convincing and, with the pictures to back him up, Mother believed him.

Uncle had taken Father on several mini-vacations, and had the photos to prove that he was an irresponsible, drunken businessman. He would say, "Let's go on vacation, you need to relax. You worry too much." Father paid for the trips. While they were there, he drank and played the slot machines. He liked them because they reminded him of his old business in Vietnam. He didn't know how to play the other games. Father had a very outgoing personality, so he would strike up conversations with people he met in the casinos. Of course, many of the women he met were casino employees or prostitutes paid to keep the customers happy. He assumed Uncle took photos for "souvenirs." Father thought he was just taking innocent pictures with the pretty girls to remember the trips. Uncle, of course, had other plans.

Father tried to explain to Mother that Uncle's stories and photos did not tell the truth of the matter, but the damage was done. He told her that Uncle did return half of the savings to him after he arrived in Hong Kong. In fact, however, when they compared notes, Uncle had only returned about a quarter of the funds. He told Father he would give Mother the rest when she came to Hong Kong, but of course he never did. Father had no way of knowing how much to expect from Uncle, and Uncle took the chance that Mother would never escape Vietnam. Father trusted Uncle to be honest, and honored Mother by deciding that if she trusted her brother, he would too. Mother was furious. She believed the worst about her brother and her husband. She had no choice but to put up with both of them, because now Uncle had her money and Father had her heart.

We noticed that our uncle often came to visit Mother only. If we were home, he didn't say much about anything regarding Father's problems. However, if he thought we were not home, he told mother stories about Father and our two older brothers living a very decadent lifestyle in Hong Kong. He even showed his "generosity" to Mother by offering her a loan to buy the sewing machine and the Pinto. She desperately needed to buy the sewing machine and a used car, so she accepted his offer. Of course, she knew she was really borrowing her own money. He never returned another dime of the money she had sent to Hong Kong. Mother's sewing machine and Pinto cost her about two million dollars.

Father admitted he had managed poorly the money Uncle had returned. He used it to buy two houses in well-to-do neighborhoods, one that Hong Kong's public transportation didn't service, which helped to keep tourists and riff-raff out. After the fall of Saigon, the stock market fell and he lost quite a bit of his investments. He invested in the Hong Kong master franchise rights to McDonald's restaurants, and sold out because the investment didn't produce quick results and each new restaurant would require additional capital. Patience was never his strongest asset. Of course, now there's a McDonalds in every Hong Kong neighborhood. He invested in a Vespa dealership which went well for a while. He also invested in the famous "Jumbo" floating restaurant, which had a secret casino operation above the deck containing the restaurant. Several people came to him saying that Mother had borrowed money from them before they left Vietnam. There was no way to verify the loans after communication with Vietnam was cut off, so he relied on their stories and repaid her debts.

Even after all those bad investments and losses, Father was able to liquidate and come up with enough cash to claim investor status and obtain a visa to work and live permanently in the United States. He admitted that his heart was not in the United States, nor in the restaurants he opened in California. His lack of interest caused him to misplace his trust in managers and exhausted his resources. Without Mother's head for business, the old model just did not work as it had in Vietnam. He was down to his last restaurant and unable to dig himself out of the depression and guilt of not knowing where his family was or whether we were alive or dead. He turned to alcohol for comfort, even contemplated suicide, and bought a handgun out of a classified ad in the newspaper to do the job.

One June night in 1974, Father had silently watched his family being deported from Hong Kong. As we were being forced up the stairs into the plane, he stood and watched. He didn't call out our names or let himself be seen by us, though it had been years since we had seen him. He was a fugitive from Vietnam, in Hong Kong without legal standing as an official resident. We had memorized our Hong Kong telephone number and made the calls from the detention center, but Father and Uncle were powerless to assist us. Uncle had no papers to say we had any right to stay in Hong Kong, and Father was already an unofficial resident. He might have been deported along with us if he had spoken up. Part of his soul died at the airport that night.

Father struggled to keep going because he had to be strong for Joe and Henry who were with him in Hong Kong. After the fall of Saigon in 1975, he cashed in all his investments and sold the fancy house to come to America. He even paid for Uncle to come to the United States as his business partner and family support system. Uncle came to the United States, but he was not much of a partner or support.

It was hard for Mother to know who was telling the truth. Uncle's version of what happened was convincing, with pictures to back him up. Father only had his version of the events as his defense. All of the money Uncle gave Father in Hong Kong was gone, and she had no way to reclaim it. Mother didn't take any action but waited for the arrival of Joe and Henry. We could feel that a storm was brewing. Knowing my Uncle Wen-Caw from our miserable stay with him, we believed Father's story, but Mother was the one we had to convince. Another reason that we believed Father's story was because we knew how much he loved Mother. He waited for her, not knowing if she was alive or dead. Father had every excuse in the world to remarry, but he did not. He chose to wait for her. We could only pray that Mother would see all this and forgive Father. Everything appeared calm and peaceful as our family went about rebuilding our lives. We paid our bills, went to school and to work; but inside, we all struggled with the strange new world and with our roles between each other, and even with our own hidden experiences as they slowly manifested in the form of bubbling anger.

At a family meeting, after Henry and Joe arrived in the United States, we all asked Mother not to leave Father. We could not allow the family to break up. It was not an option. We had struggled, fought for our lives, and worked so hard to reunite over the years, that we could not and would not let the family be apart again. We said we would all work together to rebuild our family and our lives. Mother agreed to keep the family together, not because of Father, but for the sake of us kids. She didn't know exactly how much money she had sent to our uncle in Hong Kong over the years. She told us that when he came to Vietnam from Hong Kong to visit in 1969, she asked him to open an account in Hong Kong that she could send money to. She also asked him to buy a house. She was very sure that the money she sent over the years would allow her to send her six children to Canada for a higher education and a comfortable life, and for Father and herself wherever they wanted to live. She estimated that her plans would allow her to pay for our college, and after we each graduated, she could give us each a couple hundred thousand dollars to start our lives.

Mother thought that by having Uncle open an account in Hong Kong, the money would be safer than keeping it in Vietnam, since the political situation there was very unstable and unfriendly to us at the time. She trusted that he would give her the money she put in the account when she asked him for it. Uncle did as Mother asked him. He opened the account and bought her first house in his name. She sent money to him in Hong Kong to put into the account for four years from 1969 to 1973. We kids didn't know anything about the account then. Father knew about the account and the house, but didn't know the amounts Mother sent. Buying the house was part of her plan for leaving Vietnam. After my uncle bought the house, Mother told us kids to memorize the address for future plans. She never told us the house was bought with her money. We only knew that Uncle's address would allow us to reconnect if we left Vietnam, and we all used it to reconnect with Joe and Henry from the refugee camps.

After Father, Joe, and Henry arrived in Hong Kong, they weren't able to take over the account due to non-residency. Uncle never revealed to Father exactly how much money was in the account. He gave Father some money in 1972 shortly after his escape to Hong Kong, so Father didn't question his motives or honesty. Uncle told Father he returned half the money and kept the other half for the bank to continue to pay interest on. He acted as though he was keeping the account for Mother. When Uncle and Father left Hong Kong for America, Uncle closed the Hong Kong account and put all the remaining money in accounts in his own name in the United States. He treated the money as his own. Joe and Henry knew he didn't work or have a steady job to earn income when he lived in Hong Kong after visiting Mother in 1969.

Uncle Wen-Caw lived in the house Mother asked him to buy and on the money she sent him. The house was paid for without a mortgage. Greed took over his heart. He knew if Mother made it out of Vietnam alive, he would have to account for the money and return it, so he prayed for her to die at sea. He often cursed her to die when we were living with him.

Joe and Henry told Mother that had they known the house belonged to her, they would not have paid room and board when they were living with him. Mother was very surprised. I'm not sure which was worse; that Uncle never let them know they were living in Mother's house or that they had to pay room and board in their own parents' house while they were still in junior high and high school.

A year after we all reunited in California, Uncle sold his fish and chips restaurant and moved to Reno. He bought a nice home in an upper middle-class neighborhood and paid cash for it. Of course, he bought this house with Mother's money, because after he sold the restaurant he worked as a cook. There is no way he could have afforded the house on a cook's salary. Currently he is retired and lives very comfortably on the interest earned from Mother's money. His daughters even went to medical school and law school; we assume at our expense.

In late 1986, two major events happened that revealed Uncle's lies and caused Mother to reevaluate his character. First, he was the sponsor for our grandparents when they came to the United States from China. They lived with Uncle in Reno for less than two weeks when Mother received a phone call from them asking her to move them out of Uncle's house and let them come to live with us. In Chinese culture, the sons of the family are expected to take care of their elderly parents. It would be shameful for parents to live with their married daughter if they have a son. Mother's parents were raised in the very old Chinese tradition. Although they had four sons, three of them were still in China. Uncle Wen-Caw was their only son living in the United States. It was very out of character for them to request to live with their daughter. Apparently, they were desperate to move out, though they never told her why. They let her know that if they couldn't live with her, they would rather go back to China. They only said they were not comfortable living in the United States.

Mother wouldn't say no to her parents. At the time, she was working sixteen hours a day sewing to earn a living and pay the debts she had accumulated. She told Joe, Henry, and Anna to take a vacation from work. Father, Joe, and Henry rented a van, took Mother and Anna, and drove to Reno. Our Pinto would not have been able to make the trip. They stayed two days and brought my grandparents back to southern California. Ken and I were already away at college in Northern California, so we heard about all this when we went home at Christmas. Anna told me Uncle had called Mother several times in the month it took Joe, Henry, and Anna to arrange the trip. He was desperate to move his parents out of his house. He didn't tell her the reason he couldn't take care of them. He only told Mother that if she couldn't take them to live with her, he would have to send them back to China. Mother was more concerned about her parents being able to stay in the United States than the reasons why they wanted to move out of Uncle's house.

For months, they didn't say anything about why they wanted to live with Mother rather than their son. Grandfather was a heavy smoker and loved to drink during dinnertime. Joe and Henry indulged him and always made sure he had a supply of cigarettes and liquor. One evening, Henry was serving Grandfather his meal at the dinner table, and Grandpa broke down and cried. Everyone was startled and concerned that perhaps he was not happy with us kids because we had done something wrong. Grandfather told Mother that he was very happy and surprised that

Mother's children were better than he had heard.

Grandfather told us life was hell when he lived with Uncle. He said Uncle's oldest daughter was very rude and disrespectful toward him and Grandmother. Grandfather said, "Your dogs are treated with more respect than she gave us! I am so glad I am no longer living with him!" Catching his breath, he continued: "His oldest told me that she could not stand the smoke inside the house and wanted me to smoke in the garage. She waited until I went to the garage for a smoke, then she locked the door behind me. She only let me out when her father came home from work. I planned to kill myself in the garage if I couldn't come to live with you. During dinner time, she would yell at her father for bringing your mother and me to the US. She claimed that her life was disturbed and inconvenient because we live with them. She was not happy that your mother and I saw her when she sneaked boys in her room after her parents had gone to bed and let the boys out before morning."

In late 1987, while Ken and I were still away at college, Grandfather was diagnosed with lung and liver cancer. I suppose that was what came from the smoking and drinking, but at least he enjoyed the last year of his life. The doctors told Mother he only had three months to live. She called her brother in Reno and asked him to come to see his father for the last time. He said he couldn't come. His excuse was that he couldn't take vacation from his job as a cook. He promised he would try, but never came. In the last week of Grandfather's life, Mother called her brother again and told him his father would not live more than a few days longer. He told her he couldn't afford the plane ticket to come to California on such short notice. At the last minute, Mother paid for him to come and say goodbye to his dying father. On his deathbed, Grandfather apologized to Mother. He apologized for believing his son's lies over the years. He told Mother not to believe anything Wen-Caw had said to her. He told her that when he was still in China, Uncle Wen-Caw wrote him letters telling him that Mother was a bad woman, that her sons were gangsters and good for nothing, and her daughters were prostitutes.

Grandfather praised Father in front of Mother for being a good man. He told Mother that normally no man would be willing to take care of his in-laws as if they were his own parents the way Father took care of him and Grandmother. He also thanked Father for letting him die in our home. He passed away with Mother's forgiveness for the lies he had believed which made him treat her badly over the years.

Henry had a good friend in Hong Kong who was promoted to a director's position at the bank that held Uncle's account. Uncle had closed the account in 1975 when he immigrated to the United States with Father. Henry asked his friend to search through the old records. He found that the account actively received money from Vietnam from 1969 through 1973. There was no more money deposited into the account after Mother closed the restaurant, but it continued earning interest. The total at closing was over two million U.S. dollars.

CHAPTER TWENTY-ONE:
HIGH SCHOOL BULLIES

I had my own set of problems as I started school in the U.S. I learned to speak good and bad English words, to swim, and how to fight school politics and bureaucrats. I learned to handle discrimination and turn negative situations into positive ones.

The school system in America was very different from the way I remembered it in Vietnam. There I had the same classmates in the same classroom. Different teachers came to our classroom. In America, I had to go to a different classroom for each subject. I had to start from the beginning by learning my ABCs. School in the morning was regular classes. I spoke no English, so I was assigned to a regular classroom so I could learn English by listening. People in the class would say mean things, or even just everyday comments and greetings that I didn't understand. I often felt like a living statue in a park, like I didn't exist. I couldn't understand anyone, including the teacher. Sometimes the students in the class looked at me and pretended they were talking to me in Chinese or Vietnamese, but I knew they were making fun of me. They would talk in gibberish and laugh at me.

After lunch, a school bus came to take a group of students like me to another school. We were all newcomers to America from other countries. The majority were refugees from Vietnam and Cambodia. Some students were not political refugees as we were. They were from Mexico, Latin America, Taiwan, China, or Hong Kong. Our English abilities were at different levels. Three teachers taught us English as a second language, or ESL for short. The school bus took us back to our regular schools at the end of the day.

Most of my close ESL friends were refugees. We had issues and struggles in common, such as political, economic, and social class. I met my best friend, Chulech, in ESL. She was a refugee from Cambodia. Her father died during the Khmer Rouge "Killing Fields" genocide. Her grandmother, mother, four siblings, and she escaped to Vietnam, where they lived in a refugee camp until they bribed their way to a Hong Kong camp. Her family came to the U.S. about the same time we did. After we had been friends for a few months, she noticed that I did not eat lunch at school. She didn't ask a lot of questions, but she invited me to her house after school one day. When we arrived, I smelled her mother's cooking. They welcomed me with open arms. They were obviously poor and lived very simply. Her mother was very kind and loving. She knew that I was hungry and offered me food. They did not have much to give, but they had lots of love to share. Whenever I see a stray dog or cat, I remember that I was their stray while I still lived with my uncle. I visited her family often after school. I am forever grateful for what she did for me. Chulech married a clothing manufacturer, and they still live in the old neighborhood.

Most of my classmates in the morning classes were English-speaking kids. Newcomers were not welcome. We did have a few students who came from Vietnam in 1974 or 1975. They were well integrated into the American culture, language, and lifestyle. They only talked to us or translated for us when the teachers wanted to communicate with us. They had their own group of friends they hung out with. They were more comfortable speaking English to each other than Vietnamese. They struggled with their word choices when they tried to translate for us what the teachers said.

The newcomers banded together. Some tried to integrate into the American culture, but unfortunately in a very negative way. A few friends in my group were using drugs and going to parties. The disco ball was their symbol of freedom. Some of the girls were involved in gangs. Some got pregnant and had abortions one after another, like they didn't have any idea what made it happen, or if they did, they didn't care. It was "the American way." I stayed neutral, like Switzerland. I was friendly to both the old-timer immigrants and the newcomer refugees. I was a little more acceptable to the old-timers and ABC's (American Born Chinese) because I could speak Mandarin like a Taiwanese and Cantonese like I was from Hong Kong.

To my surprise, I found school fascinating. It was hard to believe that I even liked school. I always told Anna I hated school when we were living in the refugee camp. I wasn't planning to go back to school, but intended to go to work as soon as I arrived in the United States. When Uncle said it was against the law for me not to be in school, I was disappointed that I couldn't work, but I poured my energy into my studies and made the most of the opportunity to learn.

It was a very stressful and depressing time when I started school because I was emotionally isolated in my morning classes. When I sat in the regular morning classes, I didn't talk to anyone, including the teachers. Sometimes I felt like I was back on the train in Vietnam when I had to pretend to be mute. The students in the classes really didn't tolerate me. A few accepted me, but I couldn't communicate with them to maintain their friendship. For example, Father met a French couple when he arrived from Hong Kong and became good friends with them. They had a beautiful daughter, Pasqual, and she went to the same school I did. She was very good to me, but I didn't understand English or French well enough to communicate with her. I often smiled at her just to be polite, but it was a struggle to be her friend. She was very patient and tried hard to relate to me, but I had no idea how to keep up with her. Sometimes I wanted to tell her something, but I had no words. I could tell that it was sometimes frustrating for her when she wanted to share her feelings with me and I couldn't understand or express myself back to her. I couldn't tell her how my uncle treated me or that I was hungry at lunchtime.

Some of my classmates were very mean to me in class and outside of school, and I couldn't share it with Pasqual. For example, I had to take the school bus to school and back home. Kids were cruel and wouldn't let me sit down next to them. Sometimes the bus driver yelled at me to "sit down!." I couldn't tell him the kids on the bus wouldn't let me, so I had to rely on someone to take pity on me and let me sit next to them. When the original "*Spiderman*" movie came out many years later, I could relate to Peter Parker as he was ostracized on the school bus.

One day after school, on my way to the bus stop I was waiting at an intersection to cross the street. Some students were talking mean to me in an obviously mocking tone of voice. On the bus, I noticed that some kids gave me funny looks, but I didn't know why. I found the slimy spots of spit on the back of my jacket after I got off the bus. I was so upset I threw my only jacket in a nearby trashcan and cried all the way home. When would I be accepted? Why did Americans hate me? I wished the Red Cross had let me go to Australia instead of California. At least Australia wanted me.

Mother asked what happened to my jacket when I got home, but I wouldn't tell her the story. I suspect she thought I was back to my old tomboy ways and had ripped my jacket doing something I wasn't supposed to, like fighting with boys. She didn't push me for an answer; she just sewed a new jacket for me that weekend, from scraps she had left over from her piecework.

One last incident happened that made me decide to fight back as hard as I could. Shortly after we moved out of Uncle's apartment, I got my first job at Carl's Jr. in the mall after school. Father didn't have a car yet, so I had to walk thirty minutes to the mall to go to work. I learned a shortcut, so it took only twenty minutes; however, this route required me to walk through a neighborhood where some of the kids on my bus lived. I could only pray that no one would bother me when I walked through. One day, one of the kids from my bus saw me coming and let his big German Shepherd out of his yard. His dog was vicious and snarled at me. I knew it could attack. The Americans protecting our club had used German Shepherds. I was scared but had better sense than to run. I stood still and looked at the dog's big teeth. The only thing that went through my mind was, "Damn America! Not only are the people bigger than me, even their dogs are bigger than me!" I don't remember how long I was in a standoff with that dog, but I heard an adult's voice call it. After the dog walked away, I heard some kids laughing. They yelled something I had grown to understand: "Go back where you came from!"

I heard this so often I knew what it meant by then. My heart was heavy, cold, and hard as I walked to work. I thought, "You see! No country wants me. I would leave if I could. Believe me! Your country was not my choice to come to. It was your government that brought me here! Unfortunately for you, I am here!" I wished I could tell them what I was thinking. Living with Uncle had already made me regret coming to America; now I hated it with all of my being.

The next day when I went to school, I was still angry at the whole world. It must have been written all over my face, and I was not friendly or polite to anyone around me. One of my morning teachers was Mr. Stevens who taught biology. I used to smile in his class even though I didn't understand what he was saying. I watched his body language, and laughed along with the rest of the class when he did something funny. I wasn't laughing or smiling in class that day. He noticed that I was angry, and asked a Vietnamese student to tell me that he wanted to talk to me at lunchtime. I wasn't happy with his request, but since I had no place to go or any lunch to eat, I went to his classroom. He asked me to tell him why I was sad, making the motion of a sad face. I tried my best to put into words the dog incident. My English at the time was only single words. "Run." "Dog." "Bad." "U.S." Somehow, he managed to understand that I was telling him people were very mean to me. He told me to come back the next day at lunchtime, because he wanted to show me something.

I came the following day as he had asked. He started to talk, but he must have seen the blank look on my face. I did understand when he showed me a basket of apples. They looked very red and shiny outside. He took one apple out of the basket and cut it in half. It looked kind of brown and wormy inside. He took another one from the same basket and did the same thing with it. This time the inside of the apple looked very good to eat. Then he said something to me that I could only guess. At the end, he showed me books and told me to study hard so I could talk to him and to other people. I knew he was trying to tell me that not all the apples in the basket are bad and, in the same way, not all Americans are hateful. He said I should study hard and learn to speak English so I could talk to him and other people. I thought of how he and other teachers were kind to me, how Pasqual, Steve, and Christy were kind to me even though I couldn't communicate with them. I decided I would put my energy into learning English. Someday I would tell people who I was and where I had been before I came to this country. I said to myself, "I may not have a voice now, but I will someday."

As I mentioned earlier, I learned both the good and the bad, sometimes unknowingly. Two of my swimming classmates were also my coworkers at Carl's Jr., and one of our handsome male supervisors was the idol of my female co-workers. He was a white kid named Art. I could tell he knew he was good-looking, and he was very flirtatious with the female coworkers. I couldn't speak English well enough to know what they were saying or laughing about most of the time. He began to tease me about my name, probably trying to flirt with me, but I was never in the mood.

At the time, I went by the Vietnamese translation of my Chinese name, "Dinh-Dinh." He called me "Ding-Dong" and sang it like a bell. I didn't know how to tell him to stop. I was very annoyed and frustrated by him. My two swimming classmates noticed my frustration, took me aside, and taught me to say Art's "nickname." I practiced for a while and tried not to chop it up too badly. At work, they told Art I had something to tell him during break. He walked right up to my chest and looked straight down at me up close.

I said loudly with a very clear and careful voice, "F*CK, YOU, ART!" His face turned very red and his eyes got so big they looked ready to pop out of his head. Both of my friends laughed very loudly in the background. I thought maybe I didn't say it right and that was why I sounded funny to them, which I often did. I asked him, "I not say right?" This time he answered with a smile, "Oh yes! You said it right!" After that, he stopped making fun of my name.

When I went to swimming class the next day, my swimming coach had already heard about what these two classmates had done to me. He asked if I knew what it meant. I answered that it was Art's nickname. The coach told me to bring my Chinese/English dictionary to him. He looked up the word and showed it to me. After I saw the meaning of the word, I was so embarrassed I didn't talk to either of them or Art again about anything but work. I was just glad he didn't fire me. My family needed my job.

All I could do was dogpaddle and float when I was in Vietnam, and it was still the only way I knew how to swim. When I was in school, I had to take a Physical Education class. I didn't understand any American sport but swimming. The sports in America were very different from those in Vietnam. I didn't know what to call basketball or badminton. Football in Vietnam is soccer in America. When the school counselor assigned me to P.E., I motioned, by dogpaddling in the air, to be put in swimming. When I went to the swimming class, I didn't know all the right strokes. The coach had to train me from the beginning. Most of the time, he couldn't tell me verbally. He had to show me what I did wrong and how to use the right strokes. Sometimes, we used my dictionary to communicate. He took the time to teach me and really seemed to care whether or not I understood.

As the semesters went by, I learned to speak English in broken sentences, so I was able to communicate with all my teachers. I made some good progress, although slowly. The Chinese language requires good memorization and is a "use it or lose it" kind of language. You can't just look at a new Chinese word and sound it out. You have to know what the word means in order to be able to say it. English, on the other hand, I could sound out and say a word even though I might not know the meaning.

As I began to learn English, I didn't have time to learn phonics from grade school level up, as most of the other students had. I learned English the way I learned Chinese. I memorized the meaning of each and every word as I came across it. I couldn't sound out a new word unless I knew what it meant. How I did it, I don't know. As I increased my vocabulary, I increased my language skills. When I did my homework, I relied on my Chinese and English dictionary to look up every new word. My progress might have been painfully slow, but I got there and passed all my tests. I went to summer school and took extra night classes to make up all the credits that were required for me to graduate.

At the beginning of June, 1981, summer break was just a couple of weeks away. The school sent out a notice stating that if you were eighteen or over, you could leave high school and go on to junior college without a high school diploma. I was one of those students. My academic counselor told me I could get my high school diploma equivalent, or General Education Diploma, in junior college. She also told me I was one semester short of the credits I needed for my high school diploma. I had already passed all the proficiency tests; however, the district would not allow me to stay in high school because I was already eighteen. I was very upset that I was so close to getting my diploma, and would have to leave high school without it.

I shared my predicament with Mr. Stevens at lunchtime. I often went to practice my English conversation with him after he helped me, even though I was no longer in his class. I showed him the letter my parents had received from the school. He told me I could appeal my case to the principal, and if that didn't work, I could try the superintendent. He warned me not to tell anyone he was the one who told me to do it, because he might lose his job. He said I had nothing to lose by trying.

I went to the principal's office and the secretary made an appointment for me to speak with him. When I got home, I asked Henry to come with me to meet the principal the next day. It was a big school, and the principal had never met me in person. We only knew each other's names because he signed outstanding student award letters for me every semester. The principal asked me, "Why do you want to stay?" I told him in my broken English that I understood I could go to a junior college to get my diploma, but that had no meaning to me. It would mean a lot to me if my diploma were from Orange High School. I said I loved my teachers and, most importantly, I worked very hard for my diploma. It would make me very proud to have the school name on it. All I needed was one more semester of credits to graduate. I wouldn't take up a lot of room in the school to stay for one more semester … I was small and I wouldn't make trouble in class.

The principal agreed to allow me stay to complete my diploma. I finished high school in December of 1981, but returned for the graduation ceremony with the class of 1982. I sent my graduation announcement to my uncle in Reno, just to rub it in his face, because he said I would never learn English and graduate.

CHAPTER TWENTY-TWO:
COMMUNITY COLLEGE CHALLENGES

After high school, I went on to Golden West Community College. By that time, I was barely speaking English well enough to attend. Junior College would allow me time to increase my English vocabulary before going on to university. Because it was part of California's Community College system, it was also affordable and close to home. I wouldn't need student loans to attend.

I had always loved animals and I wanted to be a veterinarian. I had completed dog-grooming training in a vocational program in high school, and I hoped to go on and become a vet, but I settled for being a nurse; the community college I attended did not offer veterinary training. However, I didn't realize biology and science are other languages in themselves, and they were very difficult subjects for me. I was still struggling to learn English; adding biology and science was like trying to reach the moon. Nevertheless, I had a big dream and refused to settle for less.

I was determined to be the first female college graduate in my family's history. My mother was deprived of an education because she was a female. Anna was deprived of a higher education because we all had to live and rebuild our lives. Of all my siblings, Anna loved learning and going to school the most. She dreamed of the opportunity to go to university. She had no choice but to make sacrifices for her family. She did take art classes two nights a week at Golden West for relaxation and a diversion – it was something creative to do after her monotonous assembly job. She was so good that her professor nominated her for an art scholarship. Chapman University offered her a nice tuition scholarship in their art department, but she had to turn it down due to our situation. She still has the award letter. If she had gone to the university, she would have had to quit her full-time job. Her sacrifice meant Ken and I had the opportunity to go to college, and not right to work after high school. Anna worked on an assembly line in an electronics company. She was such a hard worker that her employer sent her to company headquarters for a weekend every year to receive awards as one of the best employees of the year.

I wanted a higher education, not only for Mother's and Anna's sake, but also for myself. I knew Anna worked very hard at a factory, yet she was paid very little. I understood that higher education would allow us a better life, and I tried my best to get it. I received financial aid, took out student loans, and did work-study to help pay for my education. My family was still struggling. Money was tight and we were making little headway toward paying off our debts.

Mother worked sixteen hours a day, seven days a week in our hot non-insulated garage on her sewing job. She had to keep the garage door shut so the neighbors would not complain to the city about us running a business out of the garage. Father was no longer able to work, but he cut way down on his smoking and drinking. He kept up the house and the yard, raised chickens, and cared for our dogs and cats in the back yard.

He took his friends to garage sales, bargain-hunting on the weekends, and went fishing in the ocean off the rocks of Laguna Beach.

Joe worked the night shift as a check processor for a bank in Los Angeles. He had to commute from Orange County, so to save money spent on gas, he lived and slept in his minivan on the weekdays. His friends let him park his car in their driveways. Sometimes he had to park in the mall parking lot to catch up on his sleep. He showered in different friends' homes before he went to work. He went fishing, too, but one time the political divide between the east and west caught up with him. When he had just arrived, he went to Laguna Beach and fished from the rocks. He saw an abalone close to shore and added it to his catch for the day. Someone must have been watching and reported him, and the next thing he knew, a government truck with lights and siren pulled up beside the Pinto and an officer gave him a ticket and took his abalone. His lesson in protected shellfish fishing landed him a big fine.

Henry, a graduate of the prestigious Hong Kong University, found that his degree was not recognized in America. Nevertheless, he abandoned a promising career with the Hong Kong Tourism Association and stayed with us in Orange County. He had been a personal tour guide for many celebrities in Hong Kong, but he picked strawberries for a living until he finally landed a commission-only sales job at a local Oldsmobile dealership. Since it was afternoon and evening work, he went to insurance school in the mornings. He took a job as fleet sales manager at the dealership so he could talk to business people. Since the job came with an office, he conducted an unofficial financial advisor business in Chinese, Vietnamese, and French at work, unbeknownst to the manager. He was determined to survive, and even though he used the dealership as his personal office, he often won the monthly or quarterly sales contests for the number of cars sold.

Stanley went to Seattle to find his future and make his fortune. He lived with my cousins while he was in high school and looking for jobs. California would not let him in their high schools due to his age. Even though he was younger than me, because Sister had taken my identity, I was now officially younger than him. Our cousins told him that Washington would let him stay in their high school system until he was twenty-one. He came back to California, but decided to live on his own rather than back with us. He and Father did not get along well, because Stanley picked up a lot of bad habits and bad friends on his journey.

Ken started out in middle school. He struggled as I had with the school system, friends, and language. I was in better shape than he was, because I could rely on the Chinese/English dictionary to help me with new words, but he couldn't. He had very little chance to be in school and learned very little written Chinese before he came to America. He was just a baby when the war began. After 1973, he wasn't able to be in school, as the other children were, due to our family having to hide our identities and trying to escape from Vietnam. Mother tried to teach him how to read, but her education was only at the third grade level. He only learned the very basics of Chinese and math. He tried his best and worked very hard in school. He graduated with a high school diploma and moved on to college with me.

I carried a full-time class load and worked three part-time jobs. The first job was work-study, which allowed me to work on the school campus between classes during the day. My night job was sewing with mother, and my weekend job was working as an aide at a nursing home.

The nursing home job didn't last very long. I worked there because I wanted to know what it was like to be a nurse. Also, I loved working with the elderly. My first day in the nursing home was total culture shock. I hadn't realized how much I missed my grandmother in Vietnam. Working in the nursing home opened my eyes to how differently older people in America are treated from the way I knew.

In Vietnam, we didn't have nursing homes. The elderly relied on family members to take care of them. If their own children couldn't take care of them, other relatives would step up. I remembered how my parents took care of my great aunt. She was my grandmother's half-brother's wife and was blind and deaf. Grandmother's half-brother was killed during the Japanese occupation of Vietnam and her grown children were very poor. They couldn't take care of her, and so she lived with us. Her children came to our house occasionally to visit, and they would take her home during the Chinese New Year for a few weeks each year. She lived with us for over ten years and died in our home due to old age. Mother had servants to take care of her and Grandmother. My great aunt was very kind, and a fun playmate. She taught us to sing Chinese children's rhymes in our old family dialect.

My first day at the nursing home was very dramatic. One of the nurse's aides trained me that day. She showed me how to clean beds, give showers, and set up meals for the residents. As I was busy taking care of one person and then another, I saw one lady sitting on her bed not touching her food. Her name was Helen. I came back to her and encouraged her to eat. My English was not very good, but I knew she understood what I said. She looked at her food, and appeared to be having problems with the spoon. I smiled at her and offered to feed her. She was happy to eat the food on her tray with my help. My trainer came to tell me not to feed her. She said I had to clean the floor, and Helen could feed herself. I went to get the mop and I could see silent Helen looking at me as I mopped the floor. She wasn't eating and the other aides were taking away the food trays. I approached her and encouraged her to eat. The trainer was nearby and yelled at me to do my job. She also told Helen to eat her food and stop looking at me. I continued mopping the floor, and noticed that Helen looked very sad. She had big teardrops on her face. I wanted to comfort her, but the head nurse called me to her office. She talked to me about not feeding Helen. She said other residents also needed my attention and I didn't have time to take care of one person at a time. I understood about thirty percent of what she said, and understood at the end that she wanted me to do better to keep my job. She also put me to work in another wing of the facility, away from Silent Helen.

At the end of that first day, I went home after my shift ended and started to cry my heart out as soon as I walked in the house. Ken asked what was wrong with me as I went in my room. Anna and I shared a room, and she was not home yet. Mother came to see what was wrong after my nosy brother told her I was crying. I couldn't get the words out, but just cried. I didn't know why I was so upset, and I couldn't understand what I was feeling. I just felt like crying.

Mother sat with me for a long time and cried with me. I asked her why she was crying. She said, "I don't know! You were crying and you can't tell me what's wrong, so I cried with you!" We both burst out laughing through our tears, and then I told her about my first day working at the nursing home. She encouraged me to do the best I could, and know that I had tried my best. She also said the old people were lucky to have me working there so I could be there for them.

After that conversation and crying with Mother, I never went straight home after my shift was over. I went to a park next to the nursing home and cried until I felt better, then went home. I didn't want Mother to be sad. It was nice to have her empathize with me, but I hated to see her cry. I would rather see her happy. After all, she had been working hard, and she didn't need to see me that way.

In 1983, we heard a rumor that the United States and Vietnam might possibly be open to reconciliation. We were so excited at the news. We didn't care whether the news was a rumor or the truth. With Mrs. Redmond's help, Father submitted a request to immigration to sponsor Grandmother to come to the United States. He wanted her to be the first one in line if the United States and Vietnam really did reconcile. If they did, they would allow us to sponsor Grandmother to come. After waiting several months, the immigration office notified us that Grandmother was deceased. We didn't have the date she passed or know any other details, because we weren't able to communicate with our uncle and aunt in Vietnam. The two countries did not have open communication. It was very heartbreaking news to accept.

Our first year back together was very emotionally and mentally difficult for all of us. We tried to get used to our individuality, and didn't give up on each other. We continued to work hard and work together to rebuild our family. Our home might have been small and crowded, but we loved each other. Despite the damage Uncle had caused in our parent's relationship, they still loved each other. Father struggled with his alcohol problems and with learning who we were individually. When he left Vietnam, we were still young children. That image in his mind had not changed through time. Now we were all young adults who had not grown up together. It was hard for him to look at us as adults. Sometimes he forgot that we had our own feelings, our own ways of doing things and working out problems.

In Chinese culture, generally fathers and daughters are not very close and don't communicate with each other often. Our relationship with our father is very distant in comparison to Western culture. This was true in our family as well, even though my parents were exposed to and accepting of much of the Western culture. Anything Father wanted to relay to me, he communicated through Mother. Father was much closer to Anna than to me. She is the oldest girl in the family and has Mother's personality, so he was more comfortable talking to her. She understood him and had more patience than I had. She knew how to talk to Father and knew the right things to say to him to keep him calm. When Father talked to me, it was like talking to himself. We were too much alike in personality and character. He had no patience with me and I had none toward him. We didn't understand each other. Without Mother, we would not have talked to each other at all.

I joined the Asian Students Club at Golden West and met many friends. The club had lots of people who came from all different parts of Asia, such as China, Hong Kong, Taiwan, Korea, Laos, Cambodia, and Vietnam. I met another best friend, Windie, through the club. Windie was Chinese by roots, but she was born in South Korea, and spoke both Chinese and Korean. She came to the U.S. when she was ten years old, and she spoke English much better than I did. She tended to say what she thought to anyone regardless of their position of authority, like most American kids do. We communicated with each other in Chinese. I learned about Korea's culture, philosophy, and food. Through her, I learned that our cultures were very close and had many similarities. We grew so close that we felt like we were sisters from a different mother. I got along with her parents well because I was more traditional. They wanted Windie to be more like me, and I wanted to be more like Windie.

Windie's family owned a famous Chinese restaurant in Huntington Beach, and sometimes on weekends I got to visit her for lunch at the restaurant. I loved her father's sweet and sour pork, which he made especially for me without the red-dyed sweet sauce. It reminded me of our restaurant's sweet and sour pork in Vietnam. I have eaten this dish at other restaurants in America, but it is so sweet and full of red dye that it is not the same. It's funny how treats can turn into memories so easily and have so much power.

I made two male best friends, Steven and Simon, in the Asian students club. They came from Taiwan, and we got along very well. They often came to our house to pick me up or drop me off from school or club activities. Most of our male friends would take turns picking up the female friends who were in the club for school or social events. Sometimes other guys came to pick me up if Steven or Simon were not able to. Father was so worried and confused with all these male friends coming and going in our house that he finally asked Mother which boy was my boyfriend.

Mother told me about his concerns, and I told her all of them are my boyfriends. I also reassured her, "You don't have to trust me that I am friends with this many boys. You have to trust yourself that you have taught me well. I would not shame the family's name. Would you rather not know who my friends are? Steven and Simon are the ones coming more often than the others are, because they are my best friends. They are no trouble and would not dare touch me. Don't be so concerned! I am more interested in my studies. I will continue to have different male friends coming to our house as they become my friends." Father didn't like my attitude too much, but he didn't forbid my friends from coming over. I was very active with school, work, and my social life. I began to enjoy my freedom in a very positive way. I became the social committee of the club. Other students and professors in the college were also interested in learning Mandarin or joining the club, so I got to know a lot of friends through it.

One of our physics professors, Conrad Stevens, who won a "Who's Who" award for a physics paper he prepared for his Ph.D. degree, was very interested in Asian culture, and he and I became good friends. He also came to my house and met my family. He was very nice to Father. When he found out Father loved the Lakers basketball team, he took him to see some of their games. A few years later, he met a woman in Taiwan and got married in California. I was very happy for him and told my parents that I was going to go to his wedding. Mother said, "I was worried that you would be heartbroken!" I was very surprised, and said, "What makes you think that? He was my good friend! He helped me with my English and I helped him with his Chinese. I am happy that he found a nice Chinese woman to marry. Why would I not be happy for him? Shouldn't a friend be happy for a friend when they get married?" Mother looked at me and smiled. She said, "Conrad took your father to the expensive games more than twice and bought hats and things for him. I am sure he spent lots of money for those tickets, and things that he bought for your father. He also sent me two dozen roses on Valentine's Day and Mother's Day for a very good reason. That was his way of telling me he liked my daughter. Unfortunately for him, my daughter is clueless and did not have him in her heart."

Was Mother right about him? I had set my mind against getting married when I decided to go to college. My plan for the future was to get an education and get a very good-paying job to rebuild my family and help pay off our debts. Dating and marriage never crossed my mind and were not in my plans. Also, I had a deep distrust of men and an inability to even contemplate being intimate with my male friends, whether I had real romantic feelings for them or not. I just figured I was driven. I didn't realize how my attitudes had been warped by my past experiences.

In 1984, I continued to work hard and tried to get into nursing school. To motivate myself, I saved money and bought a pair of white nursing shoes. I took the nursing test, but failed miserably. I wanted to get into nursing school so badly that I even had nightmares about killing the testing officials. I didn't give up. I continued to focus on increasing my English vocabulary. I learned how to drive and got myself another weekend job. School and work were very stressful and I did not realize that I was suffering with Post Traumatic Stress Disorder (PTSD). Everyone in my family was suffering, each in their own way, but none of us understood PTSD. Anna expressed her nightmares through her painting. I was more aware of my sister's feelings than I was of my brothers, because we shared a room and I could see her feelings poured out on her homemade canvases.

One of my recurring nightmares was of flying above the mountains. These dreams didn't come now as often as when I was in Vietnam. None of us shared our nightmares or talked about our fears or feelings.

I expressed my nightmares through my health. My teeth were giving me many problems. We did not have dental care during my teen-age years. During our seclusion to an extent, and certainly during our extended "vacations" and escape attempt adventures, drinking water was very limited, our diet lacked nutrition, and brushing our teeth was often out of the question. In America, none of my family had dental insurance to take care of our teeth. I only went to the dentist when my teeth hurt. Every time I visited the dentist, the report was always, you have over ten cavities, you need six root canals, you have gum disease, blah, blah, blah. I always asked the dentist just to take care of the tooth that was currently hurting. We were focused on rebuilding our family and future; if our teeth fell out, we would just eat more soup.

Finally, not only my teeth, but my general health also began to go downhill. I developed a bleeding ulcer and was very sick. I had been sick for some time but ignored it. My stomach hurt so badly I would break out in a cold sweat and curl up like a shrimp. The pain came and went without warning. It started when I first arrived in America and living with Uncle for the first year didn't help. I did not complain to Mother because I didn't think it was serious since it wasn't consistent. Gradually, it went from bad to worse.

Mother finally forced me to see a doctor. I was able to buy cheap health insurance from the junior college student program. After the doctor did all kinds of tests, he put me on a very bland diet. He told me if I didn't take care of my health, I would not live very long … the bleeding ulcer would eat me alive. He also said I had compromised my body over the years. He told me I had six months to take care of myself. He said I had been slowly bleeding internally for some time. He recommended another drastic option, which was surgery. I refused, because I had no money for surgery. I couldn't let my family be burdened more than they already were, so I agreed to the option of a bland diet.

Mother was very worried that I would die. I lost so much weight I looked anorexic. I didn't let her know about the surgery, but told her about the diet. I was still carrying a full load of classes and working three jobs, and she demanded that I cut my weekend and night jobs. I had no choice but to cut my credits and kept only my work-study at school due to the financial aid requirements. Mother prepared my diet of boiled and steamed food for a whole year.

Although I followed the bland diet and listened to my mother and the doctor, I secretly believed I was untouchable and would not die so easily. Otherwise, I would have died during the war, in prison, in the ocean, or in the refugee camp. The ulcer would not kill me. God wanted me to suffer.

In the summer of 1985, Anh contacted me and asked if I would be her maid of honor. We had kept in touch since we came to America. I left the refugee camp before she did. Her family had a sponsor in another state when they first arrived. A year later, they moved and settled in Washington. I had never heard her talk about boys or dating, so I was very surprised when I heard she was getting married.

Her parents had arranged her marriage. She didn't meet her future husband until after the matchmaker set up the arrangement with both his and her parents. Her family lived in Washington and his family lived in Kansas. After the 1985 Chinese New Year, a friend of the family told the parents about the young people. The parents mutually approved of the arrangement and the wedding was set for the summer break. Anh told me that she only met Steve when his family had come to visit a few months before. They never asked her about the marriage-to-be. The parents made plans for the wedding after the groom met Anh and agreed to the marriage. This kind of marriage arrangement was very common back in my grandmother's generation. It was much less common in my parents' generation. I never thought I would see this practice in my generation, especially in America. I didn't share my opinion about it since she appeared to agree with the plans.

Her family paid for my ticket to Washington, and I was to accompany her from Seattle to Kansas for the wedding. We were very busy shopping for the wedding after I arrived in Washington. I didn't have a real opportunity to have a conversation with her as we were always surrounded by relatives. Finally, the night before we left for Kansas, we had a few minutes alone. I asked her what she thought of this arranged marriage business. I even told her if she wanted to run away, I would help her. Anh said she would go through with the marriage to honor her family, and she trusted her parents' choice for her. She thought I was joking about running away, but I wasn't. We laughed about what the family would do if they woke up and we were gone, and then we went to sleep.

The next day we got up early, carpooled to the airport, and boarded the plane to Kansas. Anh still wouldn't tell me what she was thinking. From the Kansas City airport, we had a four-hour drive to the groom's adopted hometown. We arrived right at dinnertime and the groom's family had dinner ready for us. It was nearly midnight when we checked into the hotel after dinner. I asked her one more time what her feelings were about the wedding, and told her if she wanted to run away, I would help her. She started to cry and said, "I don't know what to do. Part of me wants to run, but I cannot let my family down. I have to go through with it!" I asked, "Do you have any feelings for the groom?" She said, "He seems nice, he looks okay, and he's interested in me. I don't know him, but I can't leave! My father's honor would be destroyed! I just can't! Let's go to sleep and not think too much about it. I'll be fine!" I knew she struggled with her feelings, but her father and her family's honor were more important than anything else. I could only wish the best for her. I encouraged her to get some rest; tomorrow would be a big day in her life.

The wedding was very busy and traditional. I tried my best to help her get through the day. I stayed with her for one more day after the wedding. Her new brother-in-law, the second son of the family, and his family took me to the airport. Anh had married Steve, the oldest of four sons and one daughter.

During the long ride back to the airport, I fell asleep in the car. The brother-in-law and his cousin were talking throughout the trip. I ignored their conversation and caught up on some overdue napping. I did overhear the cousin's wife ask in a whisper, "Well, did you ask her? Did you tell her how you feel about her?" The brother-in-law answered, "No, I have not had the opportunity to say anything. She was too busy helping Anh and they were always together!" The wife said, "Well, you better tell her before she leaves!"

It was lunchtime, and we stopped for a break. We were all eating lunch, and the cousin's wife started the conversation. She asked me whether I had a boyfriend and my marriage plans. I told her my future plans were getting through school and working to help my family, that I wasn't interested in dating and never dated. Marriage was not an option. It never entered my mind that they would seriously consider me as a possible wife for son number two.

A month later, Anh called me and said her brother-in-law was coming to California. She asked me to be his tour guide as a favor to her. I agreed and tried my best. He came with two of his friends and I did what I had promised Anh. I showed them all of the Southern California beaches and parks. We even went to Los Angeles' Chinatown for a day. I kept my distance and thanked him for his friendship for Anh's sake. He went back to Kansas and I went back to my crazy, busy life.

A few weeks later, Father got a call from Anh's mother. She asked if Father would be interested in arranging a marriage for me. Anh would be very happy, and she and I would get along great as sisters-in-law. While Father was talking on the phone, I asked Mother to help. I had told her after I came back from the wedding that I wanted nothing to do with an arranged marriage. Besides, all my older brothers and my sister were not interested in dating or getting married. I would not be the one breaking the cultural rule by getting married first. Mother signaled to Father to turn down the marriage proposal. After he hung up the phone, he didn't say anything to me but smiled to himself. I wished I knew what he was thinking. Mother later told me he was glad to turn down the marriage proposal because he was not ready to marry me out of the family and let me go. In our old cultural practices, marriage was a demarcation and declaration of adulthood. His girl would no longer belong to her father, but to her husband's family. Father was probably glad that at least someone was interested in his ugly tomboy daughter, and maybe I wasn't hopeless after all.

All of us were so focused on rebuilding our family and paying off our debts, that none of my older siblings were thinking of themselves. They sacrificed so much to let my younger brother and me have the chance to pursue our education that I couldn't give all that up and lose my focus.

1985 was a proud year in my life. I took oral and written tests for my United States citizenship and passed without any problems. Anna, Henry, and I all passed and went together to the Los Angeles Convention Center for the swearing-in ceremony. I believe it was the largest one in

United States history at the time. More than 2,000 new citizens were sworn in at once. I remember watching the television news crews covering the event, and watching their reports later on the evening news. We were all very emotional at the ceremony, from the beginning to the end. Our feelings were intense. I'm sure Anna and Henry would agree that they felt the same way I did. I was a little sad as we waited to be sworn in, because it had taken a very long, hard journey to get there. On the other hand, I felt happy, excited, and proud that I finally had a country to call my own.

For the first time, I was glad I came to America. I no longer felt regret or wished I could be in Canada or Australia. I was proud to be accepted and could now put down my roots. I felt like I was a ship which had just sailed into harbor. Finally, I could let the anchor down and rest. While the judge conducted the swearing in, I looked at Anna and Henry with their right hands raised. I couldn't understand most of what the judge said, but the tears and smiles on their faces spoke louder than words.

At the end of the ceremony, the Convention Center played two songs: Lee Greenwood's "I Am Proud to Be an American," and the classic "God Bless America." The officials asked our opinion about which song they should use for the ceremony theme song. I loved them both and raised my hand for both of them. I might not have understood all the words back then, but my emotions are still high when I hear both of the songs today. I understand the depth of the words, "… at least I know I'm free" and "God, bless America, land that I love. Stand beside her and guide her."

My English was good enough to communicate with people, but not as good as I wanted it to be. I could only get by in a conversation about daily life issues if it wasn't too sophisticated or philosophical. I was still unable to get into the nursing program and was very frustrated by this time. My community college financial aid grants were due to end when the term ended in June of 1986. I was very concerned about my career path. It was also time for me to transfer and choose a university. I had more than enough credits for a transfer.

I met with my academic advisor, and he asked what I wanted to do when I left school. I told him I wanted to be a nurse, but hadn't been able to pass the prerequisite science classes. He asked a thought-provoking question: "Why do you want to be a nurse?" I told him I liked helping people, especially old people. He asked if I had considered being a social worker. He said they helped people without having to have the medical knowledge. Since biology and science were not for me, he thought I should consider changing my major before I transferred.

I had never heard of a social worker. In all the Asian languages I know, we do not have this concept. The closest I could come would be teacher, priest, or guide. I couldn't imagine or understand the concept of social work, or what I would be doing if I worked in the field. He encouraged me and told me that I would be very good in this field and could work with the elderly population. He had an easy job to convince me to change my major, but I had to convince my family. I weighed the stress I had put my body through, yet still being unable to get into the major I wanted. I decided I had better take his advice and I told him the next day I was ready to try something new.

The professor also helped me to choose a university. I told him I would like to go to a smaller campus rather than a big university. I had been accepted at UCLA, but I was concerned that I might get lost if I went to a university that had so many students and a huge campus. He suggested I go to Humboldt State University, and showed me on a map where it was located. It was on the northernmost coast of California, and we were on the southern end. It was over five hundred miles away from home. I wasn't sure whether I could persuade my family to let me go alone so far away. In my culture, I could move out of the family home through marriage, but not for school. I wasn't sure how to convince them it was a good idea.

I went home to have what I knew would be a long conversation with my family. Luckily, my youngest brother Ken would graduate from high school in June. He planned to go to a junior college for his general education before transferring to a four-year college. I did my homework and talked him into going with me. The College of the Redwoods was a community college a few miles down the coast from Humboldt State. He was an outdoors fanatic, and would be able to spend a lot of time in the redwood forest. If he agreed, it would be easy to convince Father to let me go so far from home. I probably outweighed my little brother by ten or fifteen pounds, but somehow I needed his testosterone to protect me. After all, I wouldn't be moving out of the family by myself. We might not be in the same school's dorms, but we would be in the same town away from home. With Ken beside me, it was easy to get my mother's, sister's, and older brothers' approval. As usual, Mother convinced Father it was a good idea despite his objections and cultural expectations.

My academic advisor happened to have a good friend who was the Admissions Director of Humboldt State University, and he asked him to come and meet me. The director was very friendly and he offered me a job working in his recruiting office. He even called the ESL director at College of the Redwoods and set up Ken's admission. I would live in the dorm at the university, Ken would be in the dorm at the junior college, and we could see each other on the weekends.

A week before school started in August, Joe, Anna, and Henry drove us to Humboldt County. They bought us a used Toyota Corolla, and we drove it and Joe's mini-van which he named "Sweet-home" because he slept in it during the week. For the first time, we left Southern California and drove the entire length of the state along beautiful Highway 101, the Pacific Coast Highway. We stayed in San Francisco for a night, and drove through beaches, farmland, mountains, meadows, and cities. We were awed by the tallest trees and biggest living things on the planet, the giant red Sequoias. We even drove the van right through a hole in one of the biggest and oldest trees in the world along the famous "Avenue of the Giants." We had never been on a vacation together before in America, and we had fun. There was something for everyone to enjoy along the 101.

CHAPTER TWENTY-THREE:
CO-ED

I began classes at Humboldt State University in the fall of 1986. I hadn't realized how complicated dorm life would be, or how far out of my comfort zone. It was another major culture shock and turning point in my life. When my academic advisor suggested I live on campus in the dorm, it sounded very appealing and logical. My plan was to live in the dorm for a year. By then we would be situated and know the area, and I could find an apartment to share with Ken.

After Joe, Anna, and Henry went home, I began my new life in the dorm. All the residents checked into the dorm a few days before classes began. I arrived at Cedar Hall on Friday, and met my assigned room-mate, Nancy Hightower, who lived up to her name. She was six feet tall and looked like a giant next to my not quite five-foot frame. Nancy was a very outgoing, social person, and she made friends in the dorm as soon she arrived.

Nancy and I had similar personalities. We were both outgoing and friendly, but we came from very different cultures and upbringings. My reserved East met her wild, wild West. Language also played a very big part in the difference of our thinking and lifestyle. On some levels, we shared common interests. For example, she liked classical, old pop, soft rock, and jazz music as I did, but she listened to the English versions. I listened to the Chinese versions. I heard a lot of American music when I was younger, but didn't understand the words. I only remembered the melodies, many of which had been turned into Chinese pop songs as well.

Nancy was much more carefree and open than I was. She could change clothes right in front of me in our room. I hid in the closet to get dressed, since it was big enough for me to use as a dressing room. I had never even dressed myself in front of my mother or sister at home. Anna and I shared a room, but we never dressed at the same time. We took turns. I had never paid attention to this issue until I lived with Nancy and I wasn't about to change my ways just because I was living in the dorm.

We got along, but were not best buddies. She had a tendency to talk very fast with lots of new words I didn't understand. I still struggled with English, and had to stop her and ask for the meaning of what she said. She was very patient with me and willing to help. I found it strange that after living with me for a day, she told everyone in our dorm that I dressed in the closet. It was a big joke around the whole dorm. I didn't see the humor in my modesty. Why would it be so important to tell?

My next-door neighbor was our building's Resident Advisor, Leslie. She was very kind, friendly, and a very pretty young girl. She always had a big smile when I saw her. What caught my attention most was her long straight brown hair, which reminded me of Crystal Gayle, and her clear complexion and big, beautiful blue eyes. She was a natural beauty who didn't need makeup, which most of my Caucasian dorm-mates overused. Blue eyes were new to me. When I talked to her and looked into her eyes, I felt like her eyes were talking, not her mouth.

They caught me like a set of blue pearls from the deep blue sea. I was so attracted and distracted by her eyes that it was hard for me to pay attention to what she was saying. I could only wonder what the boys must have thought, but most of them seemed to actually prefer the girls with lots of makeup.

The more makeup a girl wore, the more guys hung around her. Who knew what horrors they hid under all that cake? I figured not wearing makeup would be my way to keep the guys away. I didn't need men in my life. I had a degree to get, and it wasn't going to be easy.

Leslie set up a mixer in the television lounge of our building for everyone to get to know each other. After the latest episode of "Saint Elsewhere," everyone got together and played a game to help us remember each other's names. I felt very out of place because I wasn't able to understand or remember all the names of the people around me. I had never heard so many foreign names all at once. It felt like I had gone back to high school again. In high school no one gave me the time of day, but everyone was here by choice and eager to learn new things and be with people from other backgrounds. At least they all remembered my name the first time around the room.

There was another Asian girl in Cedar Hall. Joy was Japanese, but she was born and raised in Hawaii. She was nice to me, but I still felt very isolated because I couldn't understand her very well. She had spoken English all her life, so we had the same communication problem I had with everyone else.

A week later, Leslie arranged another mixer. Everyone had decorated their rooms by now, so we had an "open house." She encouraged us to visit each other's rooms. She suggested that we all set up our rooms with treats to welcome each other during visits. I cooked some fried wontons to welcome my guests. As I was cooking in the basement kitchen, Nancy was greeting our visitors. Once I brought up the crispy golden snacks, in the time it took me to go back down to the basement kitchen, clean up, and return with my clean wok, all of the wontons were gone. Nancy couldn't tell me who the culprits were. She said that as soon as the girls heard we had fried wontons in our room, everybody came at once. She was more upset than I was that she couldn't keep them from eating all of my wontons. I felt like I was living with a pack of wild dogs.

Cedar Hall stood three stories tall on a wooded, jungle-like hillside. The first and third levels were reserved for male students and the second level was for female students. At least that was the plan.

Leslie came to my room after the wontons were gone to encourage me to visit the other rooms on the first and third floors. She escorted me, but I was feeling a bit sick after peeking in the first three rooms on the first floor. I had been raised not to enter any boy's room, both to protect my virtue and out of good manners. Although I had seen my mother shake hands with coworkers and guests, contact between the sexes in my experience was extremely limited.

The posters in the boys' rooms showing girls in bikinis bent over cars, motorcycles, or just plain showing off their private parts made me uncomfortable. I couldn't express my disgust to Nancy and Leslie. I know they meant well, but it was just too much for me. After my five minute tour of the first floor, I went back to my room. I just wanted to be left alone, but they insisted we tour the third floor as well. I had seen more than I wanted to already, but I agreed to go up to the third floor just to shut them up, only if both of them came along.

Finally, I made my way up to the third floor. At the end of the halls just to the right of the stairs, I met a skinny red haired guy who had introduced himself as Randy at our previous mixer. I remembered his name because his super-curly, frizzy red hair and freckles made him look like my friend's Raggedy Ann doll. I had never talked to a red-headed boy before. He invited us to see his room. Because his room was at the end of the hall, it was a four-person suite with a living room in between two bedrooms. I quickly walked around his living room and stood at the doorway to each bedroom. I didn't go in, but glanced inside without really paying attention and walked out of the living room, completing my tour. More of the same, I figured.

Randy's next-door neighbors, David and Rhys, came out of their room as they heard Randy's enthusiastic high-pitched greetings in the hall. They were polite and invited me to see their room. I had met them at the meeting the week before, but they didn't stand out like Randy, so I couldn't remember their names, or even come close. I was a little hesitant, but I didn't want to be rude since they had been more polite to me than the other boys had. I stood by the door and looked inside. To my surprise, Rhys' side was full of pictures of wolves, and David's was full of yellow-eyed owls of every shape, size and color. I was more comfortable stepping into their room. I learned their names one more time and kept it in my memory box. I didn't leave their room for a while. I thought to myself, if I went back to my room too soon, Nancy and Leslie would talk me into seeing other rooms that I didn't want to see. I stayed and talked with both of them for as long as I could.

Rhys' and David's room was right above mine. Although I could only understand about forty percent of what they were saying, I tried my best to carry on a conversation with them and noticed that I felt safe and comfortable. I asked them about their posters. They were very patient and willing to explain to me about all their favorite wild animals. I was very impressed that Rhys appeared so knowledgeable about wolves. David, on the other hand, told me that his favorite bird was the Snowy Owl. He had been collecting owls over the years. He also had a couple of goldfish in a bowl on the desk next to his bed. I could tell he loved animals. I remembered that Mother once told me, "He who loves animals has a soft heart." After I stayed in there long enough, I went back to my room. I was glad Nancy and Leslie were not around.

Close to dinnertime, Leslie came to tell me that she had picked a name for me. She explained about an "ice breaker" game for everybody to play. I wasn't sure what she was talking about, but I went along. She told me everyone had someone's name that she picked. Randy got my name and I got David's name. Randy had to tuck me in at bedtime, and I had to tuck David in. I was glad when Leslie said we didn't have to be in bed for real, just to pretend. I wasn't sure what to expect and didn't understand how the whole game worked, but it sounded very much out of my comfort zone and culture. The reason I went along is that I didn't know how to tell her I didn't want to participate without offending her. She appeared very enthusiastic about the game.

Randy came to my room Sunday night after dinner with a small glass of milk, two cookies, and a white rose on a tray. He had to tuck me in at bedtime. It was only 7:00 p.m., and not my bedtime. I still had a few things to get ready for class the next day. Nancy was in the room and she said Randy would not be a problem for her if she wasn't a problem for him. I was glad she stayed. I was comfortable with Randy, but I had never been in a room alone with a guy before. He took a small book out of his back pocket. We all sat down and he read me a poem. It was hard for me to understand what he read but I didn't have the heart to tell him it was difficult. I waited until he finished and asked, "Do I have to do the same for David? Leslie got his name for me to tuck in tomorrow night. I don't think I can read him a poem as good as you read to me." Randy suggested that I could do anything I was comfortable doing. He asked, "What would your mother do when she put you to bed?"

I could not remember the last time Mother put me to bed. We were always asleep before she came home from the restaurant. Our nannies, older female cousins, Grandmother, or my sister put us to bed. Sometimes they sang us a bedtime song or told us a bedtime story. It depended on who put us to bed. I wasn't able to tell Randy all I was thinking. I just said, "Sing a bedtime song?" Randy said, "It's okay to sing a bedtime song if you are comfortable with that." I said, "I can only sing a Chinese song, not an English song. I don't know any." Randy laughed and said, "It would be very interesting to see what David thinks, but I am sure he would be delighted! Something different." I was glad Randy gave me some good suggestions and was friendly and not inappropriate like some of the other guys.

The next night was my turn to tuck David in. I did the same thing Randy did for me. I brought some cookies and a small glass of milk from the cafeteria, and my guitar. I didn't get him any flowers. I didn't think it would be proper for me to bring flowers. I set the cookies and the glass of milk on his table and sat down on the chair by his desk. I told him that I would sing him a Chinese song, because I didn't know any English songs. I didn't know how to read a poem, so he would have to take what I could do. He didn't look upset or object. I didn't know many songs to play on my guitar, and I had no formal musical training. I was very limited with my song choices, because I taught myself how to play the guitar. I couldn't read music to learn new songs. I learned songs by listening and watching my friend play when I was in Vietnam.

I could only sing and play the few songs I knew. He saw that I had several music sheets in my guitar case, and asked if I would play those, too. I tried, and he pretended to yawn and snore as I finished. I didn't know what he was thinking, but I did what I had to do and what I was comfortable with, as Randy had suggested. David told me he enjoyed the music. I was surprised at his remark. He didn't understand Chinese, so how could he have enjoyed it? I think he just said that to be nice. At least he was polite.

I began classes and work at school, met new friends, and tried my best to adjust to dorm life. It wasn't that bad at first. Ken came to see me on weekends. I went to the market to buy food, and cooked some home-style meals for us. We were very homesick, but we encouraged each other.

One day, Ken complained to me that the kids in his dorm ate all the food which I had made for him. We decided to teach the thieves a lesson. Rather than making fried rice with all the ingredients added already, I made Ken some plain white rice. I cooked up some pork cubes like stew meat, and made it very garlicky and salty. It could be choked down with the plain rice, just a little meat at a time, but anyone attempting to eat just the pork would get a nasty surprise. It worked; Ken's dish lasted all week and no one ever stole his food again.

I met a San Diego girl named Kathy Monnin at my work-study job in the mailroom. She was a social work major, too. Kathy was the same age as Ken, but she started at Humboldt a year ahead of us. She took to me as my protector. She saw my struggles with English and helped edit my letters to prospective students. She stood up for me when my supervisor wanted to derail my internship due to my poor English skills and explained words I didn't understand. She was the director of the Adopt-a-Grandparent Club, and encouraged me to join the club. Kathy was very excited and happy that she and I shared the same passion for working with the elderly. She helped me get an internship at the adult day care center working with her. She trained me how to interview clients, do home visits, and write reports. She was very patient and showed me step-by-step. She helped me when I had problems in classes she had already taken by telling me the important things to remember for tests.

One of the girls working in the mailroom with us was very mean to me. She often told me what to do, and was very impatient and unkind. Most of the time, I couldn't understand what she said. I wasn't able to tell her to "back off," but Kathy stood up for me and told her off. She tried to explain the meaning of the bad words my tormentor said to me, but I had had my fill of her type of person and didn't even want to understand them.

Kathy suggested we set our work schedules so we could work together. Our schedules were very flexible as long as we worked at least twenty hours per week. She lived in a townhouse apartment in town rather than the dorm, so I didn't see her after school or on the weekends. When things got unbearable in the dorm, she invited me to stay in her apartment when we had a four-day weekend, but she lived with her boyfriend. I wasn't comfortable interfering with her time off and her personal life. Through the years and across the oceans, which sometimes separate us as she travels the world, I have continued to love her as my sister.

Eventually, Kathy went on to obtain her Master's degree in social work, and married a medical student. A few years later, when now

Doctor Steve's mother was gravely ill, she told him it was not worth it to wait until retirement to pursue his dreams. He packed up his belongings, put some special things in storage, sold the house and medical practice, bought the boat and made his dream come true. They traveled the world in their sailboat for five years. Somehow, I could not take them up on their invitations to accompany them sailing, not just due to the time and money it would cost, but mostly due to my absolute commitment never to set foot on a boat in the ocean again. It's just not my idea of a relaxing time.

Back in Cedar Hall, I soon learned that many of the girls in the dorm were sleeping around. Their life choices were wild and ir-responsible. They didn't have relationships with the people they had sex with. They acted like it was nothing to sleep with a different guy every weekend. Whatever felt good at the time was okay. I didn't understand their lifestyle. In Vietnam, prostitutes were paid for their services. These girls cheapened themselves for fun. Who would want to marry them later?

Marijuana and alcohol were also big problems in the dorm, and they played a part in the students' wild behavior. Boys got drunk and fought and yelled in the hallways. Or they got high and cried a sad story to get a girl to feel sorry for them. Late at night and through the weekends, I could hear the noise of their laughing, yelling, or crying from anywhere in the dorm and even from outside in the canyon created by the dormitory complex. The ruckus started Thursday nights and kept up until early Monday mornings. I felt like a prisoner in my room.

Randy and Rhys usually came and invited me to eat at the cafeteria with them and David. I didn't mind eating with them; I felt even more out of place when I was in the dining hall eating alone. People at the tables talked and ate at the same time. I ate my food and didn't know what they were chatting about. It was as if they all spoke a secret language around me. I tried to listen, but it was too confusing. They sounded like they were speaking English, but the words didn't make any sense to me. David waited for us at the cafeteria and saved seats for us. He never came to my room. If he did come, he always asked for Nancy and talked to her. When we sat at the cafeteria table, he was always quiet but friendly. He appeared very calm and stable, not like the others ... loud and wild. He seemed out of place in this crazy environment, too.

On Tuesday nights, I often saw David come out of Leslie's room with Randy, or a group of people. Some of them carried a thick black book in their hands. I knew it was a Bible, because Simon had given me one before I left Orange County for Humboldt. I guessed they were probably having church in Leslie's room. I wasn't interested. To me, religion was just as foolish as the slutty girls. There was no god, no magic, and no salvation for the depravity of mankind. There was only selfishness and greed. Maybe there was a devil, but there was certainly no god who cared to get involved with his creation, no matter how much incense you burned or how many songs you sang.

Yumi Sato lived in the dorms in the building next to us. She was an exchange student from Japan, working on her Master's degree. We often ran into each other at the cafeteria and library. Yumi and I had the same hairstyle, and we were about the same height, but she was twenty pounds lighter in her five-foot frame. She had a thinner build and far sharper features than mine. I thought she was much more attractive than me. Somehow, Americans could not tell us apart. We both wore denim jackets regularly, and people often asked us if we were twins when they saw us walking together. I sometimes had people come up to me and call me Yumi, and she got called Ting-Ting when she walked alone.

I kept my hatred for Yumi a secret. I didn't tell her my father had been a prisoner of the Japanese during World War II. If she found out, she might have been afraid to be my friend. One night in the library, I told her what had happened to my father and how he had seen Japanese soldiers torturing the Chinese during the war when he was just a child. I told her about Nanking. She just looked at me with a blank look on her face. She didn't know any history of her people's involvement in the Second World War. She told me those stories couldn't have happened, and we got mad at each other.

A few days later, Yumi came to me and said she had been doing some research in the library. What I told her was true. They didn't teach these things in history class in Japanese schools. She said she hoped we could still be friends, but she could not undo what those people had done. Maybe our being friends would change the future. Knowing her has helped me make friends with people I might have hated before just because of who their ancestors were.

Yumi and I remained the best of friends, and I took her to visit my family in Garden Grove. I was nervous about how my father would feel about me bringing a Japanese person into his home, but to my surprise he greeted her with his usual big grin and talked with her in Japanese. He brought out his calligraphy set and sat down at the kitchen table with her and compared Japanese writing with Chinese. They got along so well, I wondered where my hatred had come from. Yumi returned to Kyoto after she finished her degree, and we kept in touch until I had my first child. She sent newborn Hunter the cutest pair of baby blue leather shoes I have ever seen, and of course I cherish them still. I hope to visit her someday, and I think my Father will look down from Heaven and smile at our reunion.

As time went on, life in the dorm got worse and worse. People were getting crazier and crazier. I was having nightmares more frequently than when I lived at home. My recurring dream was about flying outside of my body, over jungle and mountains. I began to hate nighttime. I felt I had gone back to being in the war zone again. My grade average dropped from 3.8 to 1.9. I couldn't focus, and I couldn't put all the war images out of my mind. I could smell death and dust from the gunpowder. I didn't hear voices, but I couldn't turn my thoughts around. I became more and more frustrated and angry. It was worse when there was yelling, screaming, and fighting sounds in the hallway from my dorm-mates who were drunk or high. I felt out of control, confused, and scared. Sometimes I couldn't tell whether the noises were from the past or the present. I just wanted the noise to stop. I didn't know how to tell anyone how I felt. I became very depressed, and being homesick didn't help. I found myself getting close to having a nervous breakdown as the months went by. My ulcer came back, and I had to go back to my bland diet. I didn't know if I should let anyone know what was happening to me, and didn't know why anyone would care.

I often locked myself in my room after dinner on the weekends. Nancy was hardly ever there; she was always out with her boyfriend. Her relationship with this boyfriend appeared to be very complicated. According to her story, they came from the same town, and she told me sometimes they were dating and sometimes they were not. I couldn't keep up with her to know what was what. She quoted Shakespeare and said, "To be or not to be?" I couldn't understand this kind of relationship due to my lack of knowledge and experience with dating. I wished she would stay with me more often on weekends, but most of the time I was by myself, alone in my room. Rhys worked as an ambulance attendant, Randy studied and helped out at a church, and David went fishing or worked at his dad's friend's hardware store on the weekends.

One Friday night was the last straw, the final blow to my ability to maintain my sanity in the dorm. I came back to my room from the library very late and locked myself in as usual, since Nancy was nowhere to be found. The hallway was unusually quiet and it was close to midnight. I couldn't sleep so I decided to take a shower. I didn't think anyone would still be up. The crazy girls down the hall from me had been very quiet for a long time. They must have been sleeping. The bathroom was right across from my room. I just had to step out of my room and walk two steps across the hall.

While I was in the shower, I heard voices and the noise of people coming into the bathroom. I thought some of the girls were using the toilet, so I ignored the noise. Then I heard some guys talking, shouting, and laughing at the door. They wanted to come in to use the toilet. I was holding my breath, hoping the girls would not let them in, but I was wrong. The girls told them to come in and then they walked out. When the guys came into the bathroom, they sounded drunk or high. They pushed each other and laughed even louder than when they were by the door. I tried to be very quiet, but the water was still running and I couldn't shut it off soon enough. I heard one of the guys say, "Shhh, shhh. Someone is in the shower," and then laugh. I took a deep breath and yelled out loud with all my strength, "GET OUT! ALL OF YOU GET OUT! THIS IS THE WOMEN'S BATHROOM! NOT YOURS! OUT! OUT! OUT! OUT! OUT!"

I could hear my heart beating and felt like it was about to pop out of my chest. I looked around the shower for my towel, but it was hanging outside on a hook. I had nothing with me inside the shower that I could use to hide myself. I did have my shampoo and conditioner bottles that I could use as weapons if I had to. I couldn't predict what they were going to do. I recognized their voices. This was the same group of guys I was afraid of who always hung out and slept with the wild group of girls at the other end of the hall. When they heard me yell, one of them said, "Oh, it's Ting-Ting. We better get out. Come on, guys, let's go! Hurry!" They were laughing and fighting to get out of the bathroom.

When it was quiet, I knew finally I was the only one inside. I cracked open the door, reached outside the shower stall and got my towel, wrapped it around myself, grabbed my pajamas, and ran back to my room. I wasn't finished with my shower, and I still had soap in my hair. I locked the door, hurried to the closet, and put on my pajamas. I sat down on the closet floor and cried uncontrollably. I hated being that scared. I had been that scared before and I hated being reminded of it. I decided to say something to Leslie before I completely lost it. I knew I could hurt someone when I was in this place. I was so angry. I could smell the gunpowder, and see myself standing outside my neighbors' ruined house during the Tet Offensive.

I didn't sleep that night. Early in the morning, I heard some noise in Leslie's room next door. I peeked out and saw her come out of her room. I asked her, "Did you hear what happened last night?" She said, "Not really. I didn't feel very good. I took some cold medicine and it made me sleepy. I slept like a log. I didn't hear anything. What happened? Are you okay?" She looked at me with those big eyes wide as she was talking. I took a deep breath and told her what happened. I let her know that I was very angry. Leslie assured me that she would do something about it. She told me to get some rest, because I looked terrible. I don't know what she did or said to those girls and guys, but everything around the dorm seemed very calm and quiet that day. I avoided people as much as I could. I went to the new Bayshore Mall in Eureka and to the windy beach with my brother all day, and I didn't return to the dorm until very late. When I got home I didn't even greet Nancy, I just went to bed.

The next morning, I was in the bathroom getting ready for breakfast, and heard some girls come in. I was in the last toilet stall, so I kept very quiet. They were talking about the incident. One person said, "I don't understand why Leslie made such a big deal out of the guys using the ladies bathroom. It's only the bathroom!" Another joined in, "Yeah. What's the big f****ing deal? She just wanted to show off her power." Another said, "Yeah. I was the one who let the guys come in and use our toilet. I share my bathroom with my brothers at home. I don't understand what's her f****ing problem that she had to talk like that to us. I don't f****ing care what she said, the boys can use the bathroom any time." They walked out of the bathroom continuing their profanity and left me by myself again.

I don't know how long I sat in the stall, but I could feel smoke coming out of my ears and my nose. I told myself over and over that dorm life was over for me. If I didn't leave this dorm building, I couldn't guarantee what would happen to it. The smell of dust and the bombing sounds were very clear and real to me. The sight of buildings being destroyed was also very real. I felt like the war had not left me. I brought it with me to America and into this dorm building, and I needed to tell someone about my rage before I took action. I struggled between the past and the present. I kept telling myself that the war in my neighborhood could not be happening in the dorm. I had to focus and force myself to think of my family in Southern California and my brother Ken living just a few miles down the highway.

Fortunately, I was taking a basic mental health class. I was learning about the human mind, and I decided to share my problems with my professor, Sara Turner. She was also my academic advisor. She was supportive, patient, and believed in me. My internship field instructor said I was not able to speak English well enough to be a good social worker, because my language skills would be a handicap. Sara disagreed with her and stood up for me. She believed that with time and high technology (computers were just then coming into common personal use), I would improve my English and be the best social worker she had ever trained. Of course she was exaggerating, but her confidence buoyed me when I needed it most.

Sara was clearly concerned about my story and my reaction and suggested that I seek counseling services at the school Student Health Center. Even though social work was now my major, it was hard for me to understand what counseling really meant and how it would help. In my language, we didn't have a word for counseling or therapy. Our closest word means advice, like parental advice or direction. It was difficult to accept the concept, but I went.

I didn't know what to tell my counselor during the first session. I had a hard time expressing myself due to my limited language and understanding of how the process worked. I went for a few sessions and felt so awkward. I couldn't understand why I came, nor could I expect her to understand me. I felt counseling was doing more to confuse me than help me. It was more complicated than I expected it to be, so I stopped going. I did remember that she said I was suffering from major PTSD. I did not understand what PTSD was at the time. My education so far had not taught me this diagnostic term. She also said, "Amazingly, you are functionally more normally than most people with your issues, and you are not in the state hospital." I didn't understand what the state hospital had to do with me. Wasn't a hospital for sick patients? What did that have to do with me and what I thought? Of course she meant the public mental health institution.

Halloween was just around the corner. Randy, Rhys, and David had become trusted and safe male friends in the dorm for me. I was more comfortable with them than the other guys in the dorm. We saw each other at the cafeteria and the library. Randy and Rhys came to my room to get me and walked me to the cafeteria more than David did. Yumi and I saw David at the library almost every day. He always saved seats for us and walked us back to the dorm late at night. He was still very quiet and calm. He invited Ken and me to the dorm's Halloween walk in the park.

The dorm had a late night walk in the park that most everyone was going to. Ken visited me every weekend and had become friends with my friends, so we all went as a big group. Amazingly, the walk in the woods did not trigger my fears. I was just not ready to deal with the jungle experiences, so my mind ignored the similarities between that walk and running through the jungle after escaping the train.

That night, I got to see the fun side of David. He began to loosen up. He was a real mountain man, and on the walk he was in his environment. He got along well with Ken because they both appreciated nature. David could name the trees, plants, animals, and birds, and Ken loved the rocks. He was not the distant and quiet guy I knew since school started. We played pool in the recreation room after the walk. He was more open and relaxed around us. After that night, he joked more often and was much friendlier and less shy.

Thanksgiving break approached, and David invited my brother and me to join him and Rhys at his grandparent's vacation cabin, about a two-hour drive east into the mountains. I told him we couldn't go. A good friend of mine from home was coming to visit us over the break. I met John in the Golden West College Asian Student's Club, and he continued to keep in contact with me since I came to Humboldt. He had some time off from work and wanted to visit.

Yumi, Ken, John, and I had a fun time during his visit. We went to Redwood State Park and the beach. John's visit was only during the four day Thanksgiving break, and then he went back home to Orange County. We had one more month of school before Christmas and the end of the first semester. I was glad to see John, because he came from home. I felt he brought home to me during that short time. I looked forward to going home for Christmas break.

As I thought about going home in a few more weeks, I tried my best not to get too depressed about being in the dorm. Kathy suggested that since I hated being in the dorm and wasn't doing well, I should request that the dorm committee allow me to leave. I wasn't sure how it worked, so she helped me submit my request. Leslie helped me practice what to say before I went to the committee meeting. I told the committee that my grade point average had dropped to 1.9 due to the craziness of living in the dorm. I said I was getting close to losing my mind and having a nervous breakdown. I said I had to leave the dorm or I couldn't guarantee what I would do to the building. I could not and would not come back to live in the dorm next semester. They allowed me to get out of my contract for the school year after the first semester was over, and I was very relieved.

The news went through the building like wildfire. People in the dorm were glad for me, but some were not sure. Some of the guys came to me and said, "We will miss the smell of your cooking on the weekends." Nancy and Leslie were happy for me. They saw how depressed I was. Yumi helped me connect with some of her Japanese friends that lived in an apartment building just across the freeway in town. I met the manager that same day and signed a lease for the rest of the school year on a single bedroom apartment for Ken and me for the next semester within shouting distance of the campus. I was so happy the day we signed the lease.

When I went to tell David and Rhys, they were talking. I didn't usually go to their room unless Nancy wanted some privacy. She asked if she could have the room to herself to call her family during dinnertime, so I went to tell the guys my good news. David was drinking a beer and Rhys was drinking orange juice. They welcomed me inside and I told them the news. David offered to help me and Ken find some furniture during break. They were very happy for me. I asked what they were up to. I was surprised to see David drinking beer. I had never seen him drink before. They said they were relaxing before the hectic final exams. David asked if I wanted to try his beer. I told him I could only have one sip, not a whole bottle. He handed me the beer in his hand, which was about one-third full, and opened another. I sipped on the bottle for a while, and gave the bottle back to him. I didn't mind beer, but I didn't want to drink alcohol when I was not at home. I had beer at home with my family only during special events, but never a whole bottle, only a small glass, and I shared that with Anna.

Rhys offered me his orange juice to try. I had never drank beer and orange juice at the same time. I wondered if he was trying to show me something different by having me drink these two beverages. I took two big swallows of his orange juice and gave it back to him. It had a sweet but bitter taste. I didn't know that Rhys' orange juice had alcohol in it, and that I would have a very strong allergic reaction. I tried to listen to their conversation, but in less than five minutes, I didn't feel very good. I got up from my chair and told them I was going back to my room. I walked out of their room quickly and went toward the stairs to go back down to my floor. The stairway was just across the hall from their room. The next thing I knew, the stairs were spinning around and around. I don't remember how I got back to my room, but I woke up tucked into my bed still in my jeans and sweater, with my shoes at the door. I was lucky I was in the company of gentlemen.

The school had just started construction of the foundation for a new building in the parking lot next to the dorms. A huge hammer dropped on big steel beams, pounding them into the ground. A chain hoisted the hammer back up and let it fall again and again. The noise woke me up and just about killed me as my head pounded along with the pile-driver. When I went to eat breakfast, David and Rhys told me that I must have a hangover. I didn't know what they were talking about, but I hurried to finish my breakfast and headed to class. I don't remember how I got thru the day with my big headache, but I did take Leslie up on her cold medicine remedy.

I got a letter from John later that day. It was three pages long, and that was overwhelming for me. I tried to read it, but it did not make any sense to me. I gave it to David to help me read it. By this time, David had been helping me with my English and new words when we did our homework in the library. He finished reading the letter and said without looking directly at me, "It's a love-letter. John is telling you that he likes you." I did not ask him any more questions, but he looked unhappy with me. I don't remember why Yumi didn't join us at the library that night, but I noticed that David was quiet and distant. He was not as friendly as he was when Yumi was around. He looked a bit moody for a few days. I didn't respond to John's letter. Not that I didn't want to, but because I didn't know what to say. I decided it would be better to talk to him in person when I went home for Christmas break.

On Saturday morning, Leslie saw me in the bathroom. She seemed more chatty than usual. Out of the blue she looked at me with her big, beautiful blue eyes, smiled, and said, "David really likes you!" I looked at her, "What? Are you sure? Not you, or Nancy, or Yumi? I think you are wrong!" Leslie didn't give up. She laughed and continued to say, "Yep! He really, really likes you!" This time I was very confused, "No way! He is moody when Yumi is not studying with us. He always asks for Nancy when he comes to my room. He doesn't talk to me if no one is around! He's leaving your room all the time! How can he like me?" Leslie told me she was dating George, not David. I still thought she misunderstood him. I asked if he told her himself. She said no, but she could tell. I told her if she watched him when he came to my room, she could see that he only talked to Nancy, not to me or Yumi. I went back to my room and got ready for breakfast. Either Randy or Rhys, or both of them would be coming soon and to walk with me to the cafeteria.

Randy came and we went to the cafeteria. David and Rhys were waiting, and had saved seats for us as usual. We went through the line and sat down to eat. I wasn't in the mood to listen to the table talk. Normally, they talked and talked, and I just ate my food and tried to listen and understand what they were saying. I was still thinking about the conversation with Leslie. Suddenly, I heard David tell the guys at the table, "Hey! Ting-Ting is still sitting here!" All I heard was my name. I looked at him and the people at the table. I noticed that all the people at the table were his male dorm mates and I was the only female. I had always noticed when Randy and Rhys left the table, but this time I didn't even know they were gone.

David had always been protective, but he appeared really annoyed this time, more than any time before. One of the guys said, "What? She doesn't understand what we're talking about." He turned and looked at me, "Do you understand what we're talking about?" I looked at the guy asking the question and shook my head, then looked at David. He didn't look at me, but answered the guy, "Shut up! She is here and she is a lady. If other women were here, would you be having this conversation?" I didn't know what the problem was but, judging by his body language, I could tell David was mad. I had never seen that side of him before.

I wasn't about to let a fight start on my account. I hurried and finished my food and left the table. David got up and left after me. I heard the guys still saying something, but I didn't want to know what they said. When we walked out of the cafeteria, he was very quiet and appeared not to want to talk. As we walked toward the entrance to our building, he stopped and asked me with a very serious look, "Can we go steady?" I answered, "Sure!" I went in the door and up to my room, but I noticed that he didn't follow me. I walked in and saw Nancy sitting by her desk. I asked her, "Nancy! Is the word 'study' sometimes pronounced 'steady?' I learned a new way of saying study!" Nancy looked at me and asked, "Who told you that?"

I looked out my window and saw David still standing in the same spot. I wondered why he didn't go get his books. Did he not want to study? I pointed at him and answered Nancy, "David Burford did! He asked me when we were on our way back from the cafeteria." I turned around to finish my sentence, but I found Nancy wasn't sitting by her desk. She was lying on the floor laughing so hard she couldn't catch her breath. I was surprised, and didn't know what was so funny. "What did I say wrong?" Nancy finally controlled her laughing and said, "He means he wants to go out with you! Like a boyfriend and girlfriend!" I was shocked. I told her I told him, "Sure." I thought about the conversation with Leslie. I sat down on my bed and thought about what I should do next. I gathered all my courage and went out to talk to him. I don't remember how long I sat on my bed and how long it took me to think. When I walked toward him, he looked at me with a funny smile on his face. I said, "We need to talk; let's walk!" He ran up to his room and came back with his book bag and we headed out to the small Redwood Park trail by the dorm buildings.

I'm not sure exactly what I said to him, but I did make a list of things that I would not do as a girlfriend. I had never dated anyone before and I didn't know how and what to expect. I hadn't planned to date, but if I did, I wouldn't date the American way. I told him that my culture and upbringing were very old-fashioned. I wanted to keep it that way and not compromise just because I was living in America. I wouldn't be sleeping with him like the other girls in our building slept with guys. I would like to keep our friendship the way it was, making it deeper with time. He must never hit me. If he did, I would tell my brothers and they might kill him. If he changed his mind because of my rules, I would understand. He smiled at me and said that he understood. He said, "You have nothing to worry about! All your rules are fine with me. We can just take things slow. I don't expect you to do anything you aren't comfortable with." I thought if he followed my rules, I could give dating a try.

I shared with Yumi and Kathy. Yumi was very happy for me. She said she always knew he had feelings for me, and she thought he would be a very nice, kind boyfriend for me. Kathy, on the other hand, had never met David. She was like a little, loving mother hen, so she checked him out. She asked her business-major friends about him. She invited us to her apartment for dinner. The only thing she didn't do was a criminal background check on him. Fortunately for David, Kathy's cat, Annie, took to him. She was very shy and often hid when unfamiliar people were in the house, but she took to him. David also wore a flannel shirt like her boyfriend, so he passed her test.

CHAPTER TWENTY-FOUR:
LIVING THE AMERICAN DREAM

We made our plans for the 1986 Christmas break. David only had a six-hour drive to get to San Jose. Ken and I had a thirteen-hour drive ahead of us, so David invited us to stay with his family overnight. It made for a perfect break for us on our way home. We would have to stay in the San Francisco area for the night anyway if we weren't staying with him. Ken and I followed his antique red and white Ford truck to San Jose.

We got to meet his family. I learned that he had moved out of his parents' house into his grandparents' guesthouse when he was nineteen and attending junior college. His parents were very hospitable and friendly. His mother was a nurse, his father was an engineer, and they were nice, but when I met his grandparents, it was love at first sight. His grandfather was a very tall (six feet four inches) octogenarian, a gentle giant. He was a World War I and II veteran. When he sat in a chair, he was still almost as tall as I was standing up. He had a very contagious smile. I had never met anyone as big and tall as he was. I could only hug him up to his tummy when he stood, but if he sat down, I could reach around his neck. David's grandmother was almost my size. Grandma

Alice was about five feet three inches tall. She had been a nurse, and now her nursing skills were taking good care of Grandpa Bill. She was kind and loving, the typical grandmother any child would want to have. Meeting his grandparents reminded me of my grandmother. I had not had the privilege of meeting my own grandfather, who passed away before I was born, but I was always close to my grandmother. Watching David's relationship with his grandparents, I could see they were close. Knowing he shared the same family values and love for his grandparents that I had made me fall in love with him.

In the summer of 1987, I invited Yumi, one of her friends, Kyoko, and David to visit my family. Mother's father had just passed away, and her mother was still living with us. Grandmother had never seen a white-skinned, blond-haired boy with deep blue eyes up close because she had lived her whole life in North Vietnam and China. Since she had come to America, her eyesight and health had not been good, so she rarely left the house. David looked very interesting and unusual to her. Before he met me, he knew how to use chopsticks, but not well enough to eat soup and noodles with them. I had him practice before he came to my house. Grandmother was very impressed with him when he used chopsticks in the proper, precise way. She quietly watched every move he made at mealtime. After he left, Grandmother was still talking about how impressed she was with him. In Chinese culture, we discourage the use of the left hand as soon we learn how to pick up the chopsticks. David is left-handed, so he used the chopsticks with his left hand. Grandmother asked why he was not using his right hand. I had to explain to her that American children have more freedom to choose whether they want to be right or left-handed.

Before David came, I told Mother that we were dating. When he came, Father took him fishing at Laguna Beach, which was his favorite fishing place. David came home wearing Father's favorite hat, so I knew Father approved of him. I asked him how he won my parents' hearts, and he said he was just loveable.

David drove the four of us down to San Diego to visit their famous zoo. We had a great time and even though he was surrounded by the beautiful Japanese girls, he paid attention to me. Yumi and Kyoko both told me I was safe and he was a good guy.

In November 1988, before Thanksgiving break, David popped the big question. I knew I could not say yes. I told him that in my culture, the expectation usually was that the parents on the man's side hired a match-maker to talk to the girl's parents and get permission for him to marry her. But since this was American culture in modern days, no one continued the practice and tradition, so I would not ask the impossible. Besides, it was too complicated to explain to his family. I told him he should ask his father for help. His father had to ask my father's permission for us to get married. In order to avoid my father's objection and disapproval, we needed to do it right. I didn't plan to get married without both of our parents' blessings. I didn't expect a big, fancy wedding, but I was not about to compromise my relationship with my parents. I also didn't want to think about marriage before we graduated. I told him we should wait until Christmas break to be concerned about it. We also needed to have our parents meet and get to know each other.

As I told him all this, I also prepared myself for a broken heart. I didn't think he would go along with my request or that his father would agree to take the time to go and ask my father for my hand in marriage. It was too outside of their culture and comfort zone. Our families lived three hundred miles apart, and it would take time and effort. I knew his father would not necessarily understand my culture, and I thought he would not be willing to go along with my request.

To my surprise, David arranged for his family to visit my family during the 1988 Christmas break. They stayed in Simon's family's hotel across the street from Disneyland. Father spoke enough English to get by, but Mother spoke none. Henry became both parents' translator. It was a big event for both sides of the family. Father and Mother even cooked a special welcome meal for David's family. We also went out to eat Chinese food. On New Year's Eve, we all gathered to celebrate at my parents' house. David's father surprised us all by asking my father for permission for David and me to get married, and Father was very pleased and proud. David proposed to me in front of both our families. He had saved enough money for a half-carat diamond ring, and we were officially engaged.

David finished his coursework a semester ahead of me. He didn't have to return to Humboldt after Christmas break. When I got back, I showed Kathy my engagement ring. She knew about the Eureka jewelry shop that had made it, and she said it was beautiful, but why did it have so many prongs holding in such a small diamond? I explained that David had gotten to know me pretty well, and the diamond was definitely safer locked in tight on my clumsy hand.

Kathy and her best friend Nancy (not my roommate) planned a bridal shower for me. I had met Nancy in Kathy's adopt-a-grandparent program the year before. Kathy had graduated in June of 1988, but she stayed in Humboldt for a while as she applied to graduate schools. I hadn't had a lot of opportunity to be close to Nancy. She was a local girl, whose father was a veterinarian. Naturally, she was interesting to me because of her father's job. She was very tall, and her boyfriend,

Mohammad, was a tall, dark, and handsome Egyptian man. She was closer to Kathy than to me, but we heard about each other from Kathy often.

I had never been to an American bridal shower before, and had no idea what it was. In my culture, we do not have a shower for the bride. We have a "gift show." The bride's parents arrange for relatives and friends to visit before the wedding day. They show off all the wedding gifts the family gave the bride ... the china dishes, household supplies, linens, and furniture the bride got for a good start. This is to show the relatives and friends how wealthy the family is and how much they blessed their daughter by marrying her off with all these gifts.

Kathy and Nancy went out of their way to set up the shower for me. I had no clue what to expect. They took me to a local bar. I had never been to a bar and didn't know what to order. The bartender gave me a funny look when I told him I wanted a 7Up. I almost asked for a glass of water, as I very seldom drink soda. Since I was in a bar, I thought I had better order something. They both ordered a beer, and I didn't want to put them on the spot by ordering water. The bar was full of loud college kids and cigarette smoke. I listened, but did not understand all the conversation around me. Kathy and Nancy were talking and joking with all the people they knew, smiling at me, and telling people I was getting married. I wasn't sure what they said, but I tried my best to process the chaos around me.

A young man came to our table with some balloons and a gift in his hand. He was dressed very formally in a black suit with a bow tie. He looked at me with a big smile on his face. I didn't know who he was or why he was there. I thought he must have been Kathy's and Nancy's friend, but he came and gave me the balloons and gift. Kathy encouraged me to accept it and told me the gift was from them and included him. I wasn't sure why or how he could be included in my gift. Why didn't they just give me the gift themselves, why him? Before I could process the information, he gave me a kiss on the cheek and left. I still didn't know who he was and why he was there. I heard Kathy and Nancy say something, "... not to scare her!" I wondered why he gave me their gift and how he could scare me. He looked very nice and harmless! Years later, they told me they hired the guy to give me their gift as part of an American tradition. Normally, this handsome young guy would strip-dance for me, but they told him not to scare me. I was so glad and grateful they stopped him.

In June of 1989, David came back to school and went through the graduation ceremony with me. Both our parents and his grandparents came for our big day. Father met both sets of David's grandparents and loved them at first sight must like I had. It was his proudest day. I was the first female in my whole family's history to graduate from college. Father and Mother tried very hard to hide their emotions and tears as they watched me get my diploma. I knew exactly what Mother was thinking. The result was worth the struggle. When I received my diploma on the stage, I was receiving it for Mother and all the women in her generation and before who were deprived of an education.

After graduation, we went home; David to San Jose and me to Garden Grove. We had three months to plan the wedding. As we planned, I learned my true age. One day Mother asked me about David's age. I told her that I am two years older than he is. In Chinese tradition, the husband is generally older than the wife. Because he is head of the household and protector of the family, he needs to be older and wiser to provide for them. Since I was older than David, we were pushing our luck. After Mother thought about my answer, she started to count on her fingers. She looked at me and asked, "Do you remember when you were in the same third grade class for three years? I had to hide your true age because of the war. You are actually five years older than David." I called him that night and told him to call off our marriage. He said our age difference would not matter in the long run because women usually live several years longer than men, so we would have our whole lives together. I couldn't talk him out of it.

I was breaking cultural rules by getting married first. My older siblings should have gotten married before I did. I married outside my race, and all my cousins thought I must be pregnant and I was desperate, which was why I was getting married. They predicted my marriage would fail after a year, because it was based on either desperation or curiosity. Father had only one brother and sister still living. They were younger than he was and they told him my marriage would be a flop and were very much against it. Listening from around the corner in the hall, I heard Father defend my decision. He said in a cheerful voice, unmoved by his siblings' concerns: "David's family is good. His grandparents have been married for over fifty years and are still very much in love. They hold hands and sometimes his grandfather gives his grandmother a kiss when no one is looking. It was very sweet to see how they really love each other. David's parents are also very good. He has good elders who are a good example. It is very rare to see an American family that is so close. I don't care if he isn't Chinese. He will be good for her."

In the next few weeks, we ran into other "East meets West" culture differences and clashes. Mother expected me to wear a traditional red bridal dress for the wedding and a formal sequined dress for the reception. David's mother, on the other hand, expected me to wear a white bridal gown. To my mother, red is worn for a wedding, good luck, and happy events. White is the color of death, funerals, and bad luck. For David's mom, white represents purity and red represents lust or power. Ever since David and I got engaged, Mother had been thinking about how our wedding would be set up. She longed to see me wearing traditional dresses. She had dreamed of seeing her two daughters getting married someday, but Anna had decided never to marry. Mother gave up the thought of seeing her wear these two dresses. After David and I got engaged, she had been looking forward to seeing me in them. She could have made the dresses herself, but it would have taken months and she would have had to gather the right materials.

When I told Mother about the traditional white dress I was expected to wear at the church wedding, she cried in disappointment. I decided to tell David's mother about the traditional red dresses. She burst into tears.

I had to come up with a compromise. I would wear the western style white wedding dress for the church ceremony in the morning at ten o'clock. The Chinese formal dress would be my reception dress at the church. It was hand-sewn with a rhinestone design. The base color was white and the designs were red. The designs were a phoenix bird representing the bride on my left side and a dragon representing the groom on my right side. After the reception at the church, we all went home to David's parents' house. I wore a traditional red Chinese wedding dress there for a tea ceremony. This dress was also covered with rhinestones, with lots of different designs. The designs were the phoenix, a dragon, flowers, stars, and the sun. It was a very bright, heavy dress. The tea ceremony is the symbol of the groom bringing his bride to his family and formally introducing her to her new family. All the older generations of the groom would accept tea from the bride and give her in return a piece of jewelry, or a red envelope with money inside for a blessing.

I compromised a bit on my wedding ring, too. David sold his truck to his brother to commission my wedding ring with the custom jeweler in Eureka who had made my engagement ring the year before. Unfortunately, it wasn't ready in time for the wedding. David bought a white gold band at a discount store for a temporary substitute.

I told David we would be expected at my parents' house three days after our wedding for a traditional reception with my family. That ruled out a long honeymoon. We drove down California's coast along Highway One and stopped for our first night in Carmel, then went to Big Sur. As a special surprise, David had booked a lunch on the beach in Big Sur after a three-hour horseback ride in the forest. I had never ridden a horse before, and neither of us knew what we would feel like in the morning after the ride. As I struggled down the stairs at the motel, toward David's bright red Ford Mustang painted with the words "Just Married" all over the back window, David said, "Stop walking like that! Someone's going to think I've done something terrible to you!" He had, of course, by making me take my first horseback ride on our honeymoon. Now we laugh when we tell the story, after he pretends to brag about how bow-legged I was on our honeymoon.

After we came back from our honeymoon, we lived in the guesthouse behind David's grandparents' house. It was a very small studio apartment about the size of a single car garage with a huge fireplace and a very tall ceiling. The ivy on the outside of the cement block walls had invaded the inside, and termites left their trails in the plywood ceiling. We didn't mind the inconvenience, because we had our love shack. It really was a shack, but it was our palace.

I got my first job working as a clinician at an Asian-American mental health center. The center was set up to provide mental health counseling and support services to Southeast Asian refugees who suffered mental trauma during and after the war. My job was to provide counseling, monitor clients' medications, report to the doctors about their mental condition, educate clients about mental health services, and support their emotional needs. My other main duty was working with Asian teen issues. I worked with teens and their parents, and helped them to understand and accept the gaps between their generations and the language differences.

I didn't realize working on this job would cause me to face my own PTSD. It also helped me to be grateful that what I experienced was not as bad as others had experienced. At least I didn't lose my family, or die trying to get to freedom. Many of my clients suffered worse than we had, especially those who came from Cambodia.

I met a gentleman who came to our center every week to see one of my co-workers. I noticed that he always wore a long sleeved shirt, long pants, and a scarf. The weather in California during the summer was very hot, but he seemed to have his own dress code. My co-worker never told me why he dressed this way and I didn't ask.

One day my co-worker asked for my assistance with this gentleman's visit with the doctor. We spoke our native language to each other. All the administrators, supervisors, and the doctor at the center spoke only English. The doctor was Caucasian, but most of the administrators and supervisors were American born Chinese. Part of our job was to act as interpreter between our clients and the doctor during medication sessions. I can't speak Cambodian, but he spoke Chinese. I noticed that he had to make an effort to speak. He also held his scarf when he turned his head. He seemed to try very hard to hide something under his scarf. After he left, I asked my co-worker about him at our lunch break. She told me this story:

Loung was one of the survivors of the Khmer Rouge killing fields in 1975-1979. He had moved to San Jose last year from another state. He didn't know why he survived the genocide, but his wife and five children all died. The Khmer Rouge soldiers came to the city, gathered all the men, and ordered them to dig a big hole for their own graves. One by one, the soldiers cut their throats and pushed them into the hole. Loung happened to be on top of the pile of all the wounded and dying bodies. He passed out and was unconscious after his throat had been cut. His muscles were still contracting and his body jerked and convulsed, so the soldiers stabbed his arms and legs until he stopped moving. He said most people did not die right away due to their throats being cut; they died of suffocation from being under all the bodies piled on top of them. He didn't know how long he had been unconscious. When he came to, he pushed his feet down on the pile of dead bodies beneath him and climbed out of the hole. After searching for his family and finding them all dead, he walked for two weeks before he crossed the border from Cambodia into Thailand. He slipped in and out of consciousness a few times. When he arrived in Thailand's refugee camp, he was covered with mud and blood. When he came to our office, he wore the scarf to cover the scar on his throat and the long-sleeved shirt and long pants to cover the scars on his arms and legs. He didn't want anyone to see his misfortune, because Buddhists believe bad luck is contagious. He had problems sleeping and thought about his family all the time.

I had nightmares for days after listening to his story. I couldn't imagine how he felt. I cried sometimes in my sleep or was so violent while I was dreaming that I hurt David. I felt very bad that some mornings he woke up with bruises and scratches. I was grateful that what I had gone through was not as bad as what Loung and other clients I worked with went through. My job made me very depressed. I often questioned how a human being could do such horrible things to others and live with themselves. How can a person take another person's life without any threat of harm to himself?

Some nights I came home after work and cried. The only thing that helped me feel better was taking care of David's grandparents and being around them at dinnertime. Grandma said that Grandpa was using too much salt when she cooked dinner. He was under his doctor's orders to cut down on his salt intake. I cooked for them often since I lived with them, and David and I ate dinner with them. Grandma noticed that Grandpa didn't use salt on his food when I cooked, and she asked me if I could cook more often. I am not a chef, but I managed to cook food that tasted good to him, with fried onions, garlic, and pepper instead of salt.

Six months after we got married, David came to me and said he wanted to go back to school for a law degree. His retail management career was cut short when he was fired for not keeping close enough attention to the details of the clothes on the racks and tables. He just never learned how to fold a shirt. His fencing and bookkeeping businesses were not taking off. He asked if it was okay with me if he went back to school.

I was glad to support him in whatever he wanted to do. He would be in school full time and I would work full time. David's family was surprised, but happy for him. One day, his parents' best friends asked me a very odd question: "What are you going to do since David will be in school full time?" I answered truthfully that I would be working full time to support him. I wondered to myself why this should be a question. Should not a husband and wife work together to help each other and support each other's dreams? If they heard from David's parents about him being in school full-time, why wouldn't they hear that I would work full-time to support their son? Should I be sitting at home and wait for his parents and grandparents to support me? What should I do with my education? Did I look unable to earn a living? Or should I get on a welfare program and have the government support us? I may have come to the United States the way other refugees and boat people came, but I became an immigrant as soon as I landed on American soil. Other than my uncle's steak and ketchup incident and student loans, I had never received government help since I came. Now I was a United States citizen and a college graduate, so was I unable to make a living without the government's help?

My parents were very supportive of our plan. Mother often gave me money to help our financial shortfalls without our asking. Somehow she always knew how to rescue me in my times of need. The money Father and Mother sent always came at the right time and was the right amount for our needs. I didn't understand how this worked, or how they knew what, when, and how much to send me. I tried to tell her not send me money. I felt guilty that I hadn't helped them since I graduated from school. One of the main reasons for getting a higher education was to earn a better paycheck to help my family. After I completed my education, I got married and moved away from them. They were not only supportive when I was in school, but now they helped me support my husband's dream while they still struggled to meet their own needs and pay off their debt.

Mother continued to work sixteen hour days at her sewing

machines. She saved every dime she made. Her money didn't fall from the sky or the avocado tree in her back yard, but she always gave me these answers: "It's a loan. When David can be on his own and start earning big money, you can pay me back," or "I live for these days to be able to earn this money. I don't intend to take it with me when I die. I'd better put it to good use." To this day, she never mentions the money she sent me. If I talk about it, she always says, "It has been so many moons ago that I can't remember it."

CHAPTER TWENTY-FIVE:
PTSD; THE CORNERS OF MY MIND

I never thought a happy marriage would stir up the horrific memories I had buried for over twenty-eight years. I wished for a fairytale life. The prince and princess get married and live happily ever after. In reality, David and I had no problems with love, but as time passed, we had a problem with intimacy. I couldn't stand being touched or being close to him. I became violently ill with just about everything that had to do with intimacy. I couldn't stand his smell, or look at him when we were in bed together. I became very angry and fearful when he wanted to be close to me.

My anger was not that I was mad or upset with him, but with myself. I couldn't understand why I felt this way so strongly. I wondered if maybe I had made a mistake in getting married. I thought of what Grandmother had said when I was young, that I should marry God, not man. Was this the truth? I held onto that thought for a year and a half. David was never angry with me for rejecting him. He always comforted me and cried with me when I got so frustrated with myself. He never said harsh words or forced himself on me. I couldn't stand myself any longer. I begged David for a divorce. In my mind, he should marry someone better than me. I felt I had made a mistake getting married and had ruined his happy spirit and his life. He refused to divorce me and encouraged me to give myself time and be patient.

One day my office sent me to a child abuse conference for training. There were over a hundred and fifty people in the conference room. I sat close to the back with three of my co-workers. When the speaker started to talk about children's signs and symptoms, and their reactions after having suffered sexual abuse, I felt she was talking directly to me. Each and every word that came out of her mouth hit me like a sharp knife, striking right in my heart. I felt the room was empty, and it was just me sitting there. I got violently sick and couldn't breathe. I ran to the bathroom and found myself crying out of control. I had no idea why I reacted this way. I left the conference and went back to my office. My supervisor wanted to know why I left the training and refused to go back and I couldn't tell him why. He finally calmed me down and told me to breathe. I gathered all my strength and closed my eyes.

I told him about being raped by one of my cousins. His name was Tuong Quach. His English name is George. I was nine years old, and he was ten years older. I had never told anyone before then. My supervisor sent me home for the rest of the day, and I worked up the courage to tell David what happened. He held me and cried with me. He wanted me to take my time working through this living nightmare. He assured me that he would not go anywhere because he had promised "till death do us part" when he recited our wedding vows.

In our old Chinese culture, any female who accused a man of rape would be considered a liar. Females were not valued or respected. I can't speak for the current cultural practices. I can only speak for my situation. Mother said when Cousin George called her in the early nineties after his arrival in Seattle; he said he didn't call me because we had a "misunderstanding." When she told me, I was puzzled and confused. What was he talking about? I hadn't seen him since he got married after we came back to Vietnam from Hong Kong in 1974. I heard about him from my aunt and uncle, but I hadn't seen him. I hadn't had any interaction with him.

After we left Vietnam, I hadn't heard from him until Mother told me about their conversation. What did he mean by "we had a misunderstanding?" Where had that come from? What kind of misunderstanding? My memory of the rape had not surfaced at the time Mother and I had our conversation. Now I knew what it meant and it all made sense. It was very typical that he would have considered the rape "a misunderstanding." He was nineteen and I was nine, and I would probably have been seen as the one who was lying, because I was born a female and might have seduced him.

As I prepared to write this story, I found out that my five siblings were also his victims. I told Mother about it several years after I regained my memory. She told Anna first and shared with my four brothers at different times and circumstances. They each responded by telling her that they were also his victims after they heard what happened to me. One by one, they shared their secrets with Mother over the years. She had never shared this information with any of us, and had carried the guilt with her for years until she told me what she had learned in the years since I had told her. Anna also carried the guilt that I was her replacement. She was his victim for years, and he left her alone after he turned to me.

George's mother was my father's oldest sister and our favorite aunt. His father was abusive. He beat my aunt to a pulp because she refused to give him money for opium. He even popped her eardrums, which caused her to become deaf. She and her three young children came to live with us after the ear incident put her in the hospital. Mother gathered all the women in our neighborhood, and some other relatives marched to her husband's house, armed with brooms, long bamboo sticks which were used for drying clothes, and garden tools, and removed her and her three children from his home. In those days, legal divorce was not practiced. The bamboo and garden tools did the job.

Father and Mother provided for my aunt and her children until she died a few years after we came to America. Mother said when they came to live with them, George was only three years old. His oldest brother was a young teenager, who later left Vietnam and went back to live in China on his own. His oldest sister was my favorite cousin, Mary. She was just five years younger than Mother. Mother said George had very poor health. The doctors gave him little chance to thrive and thought he would not live past four years old. He wasn't able to keep food down, and was very tiny. At the time, mother had just given birth to my oldest brother and she was nursing him. She nursed Cousin George back to health with her milk and raised him like her own son. She paid a great deal of money to the military to keep him from going to the front lines when he was drafted into the South Vietnamese army during the war. She even arranged for him to marry a nice girl and bought a house for him as a wedding present. She never imagined how she had been repaid for her kindness to him. I don't know what my aunt would have done had she ever known what he did to us. She might have killed him, or herself.

CHAPTER TWENTY-SIX:
PUTTING ANGER TO WORK

In the summer of 1992, we slept in the loft of our guesthouse with the windows open to the cool night air. The sound of Independence Day fireworks awakened me to the familiar image of a young girl's bloody death. I wondered why this image always showed up in my mind during the Fourth of July holiday. I could smell fresh blood and gunpowder when I heard the sound of fireworks. It seemed like a bad dream, but it was real. I couldn't connect this image with a place or a time.

I also thought about Xiao-Wei's death when I heard someone talking about a boat or smelled the ocean. I am very grateful for my life and my freedom, but I often feel guilty for being alive. Working with survivors of the Cambodian killing fields on my first job helped me to realize that I too had some of their PTSD symptoms. When I was in college, the counselor at the school clinic told me that did, but I wasn't sure what she meant. I refused to accept my feelings and my problems. My job forced me to face them and have a better understanding of what PTSD is.

I left the Asian American counseling job after a year because I got a better-paying job offer and needed the money to support David in law school. My second job was working as an on call crisis counselor, still in the mental health field. My duties were to respond to calls from the police, probation officers, children's shelters, school officials, and visit families who needed crisis intervention. Most of my clients were teens from the ages of eleven to seventeen. In addition, because I was multilingual, I was an interpreter for the mental health and police calls which related to problem teens and their families within San Jose's huge Asian community.

I learned that children in America who were in this age group suffered a different kind of war than I was in at their age. The conflict between generations was classic in teen problems across all ethnic groups, but the culture and language gaps were major problems among the Asian groups. The younger generation wanted to become Americanized as soon as possible, so they learned the language and culture very quickly. The older generation had more difficulty. The role of the family became reversed so that the younger generation took advantage of the older generation. There were a lot of misunderstandings and myths about American culture that the Asian community needed time, education, and effort to understand. The new generation was able to absorb education the older generation didn't have the opportunity to receive. The new generation wasn't able to communicate with the older generation because the cultural meaning of what was being said was lost in translation between English and Asian languages.

I decided I needed a higher education for this job, so I could be more effective and give myself a voice I never knew I had. I tried my best to let the new generation know they could have the best of both worlds. They didn't have to lose their culture or their language to become American. Nor did they have to look down on their parent's culture and language to have their own identity as American teenagers. I am an example of keeping the best of both worlds and not having to choose one and give up the other. I became more and more convinced that I should go back to school, but it wasn't the right time to do it. David still had one more year to complete law school, so I kept this idea to myself. Somehow he suggested on his own that I enroll in San Jose State University for a part-time program to get my Master's degree in social work. It would keep my mind occupied while he finished school and help to advance my career. I enrolled and took one night class at a time.

In my first year at San Jose State, one of the professors in my human development class was a lesbian. She appeared to be a very angry and bitter person. She was all about "women's rights" and "freedom of choice." Because she graded my papers and had the "pass or fail" power, I often kept my opinions to myself. My English had improved to the point that I could express myself by this time. I was able to understand more than before I met David. He had been a great teacher, but I still was unable to express myself the same way the professor did due to my culture and the way I was raised. Through her class, I learned how to speak up and express my opinion. I was more aware that as a female I had never been allowed to express my opinions or be heard in my culture the way American women were. I learned that speaking up without understanding the timing and how to express my thoughts could cost me greatly. It's like learning how to ride a bike. You might be able to balance, but if you didn't know how to brake, the fall would hurt badly.

I often heard people get into very heated arguments regarding the abortion issue: "freedom of choice" or "pro-life." I avoided this subject at all costs. Nonetheless, my professor assigned this subject for a class discussion. The students on both sides of the issue were very passionate about it. I kept to myself and didn't want to say anything. I knew that America allows freedom of speech, but I had been used to a system where speech was controlled by the government, and speaking out about a subject could result in imprisonment or death. I kept my opinion to myself and just listened to both sides of my classmates' arguments. The professor asked for my opinion. She wanted to know what Asian people thought about this subject, and I was the only Asian in my class. I told her I didn't represent the views of all Asians. I could only express my view, and I would rather not. I asked if she could move on to someone else. She reminded me that if I failed to participate in the discussion it could cost me a passing grade for the course.

I had no choice but to speak. I told them why I felt strongly on the subject. I had seen life being taken away, and I could not be objective. I had experienced no choice being given when life was taken from one human being by another human being. I watched guards kill prisoners based on their choice of who they wanted to kill and who they wanted to live. I watched my girlfriends from high school go through abortions more than three times due to their freedom of choice. I knew that my brother Stanley's girlfriend/wife had more abortions than she could remember because of the choices she made in her life. She chose to practice her right of "free spirit" "freedom" by sleeping around with different men without protection. She chose to use drugs while her babies were developing. She didn't want to take the chance of them being born drug-addicted, or of another race. Therefore, she felt her choice to have abortions was justified.

I also knew that millions of baby girls were aborted due to the one-child policy in China, which is based on political oppression and complicated by cultural choice. The culture itself discriminates against females, and the policy of the government to allow only one child to be born per family makes it even worse. The culture believes only the male can carry on the family name and care for the elderly. Since the Chinese government only allows one child per family, many families only wanted to keep the males. I understand that the people were under so much government control that they chose male babies over female babies. Whatever the reasons and excuses were, one human being not valuing another human being's life is wrong.

What is the difference between the guards in Vietnam, and the women who practice freedom of choice? They kill and take life based on the choices they make. These two kinds of people are no different as far as I am concerned. The only difference between the two is that one kills and takes life from an adult and the other from a baby. They have to have no conscience whatsoever, or believe against science and common sense that a fetus is not a human being, not truly alive, in order to justify the choice to end a pregnancy.

For the benefit of argument, is a fetus a human life form? In a college natural history class, I watched a video of underwater creatures found and discovered for the first time in a previously unexplored part of the Pacific Ocean. Thanks to new technology, they were able to discover this life form by using computers and special underwater cameras. When I looked at this so-called life form, it had a funny looking mushroom shape with an antenna. Yet the scientists considered it a living creature. What happened to the fetus that some doctors wouldn't consider it a life? According to them it has no life, no value, and is not worth being given the right to live. The concept of life is very confusing. If the funny looking sea-mushroom with an antenna is considered a living being deserving protection and the fetus is not, then why should human beings be considered the highest and most intelligent species on Earth?

I heard my guards say that their prisoners also had no rights as human beings. They told my sister that I was worthless. Because they said this about me, should I die too? Just because they didn't consider me a worthy human being, should I die? Since I was sick, did I lose the right to be a human being? Their reason for killing was based on their choice, their mood, and for their convenience. If choice is more important than life, I'd rather choose life over choice. That is my choice since I am alive to make it. Through tears, I told the class I had seen many people die around me, more than I could remember. Flies that were attracted to dead bodies could not top the number of people I saw die, so I'd rather choose life. The class was dead silent.

I got a "C" in the class, and had to retake it the following year. In a Master's degree program, a "B-" is a passing grade. A "C" is considered a failing grade. This professor did not like what I said and disagreed with my opinion, so she gave me a "C." It was her way of failing me with or without my participation in the discussion. She was prejudiced against any student who spoke English as a second language. This was very surprising to me, since her background was Hispanic American. She even voiced this in class at the beginning of the semester. She said, "I strongly believe all the students who speak English as a second language should not be allowed in the Master's degree program." I would have expected her to be more understanding, compassionate, and sensitive toward people who, like she did, speak English as a second language, face discrimination because of their identity and have to struggle and work hard to be recognized for their accomplishments. English is not my second language, but my sixth. I was not asking for special treatment or favors. I worked hard in every class, and earned my degree fairly like everyone else. I was not the only student she failed. All my other classmates who spoke English as a second language were failed. The majority of these students also had a Hispanic American background, the same as her. I didn't understand what her problem was, or how she could be so bitter and hateful.

The second semester, I had another professor who was also openly gay. One of his assignments was discussion in a small group. My small group had six people including me. The discussion question was, "What kind of death is most horrible?" All the people in my group came up with this answer: suicide, accidental death, and death by cancer are equally horrible. I didn't say anything. The group was divided. Everyone wanted their answer be the most horrible. I just listened to their arguments and kept quiet. When the small group got together with the big group, the answers of the other groups were also debated along with these three answers. Again, due to my silence, the professor asked for my opinion on what death was the most horrible.

At the end of the discussion, I told my classmates that none of their answers were as horrible as someone else deciding how I was going to die. They all looked at me strangely. I explained, "If I chose suicide, at least it would be my choice. I could choose to die or change my mind and live. If I decided to go through with suicide, I could choose when I wanted to take my life and how I would do it. I could use a knife, a gun, overdose, jump off a tall building or a bridge, or drown myself in the ocean. I could choose where I would like to die: in my room, in my car in the garage, in the woods, or at the park. I could choose what time I should die: morning, night, before or after a meal, after everyone left for work, or went to sleep. I could choose what day of the week, what month, what date, and what year.

"Accidental death is the quick way to die. No one knows when, where, or how it will happen. It happens and is over quickly. If I die of cancer, I could fight. Cancer can be a most painful death, but I could be prepared and fight until the end of the illness. When I know my time on this earth is short, I could be emotionally, mentally, and physically prepared. I could still make the choice to die with or without a Do Not Resuscitate order. My death is given dignity and integrity. None of these deaths are easy, without pain, or fair, but they take me instantly or allow me to make choices and give me time to process dying. If someone else chose how I will die, I would not be given a choice. The decision is dependent on someone else, not me. The deaths they chose are squarely painful and scary. However, death by the choice of another person is the most horrible death any human being has to suffer." This time, my grading experience was the opposite. Even though my argument was the same, that people's choices have consequences, and that the innocent victims of others' choices are the ones who suffer, I got an "A" in the class. I know about death and choice.

I learned that my opinion had power, both good and bad, but without higher education it had no weight. When I became pregnant, I took a leave of absence and decided to continue to pursue my Master's degree after David completed his law degree. I wasn't sure what it would allow me to do, or if it would make any difference. I only knew I was angry about all the time in my life that had been taken away without me having a voice or the right to make my own choices. I was angry about the rape ... that I was unable to speak up ... that my cousin said it was "all a misunderstanding". I was angry at how the Asian culture oppressed me and denied freedom for my gender. I wanted my voice to have a positive impact. I wanted to search for what my mission in life would be with this degree, to be able to tell the world that life is not fair, that I have the same rights as everyone else. When people tell me to "go back where I came from," I want to be able to let them know that where I came from is the same as their ancestors. We all came to America from different places, we are all from different generations, and we came at different times. I had no choice when I came, but I am here to stay. America chose me long ago, even before I came.

CHAPTER TWENTY-SEVEN:
AN UNUSUAL DEATH

When David and I were living with his grandparents, it was a happy time for both of us. He had been very close to his grandparents since he was a baby. Every morning after breakfast, we watched Grandpa Bill take a walk with our cat, Buttercup.

Buttercup adopted us when we were living in Humboldt, and we named her after Princess Buttercup in the movie, "The Princess Bride". She was a very sweet and loving cat, and she adopted David's grandparents as soon as he brought her home. Grandpa walked to the American Legion Hall facility down the street and Buttercup followed him. He picked up leaves and trash on the sidewalk as he walked, and she stopped to groom herself while waiting for him.

Grandpa had a smile that was very contagious. He didn't say much, but when he talked, you couldn't help but listen. David picked that up from him. I loved to listen to Grandpa talk about his life story, things he did as a salesman, how he talked to people, and his view of life. I loved watching him enjoy his meal at the dinner table. Looking at him made me appreciate life in a better way. Every night he gave Grandma Alice a goodnight kiss before bedtime. When we went shopping, or walked in the nearby park, he held hands with her.

Grandma Alice was a very nurturing, loving person. She could smother you to death with her love. Her life was all about nursing. She had been a nurse for special needs children, and when she retired she took care of Grandpa. David had been the apple of her eye since he was born. When we had lived with them for about three months, David and I had our first fight. Grandma told me in a very loving way that in her eyes he could do no wrong, and I couldn't tell her anything different. I didn't complain to her because she couldn't take my side. Yet, she loved and accepted me as soon as David told her about us.

Taking care of David's grandparents was very natural for me, but it wasn't natural in his culture and family. They thought I was taking advantage of them by living in their guesthouse. Money was very tight for both of us since David was in law school fulltime. His grandparents didn't charge us rent, but we paid our own living expenses. I didn't feel it was my place to tell people what I did for them, or how I took care of them. David was the one who managed and budgeted our finances, and he paid Grandma for the utility bill. His family would say, "Make sure you pay Grandma part of the electric bill." Or, "You are buying your own groceries, right?" I tried my best to understand his culture and how their expectations were different from mine. I was raised not to let money come between my relationships with my family.

In David's family, I was still an outsider. In my culture, his grandparents automatically became mine. I married him not just for the family name, but with my soul. Even his grandparents couldn't understand why I took care of them. Grandma often asked, "You are taking good care of us because you love David so much, aren't you?" I didn't understand what she meant at first. My love for David had nothing to do with taking care of them. It was my honor and duty to take care of the elderly in the family when I became a member of the family. It's just the same as when I am hungry, I eat, and when I feel sleepy, I rest. Family makes me who I am and they are part of my identity. Family gives me a sense of belonging and roots. In Chinese there is an old saying, "One who drinks water needs to know where the water came from." It means that our family allows us to know who we belong to, and where our roots came from. If we don't take good care our elders, we don't take care of our roots.

One time Grandpa Bill told me a story about how he joined two trees into one. When he described how he joined a branch from one tree onto another tree, it reminded me of David and me. Grandpa said, "I took a branch from one tree, cut a notch in it, and spliced it into another tree. Over time, the branch grew and became part of the big tree. It's called grafting. Two trees become one, and each bears fruit." When David and I were married, shouldn't we become one? Shouldn't his grandparents be my grandparents? I found it very interesting that the American culture has a hard time understanding or accepting this very simple concept, yet grafting is natural to gardeners.

In 1992, Grandpa was ninety-four years old. One morning after breakfast, I was helping Grandma clean up her kitchen. As I put the dishes away, I heard her say, "Bill, what's wrong?" I turned and looked at Grandpa. He was sitting in the same chair he had at breakfast. He looked confused. He was waving one hand in the air and holding his head with the other, leaning his elbow on the table. He wasn't answering Grandma's questions. He looked pale and uncomfortable. I called out to the guesthouse for David to help. He came running and asked, "What?" Before I could answer, he looked at Grandpa and knew something was wrong. He turned and asked him, "Grandpa! Are you alright?" Grandpa didn't answer. He continued to wave his hand in the air like he was shooing flies away. David told him, "Come on, Grandpa! I'm taking you to the hospital!" As he stood up, Grandpa was more confused and refused to let David coax him. He fought against David by grabbing the handle of the refrigerator door. He refused to let go or listen to David. Grandma tried to help calm him, but he appeared to be in his own world.

I ran out to the guesthouse and got the car keys. David and Grandma managed to talk Grandpa out of the house. I opened the car door for them. David had to force Grandpa into the car, peeling his hands off everything he tried to hang onto going down the driveway. He was still fighting and wasn't cooperative. I helped Grandma into the car and helped David try to get Grandpa seated. He held onto everything and refused to get in the car. David finally took hold of his hands and said in a very calm voice, "Grandpa! Let's all go for a car ride. We'll just go for a car ride. Look, Grandma is waiting for us and she wants to go for a ride." Grandpa turned his head toward the back seat and looked at Grandma. He calmed down and sat still in his seat. David hurried to put the seat belt around him and locked the door.

We drove like the wind and I was surprised the police didn't stop us on the road. David pulled up to the emergency entrance of the hospital and jumped out of the car as soon as it came to a stop. As I got out, I heard him call in a loud voice to the nurses, "Help! My grandfather might be having a stroke! Help! Help!" The medical staff dressed in white and light blue came running toward Grandpa. They put him in a wheel chair and took him into an examination room. I helped Grandma out of the car and told David, "Walk with her; I'll park the car."

When I came into the emergency room to look for David and

Grandma, I saw David's parents running toward the entrance. I don't remember how long we waited for the doctor to come and talk to us, but everything seemed to be moving in very slow motion. The doctor did come to tell us that Grandpa had suffered a mild stroke, and it was good that David got him to the hospital in time for them to help him. He would be admitted to the hospital. The rest of the day was spent waiting for tests and to see how he responded to treatment.

He had another, bigger stroke a few days later. We were in and out of the hospital with Grandma for ten days. Grandpa's condition was up and down like the weather. Sometimes he recognized us, sometimes not. He called my mother-in-law by my name, which made her cry. He called David "Danny," David's father's name. He talked, but his stories weren't connected to reality. He told us when he moved to San Jose, the last hanging in the state had just happened in the public square. The story was partly true, and it obviously made an impression on him, but it happened years before he came to town. The next day, the swelling in his brain grew and he didn't regain consciousness. We came back to the hospital a few times afterwards, but we all knew it was just a matter of time. David bought him a pair of slippers shaped and painted to look like trout, which made everyone laugh as they visited, because Grandpa's feet stuck out of the end of the hospital bed.

David and I continued our daily routine and checked on Grandma every day and night to make sure she was okay. She would say, "I'm glad you kids are here with me! I wouldn't know what to do without you by my side. I just can't get through my days without Bill!" They had been married for fifty-nine years, and their sixtieth anniversary was just around the corner. Grandpa passed away in his sleep during his second week in the hospital. Dealing with his death was not easy. Although so very different, his death still reminded me of the dead bodies I had seen during the war. I began to reason that death did not have to involve drama or violence. It can be a peaceful, normal process.

CHAPTER TWENTY-EIGHT:
BIRTH, AND OTHER LOSSES

After Grandpa died, we continued to live with Grandma. We all missed him. I couldn't imagine how much she missed him, but life had to go on, so we did what we could to keep her daily activities as normal as possible. Grandma often mentioned what Grandpa would like or dislike about everything we did. I tried my best to keep her busy at her own pace. She didn't like anyone touching her bed or cleaning her house. I encouraged and reminded her to do things for herself. For example, when I washed my laundry, I purposely saved my bed sheets for last. Then I would ask if Grandma wanted to wash her bed sheets with mine since the load was too small to wash by itself. At first, she hesitated, but when I asked her why, she admitted that the mattress was too heavy for her to lift to change the sheets by herself. I offered to do it with her, not for her. After that she was happy to wash her sheets with mine, and she even told me when it was time to help wash the sheets.

When I cooked meals for us, I asked Grandma if she would like to teach me her way of cooking. She taught me how to make grilled cheese sandwiches, meat loaf, spaghetti, and chicken pot pie. I was never exposed to those foods before I met David. She tried to teach me how to make her best tuna salad sandwich for David, except that I couldn't stand the smell of canned fish. It reminded me of being in the refugee camp eating canned sardines and tuna for nine months, and it turned my stomach. Grandma taught me how to read recipes and use measuring cups and spoons. When I learned to cook at home with Mother, she didn't use measuring utensils. She just showed me how to throw in all the ingredients together. She taught me how to cook relying on taste, smell, and sight. All I had to do was put in a little of this and a little of that, and my meals came out very good to eat.

Grandma also taught me how to bake cookies, cakes, and pies. This was all new to me, and it gave her something to look forward to, being able to spend time with me. When she was sick, I cooked soup and food that she was able to tolerate. Grandma and I bonded very tightly since we spent lots of time together. She always said, "You have no idea how much you mean to me, how much of a blessing you are to me." She was right. I only knew that she was my grandmother the day I said "I do" to David.

Finally, David finished law school. It was a proud time for all of us, especially for Grandma. I could tell she was happy when we were at his graduation ceremony. She would whisper to me, "Oh! If only Bill could be here to see David." Or, "Bill is smiling down from heaven at us right now." After the ceremony was over, we had a party for David at home. I have always appreciated what Grandma said to me when we kissed her goodnight. She said, "Thanks, honey, for working so hard to support David through the years. You are good for him. No one notices, or says thanks to you, but I notice. I just wanted you to know that I do, and I wanted you hear it from me." Hearing Grandma says those words made me feel like I had graduated and earned a degree that day, not David.

At the end of his first year of law school, David had to study for exams. I got sick, and he couldn't handle me being sick while he tried to study for his exams. He decided to send me home to my parents for a couple of weeks so my mother could take care of me. The night before I left for Los Angeles, he was studying and I was painting my nails. He took a break to check on me in the loft, and asked what I was doing. I asked if he would miss me and jokingly asked if I could paint his toenails just to remind him of me while I was gone. I was shocked when he took me up on my dare. He compromised and said I could only paint one toe. I painted his left big toenail bright red and took a flight to Los Angeles the next morning.

While I was at my parents' home, I got to rebuild my relationship with my father. I had never had a calm and quiet conversation with him in my whole life. One day, we were watching TV together. I started asking him lots of questions about his childhood. At first, he was impatient and very surprised. He asked, "why all these questions?" I told him we were trying to have our first child, and I wanted to be able to tell my child about his or her grandfather. I wanted to know who my father was, the places he had been, what his life was like, his regrets, and his accomplishments. He was captured and was a prisoner of war during the Japanese invasion and occupation in World War II. I wanted my child to know his or her roots.

I reminded him that I was an adult now, and I could handle his stories, both the good and the bad. We spent lots of time talking. Father and I bonded and talked like old friends catching up with the good old days. In Chinese culture, a father and a daughter are not as close as in the Western culture. Adulthood is established by marriage between the child and the person the parents choose for them to marry. Also, Father and I were separated due to the war. In his mind, he still thought of me as the same little child I had been when he left.

A week before it was time for me to go back home, David called. He called almost every day while I was with my family. This time, he asked if I was sitting down, then told me he had been in an accident. He reassured me that he wasn't hurt badly, but his motorcycle was totaled. He had been riding it to the train station to catch the train from San Jose to school in San Francisco. An old man in a big truck turned left in front of him. He didn't see the motorcycle in the oncoming lane. The motorcycle's brakes locked up and skidded, but couldn't avoid the inevitable collision with the pickup. It hit the back fender of the truck, throwing David into the oncoming lane of traffic. Luckily, he had his helmet, leather jacket, jeans, and boots on, but they had to take him to the hospital because the helmet hit the ground and had a big scrape in it. He later found out his hip had been dislocated in the accident. While he was in the hospital, the nurses had to cut his jeans open to pick some gravel out of his knee. When one of the nurses took off his boots and cut his socks off, she burst out laughing uncontrollably. The best part was that this hospital was where he was born and where his mother attended nursing school. One of the nurses was his mom's classmate. When she got the news that David was in the hospital, she came right away to see him. She came into the Emergency Room, and all the nurses couldn't wait to tell her about his big bright red toenail.

When I went home, David's right knee was bandaged and he was limping. It reminded me of all the wounded soldiers in Saigon during the war. It was hard not to think about the war seeing David walk with bandages and crutches. I tried to remind myself that he wasn't wounded by the war or by soldiers. It took many months for him to heal. The next year and a half flew by as I worked, David attended law school, and Grandma adjusted to life as a widow.

I promised Grandpa on his deathbed that I would have a child to carry on his legacy. A year of trying turned into two, and we decided to seek fertility treatments. The first step was David's. He had to be tested to rule out any problems on his side of the equation. We called the medical insurance company, who put us on the list for testing. They were booked up for about four months ahead. A week before his appointment, a collection jar showed up in the mail with some instructions for David to follow. He coarsely joked to Grandma that he could spit for a week and not fill up the huge jar. Grandma turned beet red, laughed, turned around from hanging her laundry, and went back in the house still chuckling. "Oh, my David. Oh, David," she kept saying to herself. The next morning, my ritual urine test turned up positive. We were pregnant. I don't know which David was happiest about ... not having to go through with the dreaded testing or the fact that we would be parents.

After David took the attorney's admission exam, we decided we needed a vacation. His leg had healed enough to travel, so we flew to Spokane, Washington, rented a car, and drove Grandma back to her childhood home in Kalispell, Montana, to celebrate her ninetieth birthday. It was the best trip we ever had. We took her to visit Glacier Lodge in Glacier National Park, where she and Grandpa honeymooned. I will always remember the look on her face as she sat on the leather sofa in the lobby of the lodge in front of a huge fireplace in the midst of windows looking through the porch out over a lake surrounded by mountains. I asked her if she was too cold, since she was turning red. "Are you okay, Grandma," I asked. "Never better, honey, never better," was her reply. "Grandma, what are you thinking about?" "I can't say, honey," she said with her face blushing and her grin growing. We realized we had caught her in an intimate recollection. She changed the subject, "This big fireplace was not here back then." She sat on the couch in the newly restored lobby, and looked all around the room. She said the furniture and decor were different, but the building itself looked the same as she remembered. Did she want to see one of the rooms? They had been restored as well. "Oh, Heavens, no," was her reply.

We took her to see her grandparents' cabin on the shore of Flathead Lake, in Lakeside, Montana, where she had lived during the summers when she was a girl. The current owner, an architect from Virginia, had added onto the house, but kept the old cabin intact as his living room. Grandma was very pleased to see the old house was still standing and was much as she remembered. Her childhood home was just a mile or so north, also on the lake. It was nearly unrecognizable because the lake had risen to within just few yards of the house after a dam was built. Her twenty acres of cherry trees had been subdivided and built up with fancy vacation houses. She could tell it was her house, though, because of the ancient apple trees in the yard. David got to see trees his great, great grandfather had planted.

On the way back to the West Coast, we took her to visit the Deaconess Hospital in Spokane, Washington, where she got her nursing training. The hospital staff was very kind to us and gave us a wonderful tour. They even showed us their storage area, which was a wing of the hospital filled with old-fashioned fixtures in rooms which had remained unchanged since Grandma's last visit in the forties. They put her picture and a story about our visit in their weekly newsletter. She had brought along her white starched nurse's hat, long out of fashion, to show off her Deaconess graduation hatpin.

The highlight of the trip for Grandma was staying with her niece, great-nephew, and great-niece on their farm. The farm had been in their family for over a hundred years. We were very glad we got to take her on the trip. She was able to tell us stories about her childhood growing up on the lake.

One of Grandma Alice's favorite stories was about her little sister going to sleep one summer night in a boat pulled up on the shore. A nasty storm came up and the waves pulled the boat out onto the lake. When her father realized his boat and his daughter were missing, he hiked to the neighbors on both sides of his orchard and put out the word that three-year-old Gracie Hope was out on the lake in a boat alone in the storm, and asked everyone to keep an eye out for her. Each neighbor in turn hiked to his neighbor and spread the word around the entire lake, until someone spotted the stray boat and brought it in to shore. Each neighbor then comforted and carried the cold, tired, scared little girl to the next neighbor until she finally reached her own home, all before the first telephone came to the lake. She was back in her own bed before morning.

By the fifth month of my pregnancy, I was getting very big. People always asked me if I shouldn't be in the hospital by now to have the baby, and I had to tell them I had four more months to go. I looked huge and waddled like a duck. One shopkeeper at an Asian bookstore in San Jose shooed me out of her store for fear my water would break onto her floor.

My Valentine's Day due date came and went. Two weeks later, the doctor had to induce my labor. The pain of childbirth was indescribable. I went into a trance and forgot how to speak English as soon as I started my labor pains. I repeatedly asked the nurse, David, and his mom to give me water, but no one would respond to me. I told them over and over, but no one in the room would talk to me.

After thirteen hours, my baby was born. Five doctors could not agree beforehand how big he was. He weighed eight pounds, eleven ounces and was the biggest baby born that day. At four feet eleven inches tall, I was the smallest mother on the floor. The five doctors on duty that day said to each other after they weighed the baby, "Oops. This mother is too small for this baby. We should have done a C-section." If I hadn't been so weak, and out of it due to the pain, I would have bitten their heads off! Everyone was raving about how well I did during the delivery, how I was so quiet, and they never heard me cry out. There were eighteen women in the hospital that gave birth that night, and I was the quietest one. No one knew that I had mentally checked out, which I was very good at by that time. I was trained very well how to disassociate myself from reality. I was so good at it that everybody thought I was doing really well. David's mom did worry that after the baby was born, I might not have any hair left. During the contractions, I didn't yell, but I was pulling on my hair. And the water I was asking for? I was just talking to myself. The Mandarin David had learned didn't help him with my Fujianese.

After Hunter was born, it took me six months to retrain myself and regain my English. David's father kept telling him that something was wrong with me, and he needed to take me back to the see the doctor. I was suffering from post-partum depression, trying to remember the English language, and physically trying to heal from the natural childbirth wounds. Emotionally, I was trying to understand and process the whole childbirth and life issue. I had seen life being taken away, and taken out of this world so nastily, dramatically, quickly, and easily that never in my wildest dreams could I imagine bringing life into this world. I was more in a state of shock than I could describe or express. I looked at my baby like I was looking at all the lives lost that I had witnessed and knew had been taken out of this world. Now I had brought all of them back ... all those lives like Xiao-Wei's, the girl in the rice field, the people who died in the war, and the prisoners. I became extremely protective of my baby, and did not want to let anyone near him.

I couldn't explain to David, to his parents, not even to myself why I felt the way I did. I didn't realize that my PTSD had gotten the best of me, and that was why I wouldn't let anyone near Hunter or let him be taken out of my sight. I was protective to the point that my parents-in-law couldn't understand why I acted this way, or make sense of my behavior. I was rather annoying and obnoxious to them. When David did take the baby out of my sight, even just to the main house to visit Grandma Alice, I got very mean and nasty with him.

By this time, David was thinking about starting his law practice. The insurance company for the old man that hit David on his motorcycle paid us a settlement, and we decided we needed a new start for our new family. We wanted to be able to have our own place, and David needed to begin his career. We took a trip to Colorado to visit David's brother, Steve, who had moved to Colorado Springs with his new wife, Mary, the year before. We just fell in love with Colorado! California was getting more expensive and harder for a young family like us, just starting out, to live. Two years after graduation, half of David's law school classmates, including him, were still unemployed due to a recession. We decided to move to Colorado and settle there. We went home to discuss it with Grandma. She was sad to see us move, but was very supportive of our decision. We moved twelve hundred miles to Colorado Springs in the summer of 1994, when Hunter was six months old.

The day after Thanksgiving, I called home to chat with my mother. I always called her on the weekends and every holiday. My oldest brother, Joe, answered the phone. He always wanted to talk as soon as he heard my voice, but this time he told me to wait and handed the phone to Mother. She told me that Father went to the hospital that morning. She said, "Your father was very restless last night. As usual, I let him sleep in this morning. He usually wakes up before ten o'clock, but this morning, he didn't. I went to wake him up for lunch, but he wouldn't wake up. I kept calling him, but he just kept snoring away. I called for your brother to come and help, but he wouldn't wake up. We called an ambulance and they took him to the hospital. The doctor couldn't tell us anything all day. They are still doing tests. We just came home from the hospital." The next day, the three of us caught the first available plane home. David brought the trout slippers. Father'd had a massive stroke in his sleep and never regained consciousness. He was in the hospital for about ten days and passed away. He had just turned seventy years old.

Before Father's funeral, friends and relatives from all over the world sent flowers to the viewing room at the mortuary for his memorial service and funeral, which was packed full of people. The flower shops kept bringing flower orders for days. The funeral director said that in all the time he had been in the funeral business, he had never seen this many flowers sent, even for celebrities. He was very impressed that Father was so loved and respected by this many people all over the world. He wondered who Father was and how he gained this much respect.

Father wanted to be cremated. As we were watching his body from the viewing room and from behind the cremation glass, I was reminded that David's grandfather's and my father's were the only dead bodies that I had ever seen that looked so normal and perfect. I wasn't scared or stressed out about looking at their bodies. Of course I was sad that I lost my father and David's grandfather, but I finally realized death didn't have to be a terrifying event.

After we moved out of Grandma Alice's guest house, David's parents fixed it up to make it more livable so they could have a live-in caregiver for her. They also had a housekeeper come to clean her house two hours per week. Six months after we moved away, David's mother said to me, "Thank you for taking such good care of Grandma Alice." I was surprised. She continued, "I just found out that her bed sheets have not been changed or washed for six months! We have two caregivers who can't do what you did for her." David and I felt glad that his parents finally realized we were not taking advantage of his grandparents when we lived with them. We were taking good care of them without telling his parents.

At the same time, hearing all this made us feel like we had abandoned Grandma by moving away. We felt very bad that it never crossed our minds when we left. We moved away from her at the time she needed us the most. I had a heart to heart conversation with Grandma when she came to Colorado to visit us. She was very understanding. She said, "You need to put your child's future first. David needs this opportunity to build his career. You kids did the right thing by moving away. I wouldn't have it any other way. I'm old and I'll be okay! I am well cared for by Dan and Franell, and I'm happy for you. You will always be my kids and I'm not going anywhere soon." Two months later, Grandma Alice went to be with Grandpa Bill. One morning, she got out of her bed, collapsed, and died. She was not in pain, and she wasn't sick. She went very peacefully and quickly. David's parents had a memorial service for Grandma Alice three months later. I was twelve weeks pregnant at the time.

A few weeks after we got back from the memorial service, I lost my second child. In three months' time I lost my father, David's grandma, and had a miscarriage. By this time my emotions were on overload, and I was well on my way to having a nervous breakdown. Between the two of us, David was the one that was even more emotional than I was. Losing Grandma Alice was very hard for him, and losing the baby pushed him over the edge. I saw him cry for the first time since we were married. We held onto each other with all the strength we had, and moved on to the future. To this day, I still have a reaction when I think about the miscarriage. In my mind, I hope she was a girl, grown to be a young lady now, her soul in another body raised by another lucky family.

A few months after Grandma passed away, David's parents had to decide what to do with her house and all her belongings. I told David I was not interested in participating in the process. I didn't want to get into any family fights about who gets more, or less, or what. I told him he had to speak for himself about anything he wanted from Grandma's house. I said, "I am out of this part."

Don't take this wrong, I like and appreciate nice things and family heirlooms. I understand very well about sentimental value and keepsakes. Nonetheless, my family had lost everything for each of the last three generations due to war and migration. If I had been attached to all the things that belonged to my family, I would not be alive today. I learned very well about the value of material things from the sour grandmother on my last trip on the boat out of Vietnam. She could not take anything with her. I learned and understand the core of the old sayings, "We came into this world with nothing, and when we die, we will leave this world with nothing," and "From dust we come, and to dust we shall return." I explained to Grandma that anything she gave me before she passed away, I would give to David's siblings if they asked for it. I wouldn't fight or argue with them for the sake of material things. I had seen many valuable things that belonged to my grandmother and my mother taken away and lost through the years.

David's grandparents' love and relationship with me will be with me until I die. Nothing can take their love away from me. It was hard for David's family to understand my logic, but they were happy that they didn't have to fight with me about his grandparents' things. Steve did ask me, "Don't you care about Grandma and Grandpa? Why don't you want anything?" I responded, "It is just the opposite. I don't need your grandparents' things to show my love for them. I can say loudly that the love between Grandma and Grandpa and me is deeper than the deep blue sea. If my house is destroyed by an earthquake, or a tornado, or a wildfire, or a robbery, and all your grandparents' things got destroyed or stolen, I would still have their love for me in my heart. Nothing and no one can take it away from me or destroy it. If there is anything you don't want that is left over that Mom and Dad want me to have, I'll take good care of it for David. They already gave me the love I wanted; I don't need things to represent my memories or my love for them."

CHAPTER TWENTY-NINE:
THE AWAKENING

When people talked to me about God in the past, I always smiled at them to be polite. I didn't want to be rude or mean by telling them "Shut up!" or "Are you kidding me? You have no idea what you are talking about! God is just a figment of people's imagination out of desperation. God is not real. Get it in your head!" or "Go away! You are wasting my time!" or "God, where were you when I was sitting in the bottom of the pit?" or "If God is real, he should stop mean, nasty, evil guards and human beings from doing mean, nasty, evil acts against other human beings." or "Where was God when I needed to see him the most? All I saw was evil and wickedness!"

However, if people talked to me about the devil, I knew he was real. I had seen the devil just about everywhere, and witnessed the core of his evil works in the past and present. I saw him during the war, in the prison guards, the people around our hiding places, on the boat, in the refugee camp, in people who were once our friends, co-workers, neighbors, and in my own family.

Humankind is not very kind. Humankind operates based on self-ishness, ignorance, and greed. I didn't trust people in general, and I surely didn't trust the government and politicians.

I thought I had gambled with the devil during my many escape attempts. When I was captured, I wondered when he would take my life. On my last escape attempt, I won. I made it out of Vietnam and got my freedom. I don't know why or how I survived, but I wanted to hold onto my freedom and enjoy it to the fullest. When survivor's guilt troubled my thoughts, I rationalized that I needed to live to pay my dues. I believed this earth is a very nasty, suffering, evil place. The reason I was still alive was because I hadn't suffered enough. I needed to be alive, so I could suffer more and longer. I had to continue to fight with the devil until the bitter, terrible end.

When people talked to me about Jesus, I associated him with David and America. My parents and culture had ingrained in me that as a female, I married my husband with my soul not just for his family name. Since I married David not just for his name, but with my soul, whoever and whatever his beliefs were would be mine as well. I related Christianity and Jesus with the majority of Americans' religion and culture. Calling myself a Christian would be my way of integrating into the American culture, since I was an American citizen.

Somehow, I didn't connect God with Jesus. When people tried to talk to me about being a Christian or Jesus, I told them, "I am a Christian and I know all about Jesus, thank you for sharing." Sometimes they asked me about my denomination. I was very confused, wondering, "What? What does that mean? What kind of Christian am I?" I couldn't make sense out of what they wanted from me. I didn't understand the meaning of the word "denomination." I avoided the question. To me, I was a Christian, which meant the end of the statement. I had nothing else to add.

Early in 1996, I started back to school in the Master's degree program at the University of Denver. I had completed about twenty-four units at San Jose State, and needed to complete another sixteen units to earn my Master's degree. After dealing with three deaths, I gave up the idea of going back to school, but David insisted I go back to finish my degree and my dream. My grades were good enough that the University of Denver accepted me in their part-time program. I left David with two-year-old Hunter every Friday night in Colorado Springs, drove to Denver to attend classes all day Saturday, and returned home late Saturday night after classes were over.

One day a week, I took advantage of the childcare program at David's brother's church to do my homework and study after I dropped off my son. I met a special lady at the daycare program. It was set up for all the mothers from the church to have time away from their young children, and provided free childcare for about three hours once a week. When I first noticed this tall Asian lady, I thought she was American born. After I heard her accent when she talked to people, I thought she was Asian from England. She was very tall and had a much bigger build than the majority of Chinese women. Her English was so perfect that I hesitated to say anything around her.

For some time I tried my best to avoid her, but it was hard. Something about her was attractive to me. I saw her from time to time when I dropped Hunter off at the daycare. I always tried not to talk to her, but just said "Hi." The times when I didn't see her, I missed her. It sounds crazy, and it's something I can't explain, but she grew on me even before she introduced herself.

One day, when I went to drop Hunter off at daycare, the church was late opening due to a snowstorm the night before. I stood on the steps with all the other mothers and toddlers, waiting for the doors to open. The tall Asian lady with a baby boy and a beautiful toddler daughter came toward me and the lady asked, "Are you Chinese?" I answered, "Yes." She asked, "Where are you from?" I smiled politely, ready for rejection. "I came from Vietnam, but my roots are Chinese." With a twinkle in her eye, she said, "Really! Can you speak any Cantonese?" I was delighted, and changed from English to Cantonese to answer, "Yes! I can. Where are you from?" We lost ourselves in conversation.

The door finally opened to let us check in our children. After we checked in, we continued our conversation in the parking lot for all three hours. I discovered that she was Chinese, was from Malaysia, and her name was Peng. I didn't do any research or studying that day. When I went home, I couldn't stop talking to David about her. I had mixed feelings about her. I missed having someone to talk to in my language, so I was very excited to meet her, but I was not happy with the country she came from.

She stirred up painful memories about a place I hadn't thought of for a long time. I had buried my feelings about Malaysia since coming to the United States over seventeen years ago. I avoided anything having to do with Malaysia, including people who came from there. Meeting Peng reminded me of being rejected and shot at in Malaysia, and the vow I made when I left never to set foot on Asian soil again.

The months went by so quickly that before we knew it, we had known each other for about a year. She invited me to attend an Easter play at her new church, called "The Thorn," about the crucifixion of Jesus. She said, "Please say yes! Ted and I would like you to come with us. We bought the tickets." I had seen enough prisoners being tortured and beaten to death to last me a lifetime. I wasn't interested in seeing it, or being reminded by amateur actors in a play about how prisoners were tortured. Through the years of being in church with David and being a "Christian," I heard the story about Jesus being crucified many times. I still could feel the pain and hear the sound of my fellow prisoners being beaten in the Vietnamese prison, and I *really* didn't want to see it. I tried to be polite and find an excuse for not going, but I had to ask David. He asked his brother about the church. Steve had heard it was a charismatic, crying in the aisles kind of church, and David didn't want to go. I told Peng he couldn't go because he had to work late. She wouldn't give up or take "no" for an answer.

Through the months, I had told her about my experiences in Vietnam and my escape attempts, but I didn't tell her in detail. She experienced a short-lived civil war in Malaysia when she was a child, but she didn't know the depth of my pain. She could only guess. I also hadn't told her what I thought or how I felt about her country. I tried to keep my distance and build our friendship at a slow pace. She was so enthusiastic and excited, however, that I couldn't refuse, so I finally gave in and agreed to go.

I had never been to the church before, and I didn't realize how big the building was. The worship space was a big rectangular room like a Wal-Mart. The stage was set up in the center of the worship space. All the chairs faced the stage with aisles between several sections. It had an open aisle in the center of the worship space, which ran all the way around the stage and in front of that section of chairs. Behind the aisle were more rows of chairs that continued all the way to the back where the entrance was. Peng got tickets that put us about six or seven rows back from the center horizontal aisle. I sat on the seat next to the aisle so

I could escape easily. I had Hunter, who had just turned three, on my lap. Peng sat next to me with her one year old son, Nicolas, and Ted had their nearly three year old daughter, Alana, on his lap.

Before the play began, one of the pastors gave the audience instructions about the play and an introduction to their church. I learned that this was the second year they had put on the production. There were about a thousand people in the audience. He explained that we shouldn't leave the room after the play started because in some parts the actors and actresses would use the center aisle and walk between the center aisle and the stage. He wanted to avoid any accidents.

I had never been to a play like this before and didn't know what to expect. While the pastor talked, I reminded myself not to look when the prisoner was being tortured. I felt very calm and at peace as the play began. When it got to the part where Jesus was tortured, I closed my eyes and laughed to myself about how it looked so unreal.

As the actor playing Jesus carried the cross down the center aisle, all the actors and actresses were yelling, "Crucify Him! Crucify Him!" The whole worship space was so noisy that my son was scared. I opened my eyes to see what was happening and tried to comfort him. The actor who played Jesus had just started walking up to the stage. He had the cross on his shoulder, and the noise around the sanctuary was getting louder and louder. I was a little annoyed. Then, suddenly, Jesus stopped right in front of my row. He turned toward me and said in Fujian, not English: "**YOU**! You have seen me before!" I looked around and wondered "WHAT?" I couldn't hear any more yelling. The worship space was empty, and I was in it by myself with this actor as Jesus. I didn't know where my son was. He was sitting on my lap a second ago and now he was gone. I couldn't see Peng or Ted. I didn't know what had happened to me. I only knew I was all alone with this actor. In my mind, I remembered there should be a thousand people in this sanctuary, and wondered where they all disappeared to.

The strange thing was that the actor was talking in my own dialect. He was not speaking English. I remembered he was a young Caucasian man when the play began. I thought I was losing my mind. I knew I wasn't having hallucinations, and I didn't have a delusional condition. I had PTSD, but no other mental condition or dysfunction. As I tried to make sense of what was going on, what I heard and saw, He continued to point at me and said, "Look at Me! **YOU**! Yes! I am talking to **YOU, TING-TING**! You have seen me before! I can show you where you were and where you saw me!" Then it was like looking at a series of pictures. I saw myself with Him in the war zone... in the jail cell I was in the second time I was captured... the third time with my sister crying next to me... walking on a path in the rice field... curled up like a shrimp in the tree in the jungle... on a boat on the ocean, sitting and huddling with Anna.

I saw Him sitting next to me with His hands on me, even in situations I could not yet remember in my conscious mind. I couldn't remember where it was at the time. I was on the train, sleeping on the street of the Saigon marketplace, and in the hiding places. Some places in the pictures I remembered, but had refused to think about for years, and some places I couldn't recall ever being. He continued, "I was there with you all those times. Sometimes you saw me and sometimes you didn't. When you described me to people the times you saw me, they said you had seen a ghost. It was **ME** you saw. You don't know who I am. I am Jesus! Don't forget. I am Jesus! Don't let anyone tell you differently! **My name is JESUS!**"

Suddenly, I was back with all the noise, and my son was on my lap again. The whole experience was very quick, but it felt like a century. The conversation was all in my own dialect. Only my family speaks to me in that dialect, and I had never spoken it with anyone else in Colorado. Peng could understand it, but couldn't speak it. I held my son close to me and cried uncontrollably. Peng noticed that I was crying, but she didn't say anything or ask why.

I can't explain what happened or why, I can only say Jesus came and introduced himself to me. I didn't know him from reading the Bible or listening to the pastor in Sunday church services. When I shared this story with a lady I met some time ago, she didn't believe me. She was Chinese and had believed in Buddhism all her life as I had. She said, "How can you give credit to Jesus? Maybe because you were in the church, you were thinking about him. If you were in the temple, you would say it was Buddha who appeared to you." I told her I had known and believed in the Buddhist religion all too well, that my grandma had dedicated me in the temple to be a nun when I grew up.

I never met any of the Buddhist gods the way I met Jesus. None of them showed up, or talked to me in person. I know he is as real as any person. I am very sure of this for many reasons. First, he is a personal God to me. He looked as real as He could be up close when He was talking to me. He could have spoken to me in English, Vietnamese, or any of the other Chinese dialects I spoke such as Mandarin, Cantonese, or Chao Zuo, yet he talked to me in my own dialect. Secondly, he is a purposeful God and he purposely showed up in person to introduce himself to me. He could have let someone else tell me about him or blinded me or struck me to the ground like he did Paul on the road to Damascus, or any other way he chose. Thirdly, he was punctual; he chose the timing and me. I didn't want to be there. I didn't want to have anything to do with God. I didn't understand who Jesus really was. He was just an idea, religious terminology, my husband's belief, and a cultural icon in my understanding.

Even if I had been in the temple when He came to meet me, I believe the result would still have been the same. He could have told me his name was Peng, Minh, or Jim, and I would have believed him. Yet, he told me his name was Jesus. I wouldn't have been able to come up with this name on my own. If I wanted to think of a name, it would have been a Chinese or Vietnamese god's name before a Christian name. I didn't ask him to meet me at that time and place like he did. It was all his timing and his moment, not mine. I had no idea if or where or when I would meet him. Now I can tell people that John and Peter might think they are his favorite disciples, but I know I am his favorite child. I know that he saved me not to suffer, but to live the life he gave me.

Before I met Jesus, I often wondered who I was. Where did I belong? Something about the human part of me wanted to annoy people. For example, when I was in high school, my Vietnamese was better than those Vietnamese students who came to the United States in 1975. For the longest time they thought I was Vietnamese. One day, when a conversation came up, they were very surprised to find out that I could speak Chinese. They said, "Oh! You can speak Chinese?" I answered, "Of course! It is my native tongue." They were very surprised, "I didn't know you are Chinese, not Vietnamese like us. Why didn't you ever tell us? We always thought you were Vietnamese!" I sharply answered, "You never asked! I don't tell you any more than I have to."

Another time, when we first lived with David's grandparents, there was a little Chinese restaurant near their house. It was Grandpa's favorite

Chinese restaurant. He wanted to make me feel at home, so he took us all there to eat. I walked in and began to talk to the owner in Cantonese. I could tell from the décor that he was from Canton province in China. I carried on a conversation and they thought I was from China. When they talked about landmarks or events that happened and I wasn't able to participate, they realized I wasn't. They asked where I came from, so I let them guess. I didn't want to tell them right away. They were very surprised when I let them know I was from Vietnam, not China. I had become very bitter by now, because even though I was able to speak more fluently than they could, whatever their language, I would never be accepted by them or be one of them.

Before I knew Jesus, I was always bitter and angry at being treated unjustly or misunderstood by others. For example, when I had a confrontation or an argument with other people or family members due to how unfairly they treated me or didn't understand me, I called them on their actions and told them their behavior was not okay with me. They excused their actions by blaming my past or anger issues, which had nothing to do with it. I wasn't looking for perfection in people. I know very well that human beings are not always kind and nice. I meet a very small percentage who are, but not the majority. I understand that mis-communications and misunderstandings between people are very common and can easily happen in relationships, especially when there are cultural differences, which play a very big role in arguments. When an offense occurred, I wanted to fix it and make it right so the relationships would not go from bad to worse.

When I confronted a particular family member about a misunderstanding, this would usually be the response: "You are too intimidating and have too many anger issues about your past. Your uncle is the one who mistreated you, not me. Why don't you write your anger down in a diary, put it away, and not leave it out there for everyone to listen to?" In my thoughts, I wanted to pull their tongues out as they talked.

After I met Jesus, I understood and realized that He had protected me without my knowledge. People had done me wrong and mistreated me in the past, but the abuse could have been worse, and Jesus will deal with them someday. The battle is not mine to fight; the injustice is not mine to fix. I can only do my part by staying out of his way. Also, if he forgave all my shortcomings, the least I can do is forgive the short-comings of others. I no longer need to hold onto bitterness and anger because of their selfishness.

Writing this story about my family's journey, I realized God not only kept me alive, but my whole family as well. The best part was that He did it in spite of the fact that none of us knew Him. We all made it out of Vietnam in one piece, and none were missing in action. We were separated, living in five different countries at the beginning of the seventies, and in the eighties we all came together without knowing we would ever be together again. Every time my poor mother sent us out for an escape attempt, she didn't dare to think, "Will this child make it alive to see me again?" or "Will I be alive to see this child again?" Yet, God kept her at peace without her knowing he did it. I look at all the situations in which I could have died, but I survived. Looking back on my journey, mine was not a pleasant childhood. I should have died so many times I can't even count them. I don't know how I walked away alive. I always told my friends that cats have nine lives, but I have more than fifteen lives. If the war or my past journeys couldn't kill me, nothing could kill me now. I wish during the difficult time of my journey I had known Jesus. I could have relied on his strength, not mine, and the journey would have been much easier.

A couple of days after the planes hit the twin towers at the World Trade Center in New York on September 11, 2001, I watched part of the coverage on television as President Bush addressed the crowd with a bullhorn, declaring that the people who had done this would hear from all of us Americans soon. I turned off the television and tuned the car radio back to the coverage during the commute to my boys' school. Eight-year-old Hunter, riding in the back seat, asked, "Mommy? Are we going to war?" The tone of his voice wasn't right, so I pulled the car over and stopped on the side of the road. I turned and looked at him. He looked fearful and anxious. Then I remembered the Tet Offensive in my neighborhood when I was just his age. I looked in his eyes and thought very hard before I answered him. I didn't want to lie or sugarcoat the situation or minimize his feelings. I took a deep breath and said, "Yes. We are going to war. However, Mommy is not afraid because we have God on our side."

"When Mommy was your age, Jesus protected your grandparents, Aunty, all your uncles, and me from the war. He kept all of us alive during our escapes. He gave us more blessings than we could ask for. He blessed Mommy with your daddy, your little brother, and you. I know He will protect us again because He protected me in the past. He wouldn't leave you out, because you are as special to Him as I am. I know you're scared, but pray. Pray for all the soldiers that will be going to war, their families, and us. We'll be okay! You'll see when you're scared that you can pray and give your fears to Jesus. He will carry your fears and you will feel better." I watched his face change from fear to acceptance. Even now, his cautious nature reassures me that he will be safe, even in his career as a United States Air Force Airman.

Sometimes I feel like Job in the Bible story. I don't have a good habit of reading the Bible, or remembering all the stories I read. I can only remember the stories I relate to, like Job's story. God allowed the devil to do what he wanted to Job, but not to kill him. He said Job would not curse His name. The devil caused Job to lose all he had, including his wife and children, and to be sick, but he couldn't take his life.

In my case, I was better off than Job. My family lost everything, but none of us lost our lives. The devil caused me to have so much sickness and pain in prison that I imagine that God said to him, "You can do anything to her and make her sick, but you can't take her life. She is my special child." Here I am alive all these years later, and I plan to live to a hundred and twenty.

I no longer wonder why I made it out of Vietnam alive. I miss my friends and think about all the people who died around me. I understand that bad things happen to good people. I also know that God uses bad for good. I know someday I will see my friends again in heaven. I think about my good friend Xiao-Wei. She was the one God chose to go first. I was the one chosen to do his will on the earth by telling our story. I know He caused Peng to pursue my friendship, even though I rejected her in my heart because she had come from the country I hated for shooting at me and pulling the boats full of refugees back out to sea.

I am grateful that he has healed me more thoroughly than any counseling sessions could do for me. On my third pregnancy, I was able to experience a normal childbirth. When August was born, our second son, I was able to enjoy my normal maternal experience every mother should feel. I remember when the nurse handed me the baby, I was able to feel the emotion just as people had described to me when they held their first baby in their arms. I was out of it emotionally and mentally from shock for months when Hunter was born, however, I could feel the excitement and joy when August was first put in my arms. Emotionally and mentally, I was well aware and present. I had requested the doctor to do a C-section. I was able to understand English and hear the doctors preparing me for the surgery. I could feel the doctor give me medication to numb me from the waist down. I could feel my skin stretching as he cut me. I could hear the baby refusing to come out of me and crying so loudly while he was still inside me. I noticed that the doctor said: "Wow! This baby has good lungs. He's already crying before I have to get him out and spank him." I felt the doctor pulling his wiggling, angry form out of my stomach. I only thought of life, and not death, when the nurse put him in my arms. And he has lived up to his beginning; he is the strongest boy I know. If I dropped him off alone in the jungle, he would come out wearing tiger skin.

I understand what Jesus meant when He said, "I came for the sick, not the healthy." I am not Jesus. I cannot do what he did when he was on earth, but I understand that he kept me on Earth to take care of the sick for him, not for me. I can only look forward to what I will do with the chances I was given to live, and what I need to accomplish in this life.

When I wake up every morning, I stand by my kitchen window or on my front porch, looking from my pasture across the city and plains to Pikes Peak, take a deep breath, and thank God for letting me live another day to continue what He wants me to do on this earth. It is my way of bringing a piece of heaven down to earth.

The reason the war in Vietnam lasted so long was because the government and the politicians were acting from greed on all sides. When it started, both sides were fighting for a better life. The communists were fighting for better treatment as equals in a society which had kept the poor in poverty. It turned out to be a selfish, corrupt dictatorship that oppressed many. I lived to see the corruption of both the dictatorship in South Vietnam and the corruption of the communist government from North Vietnam after they took over the South. The weak were controlled by the powerful in both systems. The main victims of the war were the soldiers fighting it and people like me caught in the middle.

As I wrote this story, a dear friend of mine, Jim McLeran, helped me get the stories on paper and provided emotional support. He is an American Vietnam veteran, and we were able to talk about the war and help each other process our memories.

One day, Jim showed me two photo albums of pictures he had taken while he was in Vietnam. The albums looked new and untouched, and were still in their original boxes. As we looked through the pictures, he told me the stories behind the pictures, page by page, picture by picture. One picture showed a huge crater made by a hundred and twenty-two millimeter rocket shot into his camp one night that just missed the barracks he was sleeping in and landed in an open area between the barracks and the camp chapel. It landed and exploded so close to his barracks that the dirt and shrapnel that came out of the crater sounded like pounding rain on the tin roof as it came down. Another time, a rocket landed behind an outhouse in his camp and blew a soldier who was sitting inside it out the door. Only his pride was wounded.

Jim showed me another picture and said, "You see the girl in this picture? She was one of the girls who came to clean our barracks every day. But the girls who came to clean by day were also often the ones who came back to shoot rockets into our camp at night. The American soldiers never understood why the girls who cleaned during the day hated us so much they reported the locations to the Viet Cong, who shot rockets and mortars at us at night."

As he told me this, I remembered hearing the Vietnamese servants who worked for us at the nightclub talking to each other. I was just a kid and didn't understand what they were talking about, but I was old enough to remember their conversation. Most of them came from different parts of the country. Due to the war, they needed to work in the city to earn a living to feed their families in the countryside and villages. I explained to Jim, "It wasn't the people from South Vietnam who hated the American soldiers. It was the people from North Vietnam." I was too young to understand the politics, but old enough to remember the things I heard and saw. I heard the servants talk about how Viet Cong soldiers came at night into their villages. They forced the village people to show them where to bomb the American bases by threatening to kill their families if they didn't cooperate.

I said to Jim, "When they had to choose between their own families and villages, or the American soldiers, who do you think they were going to choose? These girls may have helped rocket your camp, but look where the rockets hit. They worked and cleaned your camp during the day. Don't you think they knew where all your fuel and weapons were kept? What buildings in the camp were important? They could have made sure the rockets landed on an ammunition pile and caused even more damage. Yet the rockets landed in an open area during one attack and behind an outhouse during another attack. Yes, they might have lost their jobs working for the Americans if they were found out, even been sent to an American jail, but their families and villages were still safe. You, on the other hand, could always get someone else to do their job. They probably had to flee to the city to work as servants. My mother might even have hired some of them. We don't know the odds of this happening, and I'm not sure whether any of the girls who worked at your camp were hired as our servants, but I heard enough similar stories among the servants' conversations to remember it. Who knows?"

Jim said, "But what happened the times they rocketed all the right buildings and cost some of our soldiers their lives?" I responded, "Maybe it was pure luck, or the real underground Viet Cong who did it, but not them. During the war, we couldn't trust anyone but ourselves. Contrary to all the propaganda you heard, the South Vietnamese people loved the Americans and welcomed your presence in our country."

Jim's wife, Lucille, later told me he had never let anyone touch his photo albums or any of his Vietnam War memorabilia. She had been married to him for thirty-six years, and he never let anyone, including her, touch them. He never looked at them until that day. She said it had been a major breakthrough and healing for him to work on this story with me. For years, she never understood or knew anything about this part of Jim's life. He never talked openly to her about the war. It had all been a mystery to her until he helped me. As she listened to our conversations, knowing what he experienced in the war brought them closer to each other.

Jim told me that working with me on my story has given him back his patriotic spirit, and it has been a real gift to him. He felt his service in Vietnam was a big waste, because America eventually pulled out of South Vietnam and left the people to fend for themselves. It made him feel like America let the South Vietnamese people down. It was very demoralizing to him and many of the other Vietnam veterans that they participated in the only war America ever lost. He said that when the soldiers came back home to America, they were not able to wear their uniforms in public because the American people spit on them and called them "baby killers." This caused him to lose his patriotism. But working with me, a child in South Vietnam during the time the Americans were there, not a politician or a government official, and knowing the South Vietnamese people really loved the Americans but were forced by the Viet Cong to do some of the things they did to the soldiers, has restored his patriotism. For this he said he will be forever grateful.

Lucille didn't know that what she shared was very important to me. I can only pray that by sharing my family's story, I can bring healing to refugees and veterans alike, and civilians too, whether they were involved in a war like I was or just watched one on television. With God's grace, I have lived to this day to share it. I wanted to leave a legacy to the next generation not ever to take their freedom for granted.

I have learned not to trust government control. I'd rather the government would leave me alone. God will continue to protect me. I am not naive enough to believe America's government is somehow different from the rest, or that it cannot do or become evil. I am grateful that at least the people of this country still have some sense to not let the government have full power, but reserve some freedom and control to the people. It might not be a perfect system, but it is better than any other place. In America, I have the freedom to say what I want to say. People may not agree with me, but I have a voice and can express it without fear of being jailed or executed.

I am not afraid of death anymore. I am not afraid of PTSD. I know where I am going when I die. God's timing is always perfect and He will take me home. I am grateful to be alive and to have the freedom to share my journey and express my pain and sorrow and joy.

To my friends around the world who suffered the same or worse than I did, and asked how I could revisit the terrible past: I had to, and I did it. Telling it took me ten years, but I am free. My story no longer controls me, because I have set it free. You can, too.

May God continue to bless you, and may God bless the whole Earth through you, whatever your story. God bless America and all she stands for through our citizens and soldiers around the world. Thank you.

ABOUT THE AUTHOR

Ting-Ting Chan-Burford, M.S.W., was a child of the Vietnam War, who came to America as a teen speaking no English. She became the first female in her family's history with more than a grammar school education, earning her Master's degree in Social Work (M.S.W.) from the University of Denver. She now enjoys a more peaceful life as a wife and mother in Colorado Springs, Colorado, and although she is still haunted by her childhood trauma, she has led a colorful and rich life. She now has the honor of caring for her elderly mother, whose determination saw her family reunited in a new land after nearly of decade of separation.

Visit www.littlegirlbigwar.com to see pictures of the nightclub, the island prison and more.

Made in the USA
Middletown, DE
24 May 2023

31413169R00214